ROUTLEDGE **COMPANION WEBSITE**

STEPHEN BAILEY

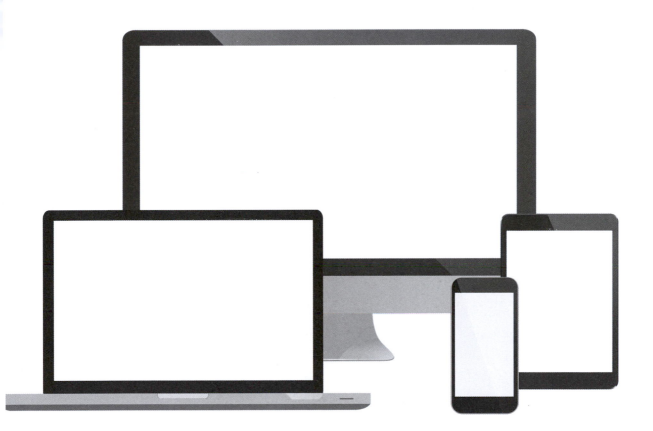

Enhancing online learning and teaching.

www.routledge.com/cw/bailey

Routledge
Taylor & Francis Group

Routledge... think about it
www.routledge.com

'*Academic Writing* is organized in a way that makes sense for teaching writing skills. The content covers a diverse body of samples from various fields, so it works wonderfully for my undergrad or graduate students. I especially like the section on common language errors, which includes extra practice for students; there is a good balance between writing instruction and discrete skill practice. It isn't easy to find a text that addresses plagiarism in a way that is clear for students to understand, and this text does the job!'

Ixchell Reyes, *University of Southern California, USA*

'This book is an excellent example of inclusive teaching. It is aimed primarily at international students, but reaches further, as it is equally useful for British students and students who come from a more practice-focused background. It is also a strong companion to books on research methods that need a solid basis for academic skills. The clear structure, accessible content, and well thought through activities in this book all give students the confidence to write effective academic work without the fear of breaking rules of plagiarism or academic malpractice. This is the book I recommend to all my students at the beginning of each academic year, independent of the subject I teach and the composition of my cohort.'

Maria Lonsdale, *University of Leeds, UK*

'*Academic Writing* is simply organised, allowing ease of access for beginner writers and specifically introducing them to the language needed to enter the conversations on academic writing.'

Djuddah Leijen, *University of Tartu, Estonia*

'The 5th edition of *Academic Writing* includes many new features which are extremely useful for all university students who are inexperienced in writing for academic purposes. The book provides both information on important aspects of academic writing and practice exercises which all students will find invaluable. It is a useful book for anyone who is new to writing for academic purposes, regardless of their level of proficiency in English.'

Radhika Jaidev, *Singapore Institute of Technology, Singapore*

Academic Writing

Now in its fifth edition, *Academic Writing* helps international students succeed in writing essays and reports for their English-language academic courses. Thoroughly revised and updated, it is designed to let teachers and students easily find the topics they need, both in the classroom and for self-study.

The book consists of five parts:

- The Writing Process
- Elements of Writing
- Language Issues
- Vocabulary for Writing
- Writing Models

The first part explains and practises every stage of essay writing, from choosing the best sources, reading and note-making, through to referencing and proofreading. The four remaining parts, organised alphabetically, can be taught in conjunction with the first part or used on a remedial basis. A progress check at the end of each part allows students to assess their learning. All units are fully cross-referenced, and a complete set of answers to the practice exercises is included.

New topics in this edition include Writing in Groups, Written British and American English, and Writing Letters and Emails. In addition, the new interactive website has a full set of teaching notes as well as more challenging exercises, revision material and links to other sources. Additional features of the book include:

- Models provided for writing tasks such as case studies and essays
- Use of authentic academic texts from a wide range of disciplines
- Designed for self-study as well as classroom use
- Useful at both undergraduate and postgraduate level
- Glossary to explain technical terms, plus index

Written to deal with the specific language issues faced by international students, this practical, user-friendly book is an invaluable guide to academic writing in English.

Stephen Bailey has taught English for Academic Purposes at the University of Nottingham and Derby University. Previously he taught students in Barcelona, Tokyo, Johor Bahru and Prague. He now lives in Derbyshire with his wife and daughter. His other books include *Academic Writing for International Students of Business* (Routledge) and *The Essentials of Academic Writing for International Students* (Routledge).

Academic Writing

A Handbook for International Students

Fifth edition

Stephen Bailey

Routledge
Taylor & Francis Group

LONDON AND NEW YORK

Fifth edition published 2018
by Routledge
2 Park Square, Milton Park, Abingdon, Oxon OX14 4RN

and by Routledge
711 Third Avenue, New York, NY 10017

Routledge is an imprint of the Taylor & Francis Group, an informa business

© 2018 Stephen Bailey

The right of Stephen Bailey to be identified as author of this work has
been asserted by him in accordance with sections 77 and 78 of the
Copyright, Designs and Patents Act 1988.

All rights reserved. No part of this book may be reprinted or reproduced
or utilised in any form or by any electronic, mechanical, or other means,
now known or hereafter invented, including photocopying and
recording, or in any information storage or retrieval system, without
permission in writing from the publishers.

Trademark notice: Product or corporate names may be trademarks or
registered trademarks, and are used only for identification and
explanation without intent to infringe.

First edition published 2003 by Routledge
Fourth edition published 2015 by Routledge

British Library Cataloguing-in-Publication Data
A catalogue record for this book is available from the British Library

Library of Congress Cataloguing-in-Publication Data
Names: Bailey, Stephen, 1947– author.
Title: Academic writing : a handbook for international students /
    Stephen Bailey.
Description: Fifth Edition. | New York : Routledge, 2018. |
    Includes bibliographical references.
Identifiers: LCCN 2017036066 | ISBN 9781138048737 (Hardback) |
    ISBN 9781138048744 (Paperback) | ISBN 9781315169996 (Ebook)
Subjects: LCSH: English language—Rhetoric—Handbooks, manuals, etc. |
    English language—Textbooks for foreign speakers. |
    Academic writing—Handbooks, manuals, etc.
Classification: LCC PE1413 .B28 2018 | DDC 808/.0428—dc23
LC record available at https://lccn.loc.gov/2017036066

ISBN: 978-1-138-04873-7 (hbk)
ISBN: 978-1-138-04874-4 (pbk)
ISBN: 978-1-315-16999-6 (ebk)

Typeset in Galliard
by Apex CoVantage, LLC

Visit the companion website: www.routledge.com/cw/bailey

Printed by Bell & Bain Ltd, Glasgow

Contents

Acknowledgements   xix
Introduction for Teachers   xx
Introduction for Students   xxii
Academic Writing Quiz   xxv
Written British and American English – A Short Guide   xxviii

Part 1
The Writing Process   1

1.1   Basics of Writing   3

The purpose of academic writing   3
Features of academic writing   3
Common types of academic writing   4
The format of short and long writing tasks   4
The components of academic writing   6
Some other common text components   7
Simple and longer sentences   7
Writing in paragraphs   8
Practice   9

1.2   Reading: Finding Suitable Sources   10

Academic texts   10
Types of text   13
Using reading lists   13
Using library catalogues   14
Using library websites to search electronic resources   15

1.3	**Reading: Developing Critical Approaches**	17
	Reading methods	17
	Titles, subtitles and text features	18
	Reading abstracts	19
	Fact and opinion	20
	Assessing internet sources critically	21
	Practice	22
	Critical thinking	23

1.4	**Avoiding Plagiarism**	26
	What is plagiarism?	26
	Acknowledging sources	27
	Degrees of plagiarism	27
	Avoiding plagiarism by summarising and paraphrasing	28
	Avoiding plagiarism by developing good study habits	30
	Practice	30
	Further practice	31
	Research	32

1.5	**From Understanding Essay Titles to Planning**	33
	The planning process	33
	Analysing essay titles	34
	Practice	34
	Brainstorming	35
	Essay length	36
	Writing outlines	37
	Practice	38

1.6	**Finding Key Points and Note-making**	39
	Finding key points	39
	Finding relevant points	40
	Practice A	41
	Why make notes?	41
	Note-making methods	42
	Effective note-making	44
	Practice B	44

1.7	**Summarising and Paraphrasing**	46
	What makes a good summary?	46
	Stages of summarising	47
	Practice A	47
	Practice B	48
	Practice C	50

Paraphrasing	51
Practice D	51
Techniques for paraphrasing	52
Practice E	52
Practice F	54

1.8 References and Quotations   **55**

Why use references?	55
Citations and references	56
Reference verbs	56
Reference systems	57
Using quotations	57
Practice	59
Abbreviations in citations	60
Secondary references	61
Organising the list of references	61

1.9 Combining Sources   **64**

Referring to sources	64
Taking a critical approach	65
Combining three sources	68
Practice	68

1.10 Organising Paragraphs   **71**

Paragraph structure	71
Practice A	72
Practice B	73
Introducing paragraphs and linking them together	74
Practice C	74
Practice D	74

1.11 Introductions and Conclusions   **76**

Introduction components	76
Introduction structure	77
Opening sentences	79
Conclusions	80
Conclusion structure	81
Practice	81

1.12 Rewriting and Proofreading   **82**

Rewriting	82
Practice A	82
Practice B	84

Proofreading	84
Practice C	84
Practice D	85
Practice E	85
Progress check 1	86

Part 2
Elements of Writing   89

2.1   Argument and Discussion   91

Discussion vocabulary	91
Organisation	92
Practice A	93
The language of discussion	93
Counter-arguments	93
Providing evidence	94
Practice B	95

2.2   Cause and Effect   96

The language of cause and effect	96
Practice A	97
Practice B	98
Practice C	99
Practice D	99

2.3   Comparison   101

Comparison structures	101
Practice A	102
Forms of comparison	103
Using superlatives	103
Practice B	103
Practice C	104
Practice D	105

2.4   Definitions   106

Simple definitions	106
Category words	106
Complex definitions	108
Practice	109

2.5	**Examples**	**110**
	Using examples	110
	Phrases to introduce examples	111
	Practice A	111
	Practice B	112
	Restatement	113
2.6	**Generalisations**	**114**
	Using generalisations	114
	Structure	115
	Practice A	115
	Practice B	116
	Building on generalisations	116
	Practice C	117
2.7	**Problems and Solutions**	**118**
	Paragraph structure	118
	Alternative structure	119
	Vocabulary	119
	Practice A	120
	Practice B	120
	Practice C	120
2.8	**Visual Information**	**122**
	Types of visuals	122
	The language of change	125
	Describing visuals	126
	Labelling	128
	Practice A	128
	Practice B	129
	Progress check 2	130

Part 3
Language Issues   **133**

3.1	**Cohesion**	**135**
	Reference words	135
	Practice A	136
	Preventing confusion	136

Practice B   137
Implied language   137
Practice C   138
Practice D   138

3.2   Definite Articles   **139**
Use of articles   139
Using definite articles   140
Practice A   141
Practice B   142

3.3   Numbers   **143**
The language of numbers   143
Percentages   144
Simplification   144
Further numerical phrases   145
Practice   147

3.4   Passive and Active   **148**
Active and passive   148
Structure   149
Use of the passive   149
Adverbs with passives   150
Practice   151

3.5   Punctuation   **152**
Capital letters   152
Full stops   153
Commas   153
Apostrophes   154
Semicolons   154
Colons   154
Quotations marks/inverted commas   155
Others   155
Practice A   156
Practice B   156

3.6   Singular or Plural?   **157**
Five difficult areas   157
Group phrases   158
Uncountable nouns   158
Practice A   160
Practice B   160

3.7	**Style**	**161**
	Developing an academic style	161
	Guidelines	162
	Practice A	163
	Avoiding repetition and redundancy	164
	Varying sentence length	165
	The use of caution	166
	Using modifiers	167
	Practice B	168
3.8	**Time Markers**	**169**
	How time markers are used	169
	Practice A	170
	Tenses	170
	Practice B	170
	Practice C	171
	Progress check 3	173

Part 4
Vocabulary for Writing   177

4.1	**Approaches to Vocabulary**	**179**
	Vocabulary issues	179
	Dealing with new vocabulary	180
	Language features	181
	Practice	181
	Confusing pairs	182
	Words and phrases from other languages	183
4.2	**Abbreviations**	**185**
	Types of abbreviation	185
	Common abbreviations	186
	Punctuation	187
	Duplicate abbreviations	187
	Abbreviations in writing	187
	Practice	188
4.3	**Academic Vocabulary: Nouns and Adjectives**	**189**
	Introduction	189
	Nouns	189
	Nouns and adjectives	191
	Confusing nouns and adjectives	191

	Practice A	192
	Similar adjectives	193
	Academic adjectives	193
	Practice B	194
	Practice C	195

4.4 Academic Vocabulary: Verbs and Adverbs **196**

	Understanding main verbs	196
	Using verbs of reference	198
	Practice A	198
	Further verbs of reference	199
	Practice B	199
	Using adverbs	199
	Practice C	201
	Practice D	201

4.5 Conjunctions **202**

	How conjunctions work	202
	Types of conjunctions	203
	Common conjunctions	204
	Practice A	204
	Practice B	205
	Confusing conjunctions	205
	Conjunctions of opposition	205
	Practice C	206

4.6 Prefixes and Suffixes **207**

	How prefixes and suffixes work	207
	Prefixes	208
	Practice A	209
	Suffixes	209
	Practice B	210
	Practice C	210

4.7 Prepositions **211**

	Using prepositions	211
	Practice A	212
	Prepositions and nouns	212
	Prepositions in phrases	213
	Prepositions of place and time	213
	Practice B	213
	Verbs and prepositions	214
	Practice C	215

4.8	**Synonyms**	**216**
	How synonyms work	216
	Common synonyms in academic writing	217
	Practice A	217
	Practice B	218
	Practice C	218
	Progress check 4	219

Part 5
Writing Models   223

5.1	**Case Studies**	**225**
	Using case studies	225
	Model case study	226
5.2	**Literature Reviews and Book Reviews**	**229**
	Literature reviews	229
	Example literature review	230
	Book reviews	232
	Model book review	232
5.3	**Writing Longer Papers**	**234**
	Planning your work	234
	Example essay	236
	Revision	241
5.4	**Reports**	**242**
	Writing reports	242
	Essays and reports	243
	Practice	244
	Scientific reports	244
	Example report: Student experience of part-time work	246
5.5	**Writing Letters and Emails**	**249**
	Letters	249
	Practice A	251
	Emails	251
	Practice B	252
	Practice C	252
5.6	**Writing in Groups**	**253**
	Why write in groups?	253
	Making group work successful	254

Dealing with problems   256
Points to remember   256

Glossary   257
Answers   261
  Part 1 – The Writing Process   262
  Part 2 – Elements of Writing   278
  Part 3 – Language Issues   287
  Part 4 – Vocabulary for Writing   294
  Part 5 – Writing Models   304
Index   310

Acknowledgements

I would like to thank all the colleagues that I have worked with over the years in different parts of the world. Always ready to share ideas, their encouragement and comments have helped me develop these materials.

My wife Rene, who has an unrivalled grasp of the finer points of academic style, has been an invaluable critic, while my daughter Sophie has helped me appreciate the other side of the academic whirl.

Introduction for Teachers

Aims

The fifth edition of *Academic Writing: A Handbook for International Students* has been written to help students who are not native speakers of English with their written academic work. In many ways writing poses the biggest challenge for these students, due to the special demands of style, vocabulary and structure met in the academic world.

This book is aimed at both undergraduate and postgraduate students, since although they are studying at different levels, the requirements of their teachers are similar – for written work that is precise, objective, accurate and fully referenced.

In addition, students may be studying in many different situations: on full-time pre-sessional courses, on part-time in-sessional classes, in subject-specific classes or in multidisciplinary courses, or studying entirely by themselves. Due to its flexible structure this book can be used in all these situations.

Structure

The organisation of *Academic Writing* is explained by this chart:

Part	Topic	Main application
1	**The Writing Process** from finding sources to proofreading	Classroom use
2	**Elements of Writing** from argument to visual information	Classroom and self-study
3	**Language Issues** from cohesion to time markers	Classroom, self-study and reference

4	**Vocabulary for Writing** from abbreviations to synonyms	Classroom, self-study and reference
5	**Writing Models** from case studies to emails	Self-study and reference

Part 1 guides students through the entire process of writing essays or similar papers, and is best taught as a series of lessons, with feedback from the practice exercises.

Part 2 teaches the related writing skills and, like Parts 3, 4 and 5, is organised alphabetically. Part 3 examines the language issues that pose particular problems for international students, and Part 4 deals with the vocabulary problems which are an understandable concern for such students.

Finally, Part 5 provides models of some of the most common types of assessed writing tasks. All the units in Parts 2–5 can be taught in conjunction with units from Part 1, or can be suggested to individual students on a remedial basis for self-study.

Full details of how units can be linked together in a teaching programme, with suggestions for suitable classroom approaches, can be found in the Teaching Notes on the companion website: www.routledge.com/cw/bailey.

Using the book

The first three units in Part 1 are designed as a basic introduction to the subject and assume a fairly low level of writing ability. With stronger students teachers may choose to progress rapidly through these to more difficult materials starting with Unit 4, Avoiding Plagiarism.

Note that *Academic Writing* uses authentic reading texts taken from a wide variety of disciplines (e.g. medicine, politics, law and engineering) that are selected to be of interest to all students. Most of the exercises can be done either individually or in pairs or groups, the latter being preferable in some cases. There is a full answer key at the end of the book, along with a glossary of academic terms and an index. Further practice exercises, mainly at a more advanced level, can be found on the companion website.

Cross-referencing to relevant sections in other units is provided like this:

> ▶ **See Units 3.4 Passive and Active and 4.5 Conjunctions**

The materials in this course have been thoroughly tested in the classroom, but improvement is always possible, so I would be grateful for any comments or suggestions from teachers for future editions.

Stephen Bailey
stephen.bailey@w3z.co.uk

Introduction for Students

The challenge of writing in English

Most international students who come to college or university to study on English-language courses can speak the language well enough for everyday activities such as shopping and travelling. But they may be surprised to find that writing notes, essays and reports in English is much more difficult. There are several reasons for this situation.

Firstly, while speaking is normally done face to face, so that you can see if the listener understands what you say, when writing we cannot see the reader, so we must write as clearly as possible to make our work easy to understand. Additionally, with academic writing, writers and readers must learn special conventions, such as using capital letters in certain places. If you do not follow these rules, your meaning may be unclear and your teacher could find it hard to assess your work. There is also the issue of vocabulary, since in most academic subjects students are expected to use a semi-formal vocabulary which is different from the idiomatic language of normal speech.

The aim of the book

The main purpose of *Academic Writing: A Handbook for International Students* is to help you succeed in the writing tasks which you may be asked to complete on your course. The kind of writing you are asked to do could be different from the work you have done before, and this may be the first time you have had to write long essays and reports in English.

Your teachers know that English is not your native language and will be sympathetic to the problems you have in your writing. But at the same time you will want to learn to write as clearly and accurately as possible, not only to succeed on your present course, but also in preparation for your future career. Most large companies and organisations now expect their staff to be able to communicate effectively in written English, as well as orally. During your studies you have an ideal opportunity to learn to write English well, and this book can help you achieve that goal.

As well as accuracy, students are generally expected to take a critical approach to their sources. This means that you are expected to question and evaluate everything you read, asking whether it is reliable and relevant. Your teachers also expect you to refer carefully to the sources of your ideas, using a standard system of referencing. *Academic Writing* will help you develop these skills.

Using the book

The organisation of *Academic Writing* is explained by this chart:

Part	Topic	Main application
1	**The Writing Process** from finding sources to proofreading	Classroom use
2	**Elements of Writing** from argument to visual information	Classroom and self-study
3	**Language Issues** from cohesion to time markers	Classroom, self-study and reference
4	**Vocabulary for Writing** from abbreviations to synonyms	Classroom, self-study and reference
5	**Writing Models** from case studies to emails	Self-study and reference

The book can be used either with a teacher or by yourself for self-study and reference. To help you get the most out of the course, note the following points:

Instructions are printed like this:

■ **Read the following text**

Cross-referencing to relevant sections in other units is provided like this:

▶ **See Units 3.4 Passive and Active and 4.5 Conjunctions**

Answers to most exercises are provided in the answer key at the end of the book. If there is no definite answer, a model answer is usually given.

The **glossary** on page 257 explains academic terms you may not be familiar with. The **index** on page 310 can be used to find specific information.

The companion website for *Academic Writing* can be found at www.routledge.com/cw/bailey. It offers extra material including further practice exercises, more challenging materials and revision quizzes, as well as links to other resources.

I hope you find this new edition helpful in progressing with your studies, and I would be glad to receive your comments and suggestions on any part of the book to help develop future editions.

Stephen Bailey
stephen.bailey@w3z.co.uk

Academic Writing Quiz

■ **How much do you know about academic writing? Find out by doing this fun quiz.**

1 The main difference between academic writing and other writing is that academic writing:
   a) uses longer words
   b) tries to be precise and unbiased
   c) is harder to understand

2 The difference between a project and an essay is:
   a) essays are longer
   b) projects are longer
   c) students choose projects' subjects

3 Teachers frequently complain about students:
   a) not answering the question given
   b) not writing enough
   c) writing in pencil

4 The best time to write an introduction is often:
   a) first
   b) last
   c) after writing the main body

5 The purpose of an introduction is:
   a) to give your aims and methods
   b) to excite the reader
   c) to summarise your ideas

6 Making careful notes is essential for:
   a) writing essays
   b) revising for exams
   c) all academic work

7 An in-text citation looks like:
   a)   (Manton, 2008)
   b)   (Richard Manton, 2008)
   c)   (Manton, R. 2008)

8 Paraphrasing a text means:
   a)   making it shorter
   b)   changing a lot of the vocabulary
   c)   adding more detail

9 Paragraphs always contain:
   a)   six or more sentences
   b)   an example
   c)   a topic sentence

10 Proofreading means:
    a)   getting a friend to check your work
    b)   checking for minor errors
    c)   rewriting

11 Teachers expect students to adopt a critical approach to their sources:
    a)   sometimes
    b)   only for Master's work
    c)   always

12. This punctuation mark (') is called:
    a)   comma
    b)   colon
    c)   apostrophe

13 A suitable synonym for 'business' is:
    a)   firm
    b)   organisation
    c)   outfit

14 'Progress' and 'research' are both nouns. What kind of noun?
    a)   countable
    b)   uncountable
    c)   proper

15 An abstract is normally found:
    a)   on the back cover of books
    b)   before journal articles
    c)   in exam questions

16 The word 'unreliable' contains:
    a)   a prefix
    b)   a suffix
    c)   both

17 When making notes you should always include:
  a) your own ideas
  b) a full reference
  c) the date

18 A pie chart is used to show:
  a) changes in time
  b) proportion
  c) structure of an organisation

19 Acknowledgements are generally used:
  a) to admit possible errors
  b) to suggest more research
  c) to thank people who helped

20 The conclusion to an article usually includes:
  a) results of the study
  b) additional data
  c) references

Answers on p. 262

Written British and American English – A Short Guide

Speakers of British and American English can usually understand each other easily, with only minor confusions due to some variations in vocabulary. However, with written academic work more differences need to be understood. The main issues are explained in this section.

NB: Academic writers in Australia, New Zealand and many other English-speaking areas tend to use British English; in Canada American English is more common.

1 Vocabulary

There are many vocabulary items which differ between British (UK) and American (US) English (e.g. *autumn* [UK] and *fall* [US]). However, these are mainly well known and widely understood. But the two main problematic variations in everyday vocabulary are:

a) words which are not commonly understood in both countries (e.g. *tap* [UK] and *faucet* [US]). Other examples: *boot* (of car) (UK) and *trunk* (US) / *nappy* (UK) and *diaper* (US).

b) words with different meanings in each country (e.g. *vest* is worn under a shirt in the UK, but in the US it is the part of a three-piece suit worn under a jacket).

For a full list of differences see: https://en.oxforddictionaries.com/usage/british-and-american-terms

2 Spelling

a) In American English the 'u' is commonly dropped from words ending in -our (e.g. *neighbour* becomes *neighbor*).

b) Words ending in -ise or -yse in British English (e.g. *sanitise*, *modernise*) change to *sanitize* and *modernize* in American English.

c)   A group of technical nouns such as *haemophiliac* and *foetus* lose the 'ae' or 'oe' in American English and become *hemophiliac* and *fetus*.

d)   British English spells the noun *practice* but the verb *practise*. In American English both forms are spelt with a 'c'.

e)   Many words ending in -re in British English (e.g. *metre*, *theatre*) become *meter* and *theater* in American English.

3 Academic language

There are many minor variations between the language of the educational systems of Britain and the US. These are some of the more important:

a)   In Britain students *read/do/study* a subject. In the US they *study* or *major* in a subject (the latter as the main part of a two-part degree).

b)   Most teaching in UK universities is done by *lecturers*, while a *professor* is a senior position. In US colleges and universities teaching is mainly done by *professors* and *assistant professors*.

c)   In Britain a *thesis* is the paper submitted for a PhD. This is called a *dissertation* in the US. (In the UK a *dissertation* may be written for a Master's degree).

d)   A *college* in the UK is usually any post-school institution which provides mainly vocational training, but doesn't award degrees (but a few universities such as Oxford are organised in *colleges*). In the US a *college* is usually part of a university and does give first degrees.

e)   Someone studying for a Master's degree in the UK is a *postgraduate*, while in the US they are a *graduate student*.

f)   Students in Britain *sit* or *take* exams, in America exams are just *taken*. Before taking an exam, British students may *revise* the subject, but in the US they *review* the topic.

UK students generally receive *marks* for their work, while American students get *grades*.

4 Punctuation

a)   In Britain quotations are shown by single quotation marks, while nested quotations (those inside quotations) use double. In the US the convention is the opposite.

UK: *As Kauffman remarked: 'His concept of "internal space" requires close analysis'.*

US: *As Kauffman remarked: "His concept of 'internal space' requires close analysis."*

Note that in British English the full stop comes after the quotation marks, while in the US it is inside.

b)   In American English the 'Oxford comma' is standard (i.e. the comma before the final 'and' in a list):

. . . typhus, cholera, tuberculosis, and smallpox were all endemic in the nineteenth-century slum.

In British English this is usually omitted:

. . . typhus, cholera, tuberculosis and smallpox were all endemic in the nineteenth-century slum.

c)   Dates are generally written with the month first in American English:

11.30.2017 = November 30th 2017

In British English dates usually begin with the day:

30.11.2017 = 30th November 2017

▶   **See Units 1.8 References and Quotations and 3.5 Punctuation**

The Writing Process

Part 1 explains and practises all the stages of producing a piece of academic writing, from analysing the title, reading the sources, note-making and referencing, through to rewriting and proofreading the final draft.

Basics of Writing

Most academic courses test students through written assignments. These tasks include coursework, which may take weeks to write, and exam answers, which often have to be written in an hour. This unit deals with:

- The names of different writing tasks
- The format of long and short writing tasks
- The structure of sentences and paragraphs

1 The purpose of academic writing

Students should be clear why they are writing. The most common reasons include:

- to report on a piece of research the writer has conducted
- to answer a question the writer has been given or chosen
- to discuss a subject of common interest and give the writer's view
- to synthesise research done by others on a topic

■ Can you suggest any other reasons?

- _____
- _____

2 Features of academic writing

Although there is no fixed standard of academic writing, and style may vary from subject to subject, academic writing is clearly different from the written style of newspapers or novels. For example, it is generally agreed that academic writing attempts to be accurate, so that instead of 'the metal was very hot' it is better to write 'the metal was heated to 65°C'. What are some of the other features of academic writing?

■ Working alone or in a group, list your ideas here.

*   *Impersonal style – generally avoids using 'I' or 'we'*

*   _____

*   _____

*   _____

3 Common types of academic writing

The main types of written work produced by students are presented in the following table.

■ Match the terms on the left to the definitions on the right.

Notes	*A piece of research, either individual or group work, with the topic chosen by the student(s).*
Report	*The longest piece of writing normally done by a student (20,000+ words) often for a higher degree, on a topic chosen by the student.*
Project	**A written record of the main points of a text or lecture, for a student's personal use.**
Essay	*A general term for any academic essay, report, presentation or article.*
Dissertation/ Thesis	*A description of something a student has done (e.g. conducting a survey or experiment).*
Paper	*The most common type of written work, with the title given by the teacher, normally 1,000–5,000 words.*

4 The format of short and long writing tasks

Short essays (including exam answers) generally have this pattern:

Introduction

Main body

Conclusion

Longer essays and reports may include:

Introduction

Main body

      Literature review

      Case study

      Discussion

   Conclusion

   References

   Appendices

▶   See Unit 5.3 Longer Essays

Dissertations and journal articles may have:

   Abstract

   List of contents

   List of tables

   Introduction

   Main body

      Literature review

      Case study

      Findings

      Discussion

   Conclusion

   Acknowledgements

   Notes

   References

   Appendices

In addition to these sections, books may also include:

   Foreword

   Preface

   Bibliography/Further reading

■   Discuss the meanings of the preceding terms.

■   Match the following definitions to terms in the preceding lists:

   a)   A short summary which explains the paper's purpose and main findings.

      _____

   b)   A list of all the sources the writer has mentioned in the text.

      _____

   c)   A section, after the conclusion, where additional information is included.

      _____

d)   A short section where people who have helped the writer are thanked.

_____

e)   Part of the main body in which the views of other writers on the topic are discussed.

_____

f)   A section where one particular example is described in detail.

_____

g)   A preliminary part of a book usually written by someone other than the author.

_____

ACADEMIC JOURNALS

There are thousands of academic journals published in English and other languages around the world. The purpose of these journals is to provide a forum for academics within a specific discipline (e.g. education or civil engineering) to share cutting-edge research. Most journals publish several issues a year and are often available either online or in a hard copy.

One important feature of journals is that the articles they publish are generally peer-reviewed. This means that when an article is submitted the editors ask other specialists in that field to read the article and decide if it is worth publishing. Reviewers may make comments that lead to the article being modified.

Students need to get to know the leading journals in their subject, which are generally available via the university library.

▶   See Unit 1.2.5 Reading: Finding Suitable Sources

5 The components of academic writing

There are no fixed rules for the layout of written academic work. Different schools and departments require students to follow different formats in their writing. Your teachers may give you guidelines, or you can ask them what they want, but some general patterns apply to most formats for academic writing.

■   Read the following text and identify the features underlined, using the words in the box.

sentence	**heading**	**subtitle**	**paragraph**	**title**	**phrase**

a)   **A Fishy Story**

b)   Misleading health claims regarding omega-3 fatty acids

c)   Introduction

d)   There has been considerable discussion recently about the benefits of omega-3 fatty acids in the diet.

e)   It is claimed that these reduce the risk of cardiovascular disease and may even combat obesity. Consequently food producers have added omega-3s to products ranging from margarine to soft drinks in an attempt to make their products appear healthier and hence increase sales.

f)   However, consumers may be unaware that there are two types of omega-3, The best (long-chain fatty acids) are derived from fish, but others (short-chain fatty acids) come from cheaper sources such as soya. This latter group have not been shown to produce the health benefits linked to the long-chain variety. According to Tamura *et al.* (2009), positive results may only be obtained either by eating oily fish three times a week, or by taking daily supplements containing 500mg of eicosapentaenoic acid (EPA) or docosahexaenoic acid (DHA).

(Source: *Health Concerns*, March 2016, p. 17)

a) _Title_ b) _____   c) _____   d) _____   e) _____   f) _____

6 Some other common text components

a)   Reference to sources using **citation**: *According to Tamura et al. (2009)*

b)   The use of **abbreviations** for convenience: *docosahexaenoic acid (DHA)*

c)   **Italics:** used to show words from other languages or add emphasis:
Medical research companies know *ex ante* that these citizens cannot afford medicines.
(= Latin for 'before the event')

d)   **Brackets:** used to give extra information or to clarify a point: *. . . but others (short-chain fatty acids) come from cheaper sources such as soya.*

7 Simple and longer sentences

■   Study the following table.

Dragon Motors – vehicle production 2013–17

2013	2014	2015	2016	2017
135,470	156,935	164,820	159,550	123,075

All sentences contain verbs:

*In 2013 the company **produced** over 135,000 vehicles.*

*Between 2013 and 2014 vehicle production **increased** by 20%.*

Simple sentences (such as the examples just given) are easier to write and read, but longer sentences are also needed in academic writing. However, students should make clarity a priority and avoid writing very lengthy sentences with several clauses until they feel confident in their ability.

Sentences containing two or more clauses use **conjunctions, relative pronouns** or **punctuation** to link the clauses:

- *In 2013 Dragon Motors produced over 135,000 vehicles,* **but** *the following year production increased by 20%.* (conjunction)
- *In 2015 the company built 164,820 vehicles,* **which** *was the peak of production.* (relative pronoun)
- *Nearly 160,000 vehicles were produced in 2016; by 2017 this had fallen to 123,000.* (punctuation – semicolon)

■ Write two simple and two longer sentences using data from the following table.

a) _____

b) _____

c) _____

d) _____

Borchester College: gender balance by faculty, 2016 (percentages)

	Law	Education	Engineering	Business	Computer sciences
Male	43	22	81	41	65
Female	57	78	19	59	35

▶ See Unit 4.5 Conjunctions

▶ See Unit 3.7 Style – Varying sentence length

8 Writing in paragraphs

■ Discuss the following questions:

What is a paragraph?

Why are texts divided into paragraphs?

How long are paragraphs?

Do paragraphs have a standard structure?

► *For answers see* **Unit 1.10 Organising Paragraphs**

■ Read the following text and divide it into a suitable number of paragraphs.

BIOCHAR

Charcoal is produced by burning wood slowly in a low-oxygen environment. This material, which is mainly carbon, was used for many years to heat iron ore to extract the metal. But when in 1709 Abraham Darby discovered a smelting process using coke (produced from coal) demand for charcoal collapsed. At approximately the same time the carbon dioxide level in the atmosphere began to rise. But a new use for charcoal, renamed biochar, has recently emerged. It is claimed that using biochar made from various types of plants can both improve soil quality and combat global warming. Various experiments in the United States have shown that adding burnt crop wastes to soil increases fertility and cuts the loss of vital nutrients such as nitrates. The other benefit of biochar is its ability to lock CO_2 into the soil. The process of decay normally allows the carbon dioxide in plants to return to the atmosphere rapidly, but when transformed into charcoal this may be delayed for hundreds of years. In addition, soil containing biochar appears to release less methane, a gas which contributes significantly to global warming. American researchers claim that widespread use of biochar could reduce global CO_2 emissions by over 10%. But other agricultural scientists are concerned about the environmental effects of growing crops especially for burning, and about the displacement of food crops that might be caused. However, the potential twin benefits of greater farm yields and reduced greenhouse gases mean that further research in this area is urgently needed.

(Source: Ronzoni, M. (2013) *Farming Futures*, p. 154)

9 Practice

■ Write two simple and two longer sentences on biochar.

a) _____

b) _____

c) _____

d) _____

Reading
Finding Suitable Sources

Students often underestimate the importance of effective reading, but on any course it is vital to be able to find and understand the most suitable relevant sources quickly. This unit:

- examines the most appropriate types of text for academic work
- explores ways of locating relevant material in the library
- explains the use of electronic resources

1 Academic texts

You may need to read a variety of sources, such as websites or journal articles, for your course. It is important to identify the most suitable texts and recognise their features, which will help you to assess their value.

■ You are studying Water Management. Read the following texts (extracts 1–3) and discuss with other students if they are suitable for academic use, and why.

Text	Suitability?
1	
2	
3	

1 WORLDWIDE PRESSURES

The global nature of the crisis is underlined in reports from many regions. In south Asia, there have been huge losses of groundwater, which has been pumped up with reckless lack of control over the past decade. About 600 million people live on the 2,000 sq. km. area that extends from eastern Pakistan across the hot dry plains of northern India and into Bangladesh, and the land is the most intensely irrigated in the world. Up to 75% of farmers rely on pumped groundwater to water their crops and water use is intensifying – at the same time that satellite images show supplies are shrinking alarmingly.

Changing precipitation and melting snow and ice are already altering hydrological systems in many areas. Glaciers continue to shrink worldwide, affecting villages and towns downstream. The result, says the Intergovernmental Panel for Climate Change, is that the proportion of the global population experiencing water scarcity is bound to increase throughout the twenty-first century. More and more, people and nations will have to compete for resources. An international dispute between Egypt and Ethiopia over the latter's plans to dam the Nile has only recently been resolved. In future, far more serious conflicts are likely to erupt as the planet dries up.

Even in high latitudes, the one region on Earth where rainfall is likely to intensify in coming years, climate change will still reduce water quality and pose risks due to a number of factors: rising temperatures; increased levels of sediments, nutrients and pollutants triggered by heavy rainfall; and disruption of treatment facilities during floods. The world faces a water crisis that will touch every part of the globe, a point that has been stressed by Jean Chrétien, former Canadian prime minister and co-chair of the InterAction Council. 'The future political impact of water scarcity may be devastating', he claimed. 'Using water the way we have in the past simply will not sustain humanity in future'.

2 A DRYING WORLD?

It is easy to think that water will always be plentiful, as it covers 70% of our planet. However, freshwater – the stuff we drink, bathe in, irrigate our farm fields with – is extremely rare. Only 3% of the world's water is freshwater, and two-thirds of that is tucked away in frozen glaciers or otherwise unavailable for our use.

As a result, some 1.1 billion people worldwide lack access to water, and a total of 2.7 billion find water scarce for at least one month of the year. Inadequate sanitation is also a problem for 2.4 billion people – they are exposed to diseases, such as cholera and typhoid fever, and other water-borne illnesses. Two million people, mostly children, die each year from diarrheal diseases alone.

Many of the water systems that keep ecosystems thriving and feed a growing human population have become stressed. Rivers, lakes and aquifers are drying up or becoming too polluted to use. More than half the world's wetlands have disappeared. Agriculture consumes more water than any other source and wastes much of that through inefficiencies. Climate change is altering patterns of weather and water around the world, causing shortages and droughts in some areas and floods in others. This situation will only get worse at the current rate of consumption. By 2025, two-thirds of the world's population may face water shortages, and ecosystems around the world will suffer even more.

3 MEASURING SCARCITY

It is surprisingly difficult to determine whether water is truly scarce in the physical sense at a global scale (a supply problem) or whether it is available but should be used better (a demand problem). Rijsberman (2006) reviews water scarcity indicators and global assessments based on these indicators. The most widely used indicator, the Falkenmark indicator, is popular because it is easy to apply and understand, but it does not help to explain the true nature of water scarcity. The more complex indicators are not widely applied because data are lacking to apply them and the definitions are not intuitive.

Water is definitely physically scarce in densely populated arid areas such as Central and West Asia, and North Africa, with projected availabilities of less than 1000 m^3/capita/year. This scarcity relates to water for food production, however, and not to water for domestic purposes that are minute at this scale. In most of the rest of the world, water scarcity at a national scale has as much to do with the development of the demand as the availability of the supply. Accounting for water for environmental requirements shows that abstraction of water for domestic, food and industrial uses already has a major impact on ecosystems in many parts of the world, even those not considered 'water scarce'.

■   The main features of academic texts are listed in the following table. Find examples of each in the preceding texts.

Feature	Examples
1 Formal or semi-formal vocabulary	
2 Sources are given	
3 Objective, impersonal style	

2 Types of text

■ The following table lists the most common types of written sources used by students. Work with a partner to consider their likely advantages and disadvantages.

Text type	Advantages	Disadvantages
Textbook	*Written especially for students*	*May be too general or outdated*
Website		
Journal article		
Official report (e.g. from government)		
Newspaper or magazine article		
E-book		
Edited book		

3 Using reading lists

Your teacher may give you a printed reading list, or it may be available online through the library website. The list will usually include books, journal articles and websites. If the list is electronic, there will be links to the library catalogue to let you check on the availability of the material. If the list is printed, you will have to use the library catalogue to find the texts.

You do not have to read every word of a book because it is on the list. Your teacher will probably suggest which parts to read. On reading lists you will find the following formats:

Books   Griffin, R.C. *Water Resource Economics: The Analysis of Scarcity, Policies, and Projects/2nd ed.* MIT Press, 2016

Journal articles   Falkenmark, M., Lundqvist, J. and Widstrand, C. (1989), Macro-scale water scarcity requires micro-scale approaches. *Natural Resources Forum*, 13: 258–267.

Websites   www.un.org/waterforlifedecade/scarcity.shtml

4 Using library catalogues

University and college libraries usually have online catalogues. These allow students to search for the materials they want in various ways. If you know the title and author's name it is easy to check if the book is available, but if you are making a search for material on a specific topic you may have to vary the search terms. For instance, if you have been given this essay title:

> *Is there a practical limit on the height of tall buildings? Illustrate your answer with reference to some recent skyscrapers.*

you might try:

Skyscraper design

Skyscraper construction

Design of tall buildings

Construction of tall buildings

If you use a very specific phrase you will probably only find a few titles. 'Skyscraper construction', for example, only produced three items in one library catalogue, but a more general term such as 'skyscrapers' found 57.

■ **You have entered the term 'skyscrapers' in the library catalogue, and the following are the first ten results. In order to answer the essay title, which would you select to study? Give your reasons.**

Full details	Title	Year	Location	Holdings
1	Building the skyline [electronic resource]: the birth and growth of Manhattan's skyscrapers/Jason M. Barr.	2016	e-Book link to resource	
2	Impossible heights – skyscrapers, flight and the master builder/Adnan Morshed.	2015	Science library	Availability
3	Best tall buildings: a global overview of 2015 skyscrapers edited by Antony Wood and Steven Henry.	2015	Main library	Availability
4	Skyscrapers: a history of the world's most extraordinary buildings/Judith Dupré; introductory interview with Adrian Smith.	2013	Main library	Availability

5	Manhattan skyscrapers/Eric P. Nash; photographs by Norman McGrath. 3rd ed.	2010	Main library	Availability
6	Art deco San Francisco [electronic resource]: the architecture of Timothy Pflueger/Therese Poletti; photography by Tom Paiva.	2008	e-Book link to resource	
7	Skyscraper for the XXI century/edited by Carlo Aiello.	2008	Science library	Availability
8	Tall buildings: image of the skyscraper/Scott Johnson.	2008	Fine Arts library	Availability
9	Skyscrapers: fabulous buildings that reach for the sky/Herbert Wright.	2008	Main library	Availability
10	Skyscrapers: a social history of the very tall building in America/George H. Douglas.	2004	Main library	Availability

Full details

If you click here you will get more information about the book, including the number of pages and a summary of the contents. If a book has had more than one edition, it suggests that it is a successful title. This may help you decide whether to borrow it.

Year

The books are listed by year of publication, with the most recent first; always try to use the most up-to-date sources.

Location

Many large universities have more than one library. This tells you which one the book is kept in.

Holdings

If you click on availability it will tell you how many copies the library holds and if they are available to borrow or out on loan.

5 Using library websites to search electronic resources

Journals are specialised academic publications produced on a regular basis containing recent research. You need to be familiar with the main journals in your subject area. They are usually available in paper or electronic formats (e-journals), although nowadays some journals are only available online.

E-journals and other electronic resources such as subject databases are becoming increasingly important. Their advantage is that they can be accessed by the internet, saving the need to visit the library to find a book. Most library websites have a separate portal or gateway for searching electronic resources.

These are the results found in one database for journal articles on 'skyscrapers':

1   Skyscrapers
     Cesar Pelli
     Perspecta, Vol. 18, (1982), pp. 134–151

2   Skyscrapers
     Robert Phillips
     The Hudson Review, Vol. 60, No. 2 (Summer, 2007), p. 276

3   Three New Skyscrapers
     MoMA, No. 25 (Winter, 1983), p. 4

4   Stars for Skyscrapers
     Lee Richard Hayman
     The Phylon Quarterly, Vol. 19, No. 3 (3rd Qtr., 1958), p. 276

5   Dawn Rises over Skyscrapers
     Deane Fisher
     Phylon (1960-), Vol. 28, No. 2 (2nd Qtr., 1967), p. 138

6   Mario Palanti and the Palacio Salvo: The Art of Constructing Skyscrapers
     Virginia Bonicatto, Chris Miller
     Getty Research Journal, No. 5 (2013), pp. 183–188

Note that many of these articles will be out of date or irrelevant, but these search engines allow you to access a great variety of material quickly. It is usually sufficient to read the abstract to find out if the article will be relevant to your work. Note that most journal websites contain a search engine to allow you to search all back issues by subject.

The best way to become familiar with these methods is to practise. Library websites usually contain tutorials for new students, and librarians are always willing to give help and advice when needed.

■ **Select a specific topic from your subject area.**

a)   *Use the library catalogue to search for relevant books. Write down the most useful titles.*

b)   *Look for a few relevant journal articles using the library portal.*

Reading
Developing Critical Approaches

Students are expected to take a critical approach to sources, which means to challenge what they read rather than accepting it as reliable. Clearly this approach requires a good understanding of written texts. This unit:

- explains effective reading methods
- examines common text features, including abstracts
- explores and practises critical analysis of texts

1 Reading methods

Reading academic texts in the quantity required for most courses is a demanding task, especially for international students. Yet students will not benefit from attending lectures and seminars unless the preparatory reading is done promptly, while most writing tasks require extensive reading.

Moreover, academic texts often contain new vocabulary and phrases, and may be written in a rather formal style. This means that special methods have to be learnt to cope with the volume of reading required, which is especially important when you are reading in another language.

Clearly, you do not have time to read every word published on the topic you are studying, so you must adopt a two-stage process of selection:

- carefully choose what you read
- assess the chosen material thoroughly and critically

The following chart illustrates the best approach to choosing suitable texts.

■ **Complete the empty boxes in the chart with the following techniques:**

- Read intensively to make notes on key points
- Scan text for information you need (e.g. names)
- Survey text features (e.g. abstract, contents, index)

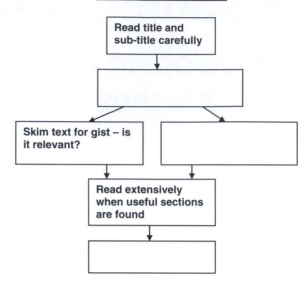

Choosing suitable texts

- Read title and sub-title carefully
- Skim text for gist – is it relevant?
- Read extensively when useful sections are found

■ **Can you suggest any other reading skills?**

- _____

- _____

2 Titles, subtitles and text features

Many books and articles have both a title and a subtitle, often divided by a colon:

> *The Right to Have Rights: Citizenship Practice and the Political Constitution of the EU*

The title is usually shorter and may aim to be eye-catching; the subtitle often gives more information about the specific focus. After finding a text relevant to your studies, it is worth checking the following text features before starting to read:

Author
Is the writer well known in his/her field? What else has she/he published?

Publication date and edition
How old is the book? Do not use a first edition if there is a (revised) second or later edition available.

Abstract
See Section 3 on page 19.

Contents
A list of the main chapters or sections. This should tell you how much space is given to the topic you are researching.

Introduction or preface
This is where the author often explains his/her reasons for writing and also describes how the text is organised.

References
This list shows all the sources used by the author and cited in the text. It should give you some suggestions for further reading.

Bibliography
These are the sources the author has used but not necessarily specifically cited. A bibliography is not required for short writing tasks.

Index
This is an alphabetical list of all the topics and names mentioned in a book. If, for example, you are looking for information about a person, the index will tell you whether that person is mentioned, and how often.

3 Reading abstracts

Abstracts are normally found in journal articles, where they are a kind of summary to allow researchers to decide if it is worth reading the full article. As a student you will not normally have to write abstracts, but it is important to be able to read them effectively.

■   Study this example:

Citizenship Norms and the Expansion of Political Participation

Russell J. Dalton

A growing chorus of scholars laments the decline of political participation in America, and the negative implications of this trend for American democracy. This article questions this position – arguing that previous studies misdiagnosed the sources of political change and the consequences of changing norms of citizenship for Americans' political engagement. Citizenship norms are shifting from a pattern of duty-based citizenship to engaged citizenship. Using data from the 2005 'Citizenship, Involvement, Democracy' survey of the Center for Democracy and Civil Society (CDACS) I describe these two faces of citizenship, and trace their impact on political participation. Rather than the erosion of participation, this norm shift is altering and expanding the patterns of political participation in America.

(Source: Dalton, R.J. (2008) *Political Studies* 56 (1) pp. 76–98)

Abstracts normally have a standard structure:

a) Background position

b) Aim and thesis of the paper

c) Method of research

d) Results of research

■   Underline and label (a-d) these components in the abstract for 'Citizenship Norms and the Expansion of Political Participation'.

4 Fact and opinion

When reading, it is important to distinguish between facts:

> *Kuala Lumpur is the capital of Malaysia.*

and opinions:

> *Kuala Lumpur is a welcoming, bustling city.*

In addition, the reader needs to decide if the facts given are true:

> *Singapore lies near the equator.*   (true)

> *Singapore was an ancient trading port.*   (false)

You need to be careful of texts that contain unsupported opinion or 'facts' that you think are wrong.

a) ■   Read the following and underline what is presented as a fact (_____) or opinion (_ _ _ _). Then decide if the 'facts' are true.

a) Sydney is the capital of Australia.

b) Australia is a dynamic, prosperous and enterprising country.

c) The majority of Australians live on sheep farms.

d) Most Australians are open-minded and friendly.

e) Australia is the largest island in the world and has extensive mineral deposits.

f) Among the 22 million Australians are some of the world's best cricket players.

b) ■   Read the paragraph on New Zealand and underline facts and opinions in the same manner as the preceding section. Then rewrite the paragraph in an objective style, correcting the 'facts' where needed.

New Zealand is a proud island nation in the southern Pacific Ocean consisting of three main islands. Nearly 1,000 miles west of Australia, it was one of the last places on Earth to be settled by man: Polynesians who arrived in about 1250 CE and who developed the fascinating Maori culture. In the eighteenth century, European settlers started to land, and in 1841 New Zealand became part of the British Empire. Due to its long period of isolation, many distinctive plants and animals evolved, such as the kiwi fruit, now the nation's symbol. Sadly, the country suffers from frequent earthquakes, such as the one that hit Christchurch in 2011, causing serious damage and loss of life.

5 Assessing internet sources critically

Internet sources are plentiful and convenient, but you cannot afford to waste time on texts which are unreliable or out of date. If you are using material that is not on the reading list, you must assess it critically to ensure that the material is trustworthy by asking several questions about each site:

- Is this a reputable website, for example with .ac. (= academic) in the URL?
- Is the name of the author given, and is she well known in the field?
- Is the language of the text in a suitable academic style?
- Are there any obvious errors in the text (e.g. spelling mistakes, which suggest a careless approach)?

■ **Using these questions, compare the following two internet texts on deforestation (the loss of forests). Which is likely to be more reliable?**

1

We are destroying the last of our vital natural resources, just as we are starting to wake up to how precious they are. Rainforest once covered 14% of the land now it's down to a mere 6%. Scientists predict that the rest could disappear in less than 40 years. Thousands of acres are cut down each second with dire consequences for the countries involved and the planet as a whole. Scientists estimate that we loose 50,000 species every year, many species every second including 137 plant types (not even species but whole groups of plant species) and as these plants disappear before science can record them so does the chance to gain helpful knowledge and possible medicines.

2

The deforestation of trees not only lessens the amount of carbon stored, it also releases carbon dioxide into the air. This is because when trees die, they release the stored carbon. According to the 2010 Global Forest Resources Assessment, deforestation releases nearly a billion tons of carbon into the atmosphere per year, though the numbers are not as high as the ones recorded in the previous decade. Deforestation is the second largest anthropogenic (human-caused) source of carbon dioxide to the atmosphere, ranging between six percent and 17 percent.

There are several aspects of 1) which should make the reader cautious: the style is very personal (We are. . .) and informal (it's down to. . .) and there is a word used wrongly ('loose' instead of 'lose'). No sources are provided. But even more disturbing is carelessness with facts. Is it really possible that thousands of acres of rainforest are being cut down *every second*? The writer also claims that many species are being lost *every second*, but if we take the figure of 50,000 per year it means one species is lost every 10 minutes. Clearly the writer is seeking to dramatise the subject, but it is quite unsuitable as an academic source.

In contrast, the second text is written in accurate, semi-formal language and mentions a source. It seems likely to be more reliable.

6 Practice

■ You are writing an essay on expanding educational provision in developing countries, titled 'Improving literacy in sub-Saharan Africa'. You find the following article on a website. Read it critically and decide whether you could use it in your work.

EDUCATING THE POOREST

How can we get the world's poorest children into school? This is a difficult question with no easy answer. In 1999 the UN adopted a set of goals called 'Education for All', but in many countries there has been little progress towards these aims. In Nigeria, for instance, the number of children not going to school has hardly changed since then. It is estimated that worldwide about 72 million children never attend school, 45% of whom are in sub-Saharan Africa. Even when schools and teachers are provided, there's no guarantee that teaching is being done: World Bank research in India shows that a quarter of teachers don't attend school on any one day.

Several proposals have been made to improve matters. A British academic, Pro-fessor Tooley, argues that low-cost private schools are more effective in delivering education to the poor since parental pressure, owing to the payment of fees, helps to maintain good standards. State schools could also relate pay to performance: research by Muralihadan and Sundararaman (2011) in India found that this improved students' test performance far more significantly than spending the same money on teaching materials.

One constant difficulty for educationalists is the problem of comparing pupil per-formance between countries. Devising reliable and objective methods of assessment is challenging even in rich countries; far more so across the global spectrum. In many places accurate data on the numbers of school-age children is unavailable or unreliable, let alone accurate measures of literacy or numeracy.

(Source: www.educationworld.com)

Positive aspects: _____

Negative aspects: _____

7 Critical thinking

Even when you feel that a text is reliable and that you can safely use it as a source, it is still important to adopt a critical attitude towards it. This approach is perhaps easiest to learn when reading, but is important for all other academic work (i.e. listening, discussing and writing). Critical thinking means not just passively accepting what you hear or read but instead actively questioning and assessing it. As you read you should ask yourself the following questions:

a) What are the key ideas in this?

b) Does the argument of the writer develop logically, step by step?

c) Are the examples given helpful? Would other examples be better?

d) Does the author have any bias (leaning to one side or the other)?

e) Does the evidence presented seem reliable, in my experience and using common sense?

f) Do I agree with the writer's views?

■ **Read critically the following two articles on universities, using the preceding questions.**

A COLLEGE CONCERNS

Despite their dominance of global league tables (e.g. Shanghai Rankings Consultancy) American universities currently face significant criticism. The American Enterprise Institute (AEI) and the Goldwater Institute have recently published negative reports on US universities, while a highly critical book *Higher Education?* (Hacker and Dreifus) was published in 2010. The critics focus on the rising costs of American higher education, which have increased at a much faster rate than inflation, resulting in a situation where even middle-class families are finding the expense unsupportable.

In the past, many American students paid for their education by working part-time while studying, but now the higher fees mean that students finish their education with significant levels of debt. This debt can be a serious burden at the start of their working lives, when they may be hoping to get married or buy a property.

Another target of criticism is the focus on research at the expense of teaching. Students rarely meet the 'star' professors, being taught instead by badly-paid graduate students, who work on short-term contracts. It is claimed that in one year nearly half of Harvard's history professors were on sabbatical leave. As a consequence, students work less; according to the AEI they currently study for 14 hours per week, whereas 50 years ago the figure was 24 hours per week. Despite this the proportion of students gaining a first or 2.1 degree has increased significantly: a situation described by the critics as 'grade inflation'. It seems incredible that working less should really be rewarded by better grades.

(Source: *Atlantic Digest*, July 2014, p. 119)

B A BRIGHTER TOMORROW?

There is little doubt that a university degree is the key to a better future for any student. Despite the costs involved in terms of fees, it has been calculated that the average UK university graduate will earn £400,000 ($600,000) more over his or her lifetime compared to a non-graduate. Possession of a degree will also assist a graduate to find a satisfying job more quickly and give greater prospects for promotion inside the chosen career. A degree from a British university is recognised all over the world as proof of a high quality education.

A university course will not only provide students with up-to-date knowledge in their subject area, but also provide practice with the essential skills required by many employers today, such as the ability to communicate effectively using ICT, or the skills of team working and problem solving. In addition, living away from home in an international atmosphere gives the opportunity to make new friends from all over the world and build networks of contacts that may be invaluable in a future career.

Studying at university is a unique opportunity for many young people to develop individually by acquiring independence, free from parental control. They will learn to look after themselves in a secure environment, and gain useful life skills such as cooking and budgeting. Most graduates look back at their degree courses as a valuable experience at a critical period of their lives.

(Source: *Borchester University Prospectus*, 2015, p. 5)

■ List any statements from the articles that you find unreliable and add comments to explain your doubts in the next table. Then decide which article you find more reliable overall.

Statements	Comments
A	
B	

▶ See Unit 2.1 Argument and Discussion

UNIT
1.4

Avoiding Plagiarism

Plagiarism is a concern for both teachers and students, but it can be avoided by clearly understanding the issues involved. In the English-speaking academic world it is essential to use a wide range of sources for your writing and to acknowledge these sources correctly – otherwise there is a risk of plagiarism.

This unit introduces the techniques students need to do this. Further practice is provided in Units 1.7 Summarising and Paraphrasing and 1.8 References and Quotations.

1 What is plagiarism?

Basically plagiarism means taking ideas or words from a source (e.g. a book or journal article) without giving credit (acknowledgement) to the author. It is seen as a kind of theft and is considered to be an academic crime. In academic work, ideas and words are seen as private property belonging to the person who first thought or wrote them. Therefore it is important for all students, including international ones, to understand the meaning of plagiarism and learn how to prevent it in their work.

   This situation may appear confusing, since students are expected:

a) **to show that they have read the relevant sources on a subject (by giving citations)**

   BUT

b) **to explain these ideas in their own words and come to their own conclusions.**

However, mastering this requirement is vital to achieve success in the academic community. Reasons why students must avoid plagiarism include:

- copying the work of others will not help them develop their own understanding
- plagiarism is easily detected by teachers and computer software
- plagiarism may lead to failing a course or even having to leave college

2 Acknowledging sources

If you borrow from, or refer to, the work of another person, you must show that you have done this by providing the correct acknowledgement.

■ **Read this paragraph from a book called *Power and the State* by Martin Smith (2009):**

> The point is not that the state is in retreat but that it is developing new forms of power which change the way it operates, how it affects citizens, and how it delivers policy. The foundations of the modern state are still in place but states are operating in new and diverse ways which create complex relationships with civil society.

There are two ways to use this idea in your work and acknowledge the source:

1   Summary and citation

Smith (2009) claims that the modern state wields power in new ways.

2   Quotation and citation

According to Smith: 'The point is not that the state is in retreat but that it is developing new forms of power. . .' (Smith, 2009:103).

These in-text **citations** are linked to a list of **references** at the end of the main text which includes the following details:

Author	Date	Title	Place of publication	Publisher
Smith, M.	(2009)	*Power and the State*	Basingstoke:	Palgrave Macmillan

The citation makes it clear to readers that you have read Smith and borrowed this idea from him. This reference gives readers the necessary information to find the source if they want to study the original.

▶   **See Unit 1.8 References and Quotations**

3 Degrees of plagiarism

Although plagiarism essentially means copying somebody else's work, in some situations it can be difficult to decide if plagiarism is involved.

■ **Working with a partner, consider the following academic situations and decide if they are plagiarism or not.**

	Situation	Plagiarism?
1	Copying a paragraph but changing a few words, not giving a citation.	Yes
2	Cutting and pasting a short article from a website, with no citation.	Yes
3	Taking two paragraphs from a classmate's essay, without citation.	Yes
4	Taking a graph from a textbook, giving the source.	No
5	Taking a quotation from a source, giving a citation but not using quotation marks.	Yes.
6	Using something that you think of as general knowledge (e.g. Earth's climate is getting warmer).	No
7	Using a paragraph from an essay you wrote and had marked the previous semester, without citation.	1. Yes
8	Using the results of your own unpublished research (e.g. from a survey you did) without citation.	1. No
9	Discussing an essay topic with a group of classmates and using some of their ideas in your own work.	No
10	Giving a citation for some information but misspelling the author's name.	Yes

This exercise shows that plagiarism can be accidental. For example, situation (10) in the chart, when the author's name is misspelt, is technically plagiarism but really carelessness. In situation (9) your teacher may have told you to discuss the topic in groups and then write an essay on your own, in which case it would not be plagiarism. Self-plagiarism is also possible, as in situation (7). It can be difficult to decide what is general or common knowledge (situation 6), but you can always try asking colleagues.

However, it is not a good excuse to say that you didn't know the rules of plagiarism or that you didn't have time to write in your own words. Nor is it adequate to say that the rules are different in your own country. In general, anything that is not common knowledge or your own ideas and research (published or not) must be cited and referenced.

4 Avoiding plagiarism by summarising and paraphrasing

Quotations should not be overused, so you must learn to paraphrase and summarise in order to include other writers' ideas in your work. This will demonstrate your understanding of a text to your teachers.

- Paraphrasing involves rewriting a text so that the language is significantly different while the content stays the same.
- Summarising means reducing the length of a text but retaining the main points.

▶ **See Unit 1.7 Summarising and Paraphrasing**

Normally both skills are used at the same time, as can be seen in the examples (a-e) below.

■ **Read the following text and then compare the five paragraphs which use ideas and information from it. Decide which are plagiarised and which are acceptable, and give your reasons in the table on page 30.**

RAILWAY MANIA?

In 1830 there were a few dozen miles of railways in all the world – chiefly consisting of the line from Liverpool to Manchester. By 1840 there were over 4,500 miles, by 1850 over 23,500. Most of them were projected in a few bursts of speculative frenzy known as the 'railway manias' of 1835–7 and especially in 1844–7; most of them were built in large part with British capital, British iron, machines and know-how. These investment booms appear irrational, because in fact few railways were much more profitable to the investor than other forms of enterprise, most yielded quite modest profits and many none at all: in 1855 the average interest on capital sunk in the British railways was a mere 3.7 per cent.

(Source: Hobsbawm, E. (1995) *The Age of Revolution*, p. 45)

---

a) Between 1830 and 1850 there was very rapid development in railway construction worldwide. Two periods of especially feverish growth were 1835–7 and 1844–7. It is hard to understand the reason for this intense activity, since railways were not particularly profitable investments and some produced no return at all (Hobsbawm, 1995:45).

b) There were only a few dozen miles of railways in 1830, including the Liverpool to Manchester line. But by 1840 there were over 4,500 miles and over 23,500 by 1850. Most of them were built in large part with British capital, British iron, machines and know-how, and most of them were projected in a few bursts of speculative frenzy known as the 'railway manias' of 1835–7 and especially in 1844–7. Because most yielded quite modest profits and many none at all these investment booms appear irrational. In fact, few railways were much more profitable to the investor than other forms of enterprise (Hobsbawm, 1995:45).

c) As Hobsbawm (1995) argues, nineteenth-century railway mania was partly irrational: 'because in fact few railways were much more profitable to the investor than other forms of enterprise, most yielded quite modest profits and many none at all: in 1855 the average interest on capital sunk in the British railways was a mere 3.7 per cent'. (Hobsbawm, 1995:45).

d) Globally, railway networks increased dramatically from 1830 to 1850; the majority in short periods of 'mania' (1835–7 and 1844–7). British technology and capital were responsible for much of this growth, yet the returns on the investment were hardly any better than comparable business opportunities (Hobsbawm, 1895:45).

e) The dramatic growth of railways between 1830 and 1850 was largely achieved using British technology. However, it has been claimed that much of this development was irrational because few railways were much more profitable to the investor than other forms of enterprise; most yielded quite modest profits and many none at all.

	Plagiarised or acceptable?	Reason
a		
b		
c		
d		
e		

5 Avoiding plagiarism by developing good study habits

Few students deliberately try to cheat by plagiarising, but some develop poor study habits which result in the risk of plagiarism.

■ **Working with a partner, add to the list of positive habits.**

* Plan your work carefully so you don't have to write the essay at the last minute.
* Take care to make notes in your own words, not copying from the source.
* Keep a full record of all the sources you use (e.g. author, date, title, page numbers, place of publication, publisher).
* _____
* _____

6 Practice

■ **Read the text on the link between Olympic success and national prosperity. Then add a citation to the summary and quotation which follow.**

Wealth is an important advantage in pursuing Olympic medals. Clearly, a large population also has benefits, since this is more likely to include people with sporting abilities. But countries must be able mobilise their human resources: in the London Olympics in 2012 India, with its huge population, only won six medals, while New Zealand (with only 4 million) won 13. When many people are affected by poverty and illness it is not easy to be ordinarily healthy, let alone be an Olympic athlete. In fact richer countries have both healthier populations and can also spend more on encouraging sport. China won only 58 medals in 2000, when its GDP per person was under $4,000. But at the 2012 London Olympics, when its GDP figure had risen to $16,000, China won a total of 88. Governments are also finding that there are benefits in focusing efforts on a limited number of sports in which there is less competition: this was the tactic that led to British success in the cycling events in 2016.

(Source: Kaufman, S. (2017) *Gold, Silver, Bronze*, p. 3)

(Summary)

Kaufman argues that wealth (expressed as GDP per head) rather than size of population is the key to national success in the Olympics.

(Quotation)

Large populations alone do not guarantee good national results at the Olympics. Countries must also be wealthy enough to have healthy citizens and be able to provide resources for training. As Kaufman points out: 'When many people are affected by poverty and illness it is not easy to be ordinarily healthy, let alone be an Olympic athlete'.

7 Further practice

■ Revise this unit by matching the words on the left with the definitions on the right.

a **Source**	To gain advantage dishonestly
b Citation	**The origin of ideas or information**
c To summarise	To reduce the length of a text while keeping the main points
d Quotation	Short in-text note giving the author's name and publication date
e Reference	Using different words or word order to restate a text
f To cheat	Using the exact words of the original text in your work
g Paraphrase	Full publication details of a text or other source

8 Research

Look on your college or university website to find out the policy on plagiarism. It may raise some issues that you want to discuss with colleagues or your teachers.

If you can't find anything for your particular institution, try one of these sites:

http://owl.english.purdue.edu/owl/resource/589/01/

www.uefap.com/writing/plagiar/plagfram.htm

From Understanding Essay Titles to Planning

In both exams and coursework it is essential for students to understand what an essay title is asking them to do. When the focus of the task is clear, a plan can then be prepared which should make sure the question is answered fully. This unit looks at:

- key words in titles
- essay length and organisation
- alternative methods of essay planning

1 The planning process

Teachers frequently complain that students do not understand what they are asked to do, but this can be avoided by more care at the start of the process. Planning is necessary with all academic writing, but clearly there are important differences between planning in exams, when time is short, and for coursework, when preparatory reading is required. However, in both cases the process of planning should include these three steps:

a) analyse the title wording

b) decide how much space to give to each part of the answer

c) prepare an outline using your favoured method

When writing coursework, your outline will probably be revised as you read around the topic and develop your ideas.

▶ **See Unit 5.3 Longer Essays**

2 Analysing essay titles

Titles contain instruction words which tell the student what to do. Note that titles often contain two (or more) questions:

What is meant by a demand curve and why would we expect it to slope downwards?

In this case 'what' is asking for a description and 'why' for a reason or explanation.

■   Match the instruction words on the left to the definitions on the right.

Analyse	Give examples
Assess/Evaluate	Deal with a complex subject by reducing it to the main elements
Describe	**Divide into sections and discuss each critically**
Discuss	Break down into the various parts and their relationships
Examine/Explore	Make a proposal and support it
Illustrate	Look at various aspects of a topic, compare benefits and drawbacks
Outline/Trace	Give a detailed account of something
Suggest/Indicate	**Explain a topic briefly and clearly**
Summarise	Decide the value or worth of a subject

Many essay titles also include a context, such as a time period or geographical area:

Instruction	Subject	Context
Discuss	*the growth of nationalism*	*in nineteenth-century Western Europe*
Compare	*the effects of privatisation on the economies*	*of Poland and Hungary 1990–2000*

Clearly, it is important to limit your answer to the given context. You will lose marks if you ignore this limitation.

3 Practice

■   Underline the instruction words in the following titles and consider what they are asking you to do. Then decide if any context is given.

a)   Summarise the main reasons for the growth of e-commerce since 2010 and discuss the likely results of this.

b)   Describe some of the reasons why patients do not always take their medication as directed.

c)   What are the benefits of learning a second language at primary school (age 6–10)? Are there any drawbacks to early language learning?

d)   What are the most significant sources of renewable energy? Evaluate their contribution to the reduction of carbon emissions in the last 15 years.

e)   Discuss the response of buildings and soil to earthquakes, indicating what measures can be used to ensure structural stability.

4 Brainstorming

When time is limited (e.g. in an exam) it may be helpful to start thinking about a topic by writing down the ideas you have, in any order. Taking title 3d) in the preceding section, you might collect the following points:

Sources of renewable energy

- Wind
- Solar
- Thermal
- Wave/tidal
- Biomass

Contribution to reducing CO_2 emissions

- Solar significant in sunny areas but not at night
- Wind power available day and night
- Wave and tidal power still in development

■ **Working with a partner, brainstorm ideas for the title 3c). Remember to deal with both parts of the question.**

What are the benefits of learning a second language at primary school (age 6-10)? Are there any drawbacks to early language learning?

5 Essay length

Coursework essays usually have a specified length, normally between 1,000 and 5,000 words. You must keep to this limit, although 5% more or less is generally acceptable. However, at the planning stage you need to consider what proportion of the essay to give to each part of the question.

As a basic guide, 20% is usually sufficient for the introduction and conclusion together (references are not usually included in the word count). Therefore, in a 2,000-word essay the introduction and conclusion would have about 400 words and the main body approximately 1,600 words.

If this was the length given for title 3c) on page 35, you might decide on the following approximate allocation:

Introduction	250 words
Benefits – young children less inhibited, more open-minded	400 words
– young appear to have better memories	300 words
– may improve understanding of their first language	200 words
Drawbacks – may not understand the grammar involved	400 words
– may not understand the cultural context	300 words
Conclusion	150 words
Total	**2,000 words**

This calculation is useful since it can guide the amount of reading you need to do, as well as provide the basis for an outline. Moreover, it prevents you from writing an unbalanced answer in which part of the question is not fully dealt with.

Essays in exams do not have a word limit, but it is equally important to plan them in similar terms (e.g. Part 1: 40%, Part 2: 60%).

■ **Underline the instruction words and the context in the following titles and decide what percentage of the main body to give to each part of the answer.**

Title	Part 1 (%)	Part 2 (%)
a) Describe the typical social, cultural and environmental impacts experienced by tourist destinations in developing countries. How can harmful impacts be reduced or avoided?		
b) How can schools make better use of IT (information technology)? Illustrate your answer with examples from one country.		

c) Outline the main difficulties in combating malaria in Southeast Asia. Suggest possible strategies for more effective anti-malaria campaigns.		
d) What is 'donor fatigue' in international aid, and how can it be overcome?		

6 Writing outlines

An outline should help the writer to answer the question as effectively as possible. Care at this stage will save wasted effort later. The more detail you include in your outline, the easier the writing process will be. With coursework, the outline will normally be written when you start reading about the subject, and it may be modified as you read more.

Note that for coursework it is usually better to write the main body first, then the introduction, and finally the conclusion. Therefore you may prefer to outline just the main body at this stage.

There is no fixed pattern for an outline; different methods appeal to different students. For example, with the first part of title 3d) on p. 35:

What are the most significant sources of renewable energy?

a)   The outline might be a list:

Significant sources

- Wind – best sites often remote
- Solar – costs have reduced sharply
- Thermal – limited application
- Wave/tidal – still unproven
- Biomass – uses scarce land

b)   An alternative is a mind map:

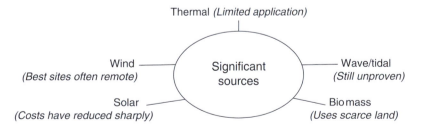

■   **Discuss the advantages and drawbacks of each method with a partner.**

7 Practice

■ You have to answer title 3a) 'Summarise the main reasons for the growth of e-commerce since 2010 and discuss the likely results of this'. In preparation, read the following text.

BRITISH SHOPPERS GO ONLINE

People in Britain do more of their shopping (currently 16%) through the internet than in most other countries. This figure, which is increasing rapidly, is having significant effects on many industries. Britain's geography makes it ideal for the spread of e-commerce, due to it being a small and densely populated country, so that most households can be easily reached from giant warehouses in the Midlands. The popularity and convenience of smartphones is also encouraging internet shopping.

The result is that retailers have had to focus on logistics to compete for trade. The efficient management of parcels is the key to success: over a billion packages were sent out in 2016. One effect has been a revival in the fortunes of the Royal Mail, which had been suffering from a decline in its letter business. Most internet orders are sent from huge 'fulfilment centres' in central England; these structures now cover 40 million square metres. However, intense competition on delivery times has recently led to a trend to build warehouses on the edge of cities, especially London, to be near customers. As a result, the cost of rents for these has risen sharply, since this land is also in demand for housing.

Another concern for internet retailers is the legal obligation to accept returned goods within two weeks of sale. This amounts to about 6% of sales overall, but as much as 40% with items of clothing. This increases costs for the seller, but has also created a new niche business in dealing with these goods. The volume of parcel deliveries, coupled with the food delivery services run by the major supermarkets, has led to more traffic on the roads. In addition, there is a shortage of drivers for the trucks and vans involved, since this work is demanding and low-paid. One solution may be to use driverless vehicles, and trials of these could begin in 2017.

At the moment about 3 million people work in UK shops, but the increase in e-commerce and the inevitable closure of many shops may lead to the loss of about a third of these jobs within the next ten years. Some of the closed stores may re-open as cafés, bars or restaurants, other may develop into 'shopping experiences' which give customers a taste of the product instead of just selling it. In any case it is likely that Britain's high streets will drastically change their character in the years to come.

(Source: Kuyper, J. (2017) *Tomorrow's Cities*, p. 232)

■ **Prepare an outline to answer the question as fully as possible, using either method.**

Finding Key Points and Note-making

After finding a suitable source, identifying relevant sections of text and preparing an outline, the next step in the writing process is to select the key points that relate to your topic and make notes on them. This unit explains and practises these stages, which also involve skills further developed in Unit 1.7 Summarising and Paraphrasing.

1 Finding key points

Before making notes you need to find the main ideas in a text.

■ **Read the following article about the growth of treasure hunting in Britain and underline two key points. Then choose a title for the article.**

Title:_____

Many people dream of finding buried treasure such as gold or silver in the ground, and in Britain thousands of people are doing that every year. Treasure hunting has become a popular hobby, with most hunters using electric metal detectors. The best areas to find treasure are England's eastern counties, such as Lincolnshire and Norfolk, which were the most densely-populated regions in the Middle Ages: over 60% of finds are dated to pre-1500 CE. These counties are also still mainly agricultural; as a result the soil is regularly disturbed by farming.

In 1996 the law on finding treasure was clarified by the Treasure Act, which imposed severe penalties for not reporting new finds to the local coroner. This has been helpful to professional archaeologists, who can build up a better picture of historical settlement using new discoveries. It also allows most finders to keep the objects found, if museums are not interested in buying them. However, the hunters known as 'nighthawks', who operate without permission on private land, are now liable to heavy fines. Despite this, the majority of 'detectorists' are keen historians who enjoy the excitement of the search.

(Source: *History Now*, August 2012, p. 61)

Note that the key points are often (but not always) found in the first part of a paragraph. They tend to be followed by examples or further information.

2 Finding relevant points

When preparing to write an essay, you have to search for information and ideas relevant to your subject. Therefore, the key points that you select must relate to that topic.

You are given an essay title: 'What are the most effective methods of reducing global warming?'

■ **Read the following article and underline five key points that relate to your essay subject (the first one has been done).**

A NATURAL REMEDY FOR GLOBAL WARMING?

The Earth seems to be getting greener: photographs of the planet taken from satellites show that over the last thirty years an area of 18 million square kilometres has become covered in new vegetation. This growth is largely in regions, mainly above the Arctic Circle, that were previously too cold for plant life, but which, as a consequence of global warming, are now able to support it. Recent research by scientists from the Lawrence Berkeley National Laboratory in the US suggests that this additional plant growth may be reducing the effects of global warming.

It is known that currently over 35 billion tonnes of carbon dioxide are added annually to the atmosphere, and this quantity increased steeply in the second half of the twentieth century, from only six billion tonnes in the 1950s. As a result, the concentration of CO_2 in the air has risen to over 400 parts per million (ppm), compared with about 300 ppm 60 years ago. But since the start of the twenty-first century this level has hardly changed, making scientists believe that some process is extracting the extra CO_2 from the air.

Photosynthesis converts carbon dioxide into plant matter, aided by water and sun-light. If there is more carbon dioxide in the air the process of photosynthesis acceler-ates, causing plants to grow faster and larger. This appears to be a likely reason for the CO_2 concentration levelling off and might be seen as a check on global warming, as previously barren sub-polar regions become home to grasses and trees. Although this could be regarded as a possible solution to the problem of global warming, the effects are likely to be temporary, since plant growth is also dependent on water, and as rainfall patterns change, droughts and floods are likely to become more severe.

Other researchers claim that further consequences of human activity, such as the loss of tropical forests, will counter the beneficial effects of extra plant growth in polar areas by releasing the CO_2 stored in the rainforests. They argue that the only certain way to prevent an acceleration of warming is to reduce human use of fossil fuels, which are the source of much of the unwanted carbon dioxide.

(Source: Suarez, M. (2016) *Earth Matters* (3) p. 176)

3 Practice A

■ Complete the notes for 'A natural remedy for global warming?' using the key points underlined in section 2) above. Add a suitable title.

Title:_____

1) New research : extra plant growth ⟶ slowing global warming

2)

3)

4)

5)

(Source: Suarez, M. (2016) *Earth Matters* 3:176)

4 Why make notes?

It is important to learn to make notes in English as a preparation for various academic tasks. Effective note-making requires concentration but will save time and increase accuracy in the long run.

■ What are the main reasons for note-making in academic work? Discuss with a partner and add to the following list.

a) *To prepare for essay writing*

b) _____

c) _____

d) _____

e) _____

5 Note-making methods

■ You are looking for information on the everyday effects of technological change. Study the text in this section (key points underlined) and the notes in the box. What do you notice about the language of the notes?

• _____
• _____
• _____
• _____

A CASHLESS CONTINENT?

There are significant differences between payment methods among European countries. In Scandinavia many shops and cafés no longer accept cash: all payments are made with credit or debit cards. By contrast, in Italy and other southern states the majority of transactions are still made in cash. The reasons for the variations are both historic and cultural.

Sweden is the leader in the 'plastic revolution', with about 95% of all payments (by value) made by card. This method is seen as quicker and more convenient for both customers and businesses, and also cheaper for the latter, since bank notes need to be sorted, checked and protected. It is also thought that the use of cash encourages tax avoidance, while banks are forced to maintain a large branch network to provide ATM facilities and also accept cash deposits. A further argument against cash use is that cashless shops are less likely to be robbed, so that the staff feel more secure.

In contrast, people in both Italy and Germany are far less enthusiastic about a cashless society: here more than 75% of transactions are still made in cash. Their banks charge more to handle card payments, so that shop keepers are less keen to accept them. In Germany there also seem to be fears about security and privacy, perhaps as a legacy of state control in the past, while some Italians apparently prefer to keep their transactions hidden from the government.

Everywhere there are poorer people who have no bank account and consequently need to operate in cash, and ultimately cash provides security in case the system breaks down. But despite these considerations, cultural as well as economic, the benefits of a cashless economy seem likely to result in a steady shift towards the use of plastic cards across Europe.

(Source: *East-West Monthly*, December 2017, p. 112)

EUROPEAN PAYMENT TRENDS

1   Wide variation in payment methods in Europe – historic & cultural causes

2   In Scandinavia (esp. Sweden) most payments by card:

Reasons

    a)   fast and convenient + saves outlets money

    b)   prevents tax evasion

    c)   safer for shops

    d)   banks need fewer branches

3   In Germany & Italy most payments in cash:

    a)   higher bank charges for cards

    b)   security concerns

    c)   worries re. govt. interference

4   Cash needed by poor (no bank accounts) and for back-up but general trend > cashless economy

(Source: *East-West Monthly*, Dec. 2017, p. 112)

6 Effective note-making

Notes are for your personal use, so you should create your own style. Your teachers will not read or mark them, but you need to make sure you can still understand your notes months after reading the original book or article.

a)   To avoid the risk of plagiarism you must try to use your own words and not just copy phrases from the original.

b)   The quantity of notes you make depends on your task: you may only need a few points or a lot of detail.

c)   Always record the source of your notes. This will save time when you have to write the list of references.

d)   Notes are often written quickly, so keep them simple. Do not write sentences. Leave out articles (a/the) and some prepositions (of/to).

e)   If you write lists, it is important to have clear headings (<u>underlined</u>) and numbering systems (a, b, c, or 1, 2, 3,) to organise the information. Do not crowd your notes.

f)   Use symbols (+, >, =) to save time.

g)   Use abbreviations (e.g. govt. = government). You may need to make up your own abbreviations for your subject area. But do not abbreviate too much, or you may find your notes hard to understand in the future!

▶   **See Unit 4.2 Abbreviations**

7 Practice B

You have to write an essay entitled 'Improving student performance: an outline of recent research'.

■   **Read the following text, underline the relevant key points and make notes on them.**

SLEEP AND MEMORY

In many countries, especially in hot climates, it is the custom to take a short sleep in the afternoon, often known as a siesta. Now it appears that this habit helps to improve the ability to remember and therefore to learn. Researchers have known for some time that new memories are stored short-term in an area of the brain called the hippocampus, but are then transferred to the pre-frontal cortex for long-term storage. They now believe that this transfer process occurs during a kind of sleep called stage 2 non-REM sleep. After this has occurred the brain is better able to take in new information, and having a sleep of about 100 minutes after lunch seems to be an effective way to permit this.

Research by a team from the University of California aimed to confirm this theory. They wanted to establish that a short sleep would restore the brain's ability to learn. A group of about 40 people were asked to take part in two 'lessons'; at 12 noon and 6 p.m. Half the volunteers were put in a group which stayed awake all day, while the others were encouraged to sleep for an hour and a half after the first session. It was found that in the evening lesson the second group were better at remembering what they had learnt, which indicates that the siesta had helped to refresh their short-term memories.

The most effective siesta seems to consist of three parts: roughly 30 minutes of light sleep to rest the body, followed by 30 minutes of stage 2 sleep which clears the hippocampus, and finally 30 minutes of REM sleep which is when dreams are experienced: possibly as a result of the new memories being processed as they are stored in the pre-frontal cortex. This process is believed to be so valuable that some researchers argue that a siesta can be as beneficial as a full night's sleep.

(Source: Kitschelt, P. (2006) *How the Brain Works*, p. 73)

Summarising and Paraphrasing

Summarising and paraphrasing are normally used together in essay writing. Summarising aims to reduce information to a suitable length, allowing the writer to condense lengthy sources into a concise form, while paraphrasing means changing the wording of a text so that it is significantly different from the original source, without changing the meaning. Both are needed to avoid the risk of plagiarism, and this unit practises them separately and jointly.

1 What makes a good summary?

Summarising is a common activity in everyday life. It is used to describe the main features of the subject in order to give a clear and simple impression. For example, if you have been to Tokyo, you might tell a friend:

Tokyo is a huge city with mainly modern buildings and a dense network of public transport. It has many busy shopping centres which are crowded day and night.

■ Write a short description of one of the following topics in no more than 30 words.

    a)   A book you have enjoyed

    b)   A town or city you know well

    c)   A film you have recently watched

■ Compare your summary with others in your class. Discuss what is needed for a good summary.

- _____
- _____
- _____

2 Stages of summarising

Summarising is a flexible tool. You can use it to give a one-sentence outline of an article, or to provide much more detail, depending on your needs. Generally a summary focuses on the main ideas and excludes examples or supporting information. When writing a summary, the same basic steps need to be followed in order to meet the criteria discussed on page 46.

■ **Study the following stages of summary writing, which have been mixed up. Put them in the correct order (1–5).**

  a) Write the summary from your notes, reorganising the structure if needed.

  b) Make notes of the key points, paraphrasing where possible.

  c) Read the original text carefully and check any new or difficult vocabulary.

  d) Mark the key points by underlining or highlighting.

  e) Check the summary to ensure it is accurate and nothing important has been changed or lost.

3 Practice A

■ **Read the following text and the summaries which follow. Which is best? Put them in order 1–3 and give reasons.**

MECHANICAL PICKERS

Although harvesting cereal crops such as wheat and barley has been done for many years by large machines known as combine harvesters, mechanising the picking of fruit crops such as tomatoes or apples has proved more difficult. Farmers have generally relied on human labour to harvest these, but in wealthy countries it has become increasingly difficult to find people willing to work for the wages farmers are able to pay. This is partly because the demand for labour is seasonal, usually in the autumn, and also because the work is hard. As a result, in areas such as California part of the fruit harvest is often unpicked and left to rot.

There are several obvious reasons why developing mechanical pickers is challenging. Fruit such as grapes or strawberries comes in a variety of shapes and does not always ripen at the same time. Outdoors, the ground conditions can vary from dry to muddy, and wind may move branches around. Clearly each crop requires its own solution: machines may be towed through orchards by tractors or move around by themselves, using sensors to detect the ripest fruit.

This new generation of fruit harvesters is possible due to advances in computing power and sensing ability. Such devices will inevitably be expensive, but will save farmers from the difficulty of managing a labour force. In addition, the more intelligent mechanical pickers should be able to develop a database of information on the health of each individual plant, enabling the grower to provide it with fertiliser and water to maintain its maximum productivity.

(Source: *Computing Digest*, January 2016, p. 90)

a) Fruit crops have usually been picked by hand, as it is difficult to mechanise the process. But in rich countries it has become hard to find affordable pickers at the right time, so fruit is often wasted. Therefore intelligent machines with advanced computing power have been developed which can overcome the technical problems involved and also provide farmers with useful data about the plants.

b) Developing machines that can pick fruit such as tomatoes or apples is a challenging task, due to the complexity of locating ripe fruit in an unpredictable outdoor environment, where difficult conditions can be produced by wind or water. But recent developments in computing mean that growers can now automate this process, which should save them money and so increase their profits.

c) Apples, tomatoes, strawberries and grapes are the kinds of crops that have always been hand-picked. But many farmers, for example in California, now find it increasingly difficult to attract enough pickers when the fruit is ripe. However, computing advances have produced a solution to this problem which will save farmers from worrying about the pickers and also collect vital data.

1 _____

2 _____

3 _____

4 Practice B

a) ■ Read the following text and underline the key points.

AFRICA CALLING

In many African countries mobile phone ownership is aiding new businesses to get started. Farmers can easily find current market prices for their crops, and traders can use mobile money services to make payments. It seems clear that as more people use these phones, national GDP rises, but it is difficult to quantify this precisely. Ten years ago there were only 130 million mobile users in the entire continent: now the number is nearly one billion. However, this figure is deceptive: many Africans have two or more SIM cards, and in reality only about half of Africa's 1.2 billion people have access to a mobile phone.

Inevitably, the Africans who have phones tend to be better-educated urban dwellers, but even these are often unable to access the internet, according to an estimate by the International Telecommunications Union (ITU). They claim that 75% of Africans are unable to use the net, with figures as high as 95% in places like Chad. This is because much of the continent is rural and sparsely populated, so that providing mobile phone masts in these districts is uneconomic. Even fewer people can receive a fast 4G signal, and when available, costs are high.

But the situation may be improving, due to advances in technology. New cables are facilitating the connection with other continents, and fibre optic networks are being installed in major cities. Modern satellites are also lowering transmission costs, and solar powered phone masts are cheaper to run in remote villages. But one significant obstacle to these developments is the heavy taxation many governments impose on the telecom companies, which can be as high as 50% in places such as Tanzania.

(Source: Weiss, J. and Evans, P. (2015) *African Perspectives*, pp. 213–4)

▶ **See Unit 1.6 Finding Key Points and Note-making**

b) ■ **Complete the notes of the following key points.**

    i)   Mobile phones have helped _____

    ii)   Link between higher phone ownership _____

    iii) Only half of Africans _____

    iv) New developments _____

    v)   But _____

c) ■ **Join the notes together and expand them to make the final summary in about 70 words. Check that the meaning is clear and no important points have been left out. Find a suitable title.**

*Title:*_____

d) ■ This summary is about 25% of the original length, but it could be summarised further.

■ Summarise the summary in no more than 30 words.

5 Practice C

■ Summarise the following text in about 50 words.

THE LAST WORD IN LAVATORIES?

Toto is a leading Japanese manufacturer of bathroom ceramic ware, with annual worldwide sales of around $5 bn. One of its best-selling ranges is the Washlet lavatory, priced at up to $5,000 and used in most Japanese homes. This has features such as a heated seat, and can play a range of sounds. This type of toilet is successful in its home market since many Japanese flats are small and crowded, and bathrooms provide valued privacy. Now Toto hopes to increase its sales in Europe and America, where it faces a variety of difficulties. European countries tend to have their own rules about lavatory design, so that different models have to be made for each market. Although Toto claims that its Washlet toilet uses less water than the average model, one factor which may delay its penetration into Europe is its need for an electrical socket for installation, as these are prohibited in bathrooms by most European building regulations.

(Source: *Far Eastern Review*, June 2017, p. 60)

6 Paraphrasing

Paraphrasing and summarising are normally used together in essay writing, but while summarising aims to **reduce** information to a suitable length, paraphrasing attempts to **restate** the relevant information. For example, the following sentence:

> *There has been much debate about the reasons for the Industrial Revolution happening in eighteenth-century Britain, rather than in France or Germany.*

could be paraphrased:

> *Why the Industrial Revolution occurred in Britain in the eighteenth century, instead of on the continent, has been the subject of considerable discussion.*

Note that an effective paraphrase usually:

- has a different structure to the original
- has mainly different vocabulary
- retains the same meaning
- keeps some phrases from the original which are in common use (e.g. 'Industrial Revolution')

7 Practice D

■ Read the following text and then rank the three paraphrases in order of accuracy and clarity, giving reasons.

THE CAUSES OF THE INDUSTRIAL REVOLUTION

Allen (2009) argues that the best explanation for the British location of the Industrial Revolution is found by studying demand factors. By the early eighteenth century high wages and cheap energy were both features of the British economy. Consequently, the mechanisation of industry through such inventions as the steam engine and mechanical spinning was profitable because employers were able to economise on labour by spending on coal. At that time, no other European country had this particular combination of expensive labour and abundant fuel.

---

a) A focus on demand may help to explain the UK origin of the Industrial Revolution. At that time British workers' pay was high, but energy was cheap. This encouraged the development of mechanical inventions based on steam power, which enabled bosses to save money by mechanising production (Allen, 2009).

b)   The reason why Britain was the birthplace of the Industrial Revolution can be understood by analysing demand in the early 1700s, according to Allen (2009). He maintains that, uniquely in Europe, Britain had the critical combination of cheap energy from coal and high labour costs. This encouraged the adoption of steam power to mechanise production, thus saving on wages and increasing profitability.

c)   Allen (2009) claims that the clearest explanation for the UK location of the Industrial Revolution is seen by examining demand factors. By the eighteenth century cheap energy and high wages were both aspects of the British economy. As a result, the mechanisation of industry through inventions such as the steam engine and mechanical spinning was profitable because employers were able to save money on employees by spending on coal. At that time, Britain was the only country with significant deposits of coal.

1) _____

2) _____

3) _____

8 Techniques for paraphrasing

a)   Changing vocabulary by using synonyms:

argues > claims/eighteenth century > 1700s/wages > labour costs/economise > saving

b)   Changing word class:

explanation (n.) > explain (v.)/mechanical (adj.) > mechanise (v.)/profitable (adj.) > profitability (n.)

c)   Changing word order:

. . . the best explanation for the British location of the Industrial Revolution is found by studying demand factors.

> A focus on demand may help explain the UK origin of the Industrial Revolution.

Note that in practice all these three techniques are used at the same time. Do not attempt to paraphrase every word, since some have no true synonym (e.g. demand, economy).

▶   **See Units 4.3 and 4.4 Academic Vocabulary and 4.8 Synonyms**

9 Practice E

■   **Read the following text:**

BRAINS AND SEX

It is widely agreed that men and women think and act in different ways. In general women appear to have better memories, better social skills and are more competent at multi-tasking. Men, in contrast, seem to focus better on single issues and have superior motor and spatial skills, although clearly many people are exceptions to these patterns.

These differences have been explained as behaviour adopted thousands of years ago, when the men went hunting while the women stayed at home and cared for their children. But another approach is to see the behaviour as a result of the way our brains function.

Recent research by Ragini Verma's team at the University of Pennsylvania has used brain scans to compare 428 men and 521 women. They tracked the pathways of water molecules around the brain area and found fascinating differences.

The top half of the brain is called the cerebrum, and it is divided into a left and a right half. The left hemisphere is thought to be the home of logic and the right is the centre of intuition. Dr Verma found that with women most of the pathways of the water molecules went between the two halves, while with men they stayed inside the hemispheres. She believes that these results explain the gender differences in ability, such as women's social competence compared to men's more intense focus on single issues.

(Source: *Living Today*, Winter 2015, p. 90)

---

a) ■ **Find synonyms for the words underlined. Rewrite the paragraph using these.**

It is <u>widely agreed</u> that <u>men and women</u> think and <u>act</u> in different ways. Women <u>appear</u> to have <u>better</u> memories, better social <u>skills</u> and are more <u>competent</u> at multitasking. Men, <u>in contrast</u>, seem to focus better on single <u>issues</u> and have superior motor and spatial <u>skills</u>, although <u>clearly</u> many people are <u>exceptions to</u> these patterns.

b) ■ **Change the word class of the underlined words in the next paragraph. Rewrite the paragraph using the changes.**

These differences <u>have been explained</u> as <u>behaviour</u> adopted thousands of years ago, when the men <u>went hunting</u> while the women stayed at home and <u>cared</u> for their children. But another approach is to see the behaviour <u>as a result of</u> the way our brains function.

c) ■   Change the word order of the following sentences, rewriting the paragraph so that
        the meaning stays the same.

   Recent research into brain functioning by Ragini Verma's team at the University
   of Pennsylvania has used brain scans to compare 428 men and 521 women.
   They tracked the pathways of water molecules around the brain area and found
   fascinating differences.

d) ■   Combine all three techniques to paraphrase the final paragraph.

   The top half of the brain is called the cerebrum, and it is divided into a left and
   a right half. The left hemisphere is thought to be the home of logic and the
   right is the centre of intuition. Dr Verma found that with women most of the
   pathways of the water molecules went between the two halves, while with men
   they stayed inside the hemispheres. She believes that these results explain the
   gender differences in abilities, such as women's social competence compared
   to men's more intense focus on single issues.

10 Practice F

a) ■   Use the same techniques to paraphrase the following text.

THE PAST BELOW THE WAVES

More than three million shipwrecks are believed to lie on the sea bed, the result of
storms and accidents during thousands of years of sea-borne trading. These wrecks
offer marine archaeologists valuable information about the culture, technology and
trade patterns of ancient civilizations, but the vast majority have been too deep
to explore. Scuba divers can only operate down to 50 metres, which limits opera-
tions to wrecks near the coast, which have often been damaged by storms or plant
growth. A few deep sea sites (such as the *Titanic*) have been explored by manned
submarines, but this kind of equipment has been too expensive for less famous subjects. However, this situation has been changed by the introduction of a new kind of
mini submarine: the automatic underwater vehicle (AUV). This cheap small craft is
free moving and does not need an expensive mother-ship to control it. Now a team
of American archaeologists are planning to use an AUV to explore an area of sea
north of Egypt which was the approach to a major trading port 4,000 years ago.

(Source: *History Now*, April 2009, p. 9)

---

b) ■   Summarise the same text in 50 words.

References and Quotations

Academic work depends on the research and ideas of others, so it is vital to show which sources you have used in your work, in an acceptable manner. This unit explains:

- the format of in-text citation
- the main reference systems
- the use of quotations
- the layout of lists of references

1 Why use references?

There are three principal reasons for providing references and citations:

a) to show that you have read some of the authorities on the subject, which will give added weight to your writing

b) to allow readers to find the source, if they wish to examine the topic in more detail

c) to avoid plagiarism and show that you understand the rules of the academic community.

▶ See Unit 1.4 Avoiding Plagiarism

■ Decide if you need to give a reference in the following cases.

	Yes/No
a) Data you found from your own primary research	_____
b) A graph from an internet article	_____
c) A quotation from a book	_____

d) An item of common knowledge (e.g. exercise is good for you)   _____

e) A theory from a journal article   _____

f) An idea of your own based on reading several sources   _____

g) A comment made by a person you interviewed for your project   _____

2 Citations and references

It is important to refer correctly to the work of other writers which you have used. You may present these sources as a summary or paraphrase, as a quotation, or use both. In each case a citation is included to provide a link to the list of references at the end of your paper:

Smith (2009) argues that the popularity of the Sports Utility Vehicle (SUV) is irrational, as despite their high cost most are never driven off-road. In his view 'they are bad for road safety, the environment and road congestion' (Smith, 2009:37).

References
Smith, M. (2009) *Power and the State*. Basingstoke: Palgrave Macmillan

---

■ **Underline the citations in the example above. Which is for a summary and which a quotation? What are the advantages of each?**

Giving citations

A quotation	Author's family name, date of publication, page no.	(Smith, 2009:37)
A summary	Author's family name, date of publication	Smith (2009)

3 Reference verbs

Summaries and quotations are usually introduced by a reference verb:

Smith (2009) **argues** *that . . .*

Janovic (1972) **claimed** *that . . .*

These verbs can be either in the present or the past tense. Normally the use of the present tense suggests that the source is recent and still valid, while the past indicates that the source is older and may be out of date, but there are no hard and fast rules. In some disciplines an older source may still be relevant.

▶ **See Unit 4.4 Academic Vocabulary: Adverbs and Verbs – Verbs of reference**

4 Reference systems

There are various systems of referencing employed in the academic world, each used by different subjects. Some disciplines (e.g. law) have their own special system (OSCOLA). Your teachers will normally give you guidelines about which system you are expected to use, or you may find these on your library website. With any system, the most important point is to be consistent (i.e. to use the same font size and punctuation) throughout your work.

Each system specifies how to reference a wide variety of sources, not only books and journals but also films, music, blogs and oral testimony. Referencing is a complex subject, and students should use an online reference guide for detailed information.

Sussex University provides a convenient guide to the different systems at:

www.sussex.ac.uk/library/infosuss/referencing/index.shtm

These are some of the principal systems:

a)   **Harvard**, generally used in the UK for Social Sciences and Business, illustrated in Section 2 on page 56.

b)   **MLA** is similar to Harvard but more common in the US for the Arts and Humanities. In this, the year of publication is at the end of the reference.

c)   **APA** is widely used in the US in the Social Sciences.

d)   **Vancouver** is commonly employed in Medicine and Science. Numbers in brackets are inserted after the citation and these link to a numbered list of references:

Jasanoff (5) makes the point that the risk of cross-infection is growing.

(5) Jasanoff, M. *Tuberculosis: A Sub-Saharan Perspective.* New York: Schaffter (2001)

e)   **Footnote/endnote systems**, commonly used in the Humanities, in which sources are listed either at the bottom of the page or at the end of the paper. The numbers in superscript run consecutively throughout the paper.

The effects of the French Revolution were felt throughout Europe.[3]

3   Karl Wildavsky, *The End of an Era: Spain 1785–1815* (Dublin: University Press, 2006) p. 69.

5 Using quotations

■   **Discuss with a partner reasons for using quotations in your written work.**

Using a quotation means bringing the original words of a writer into your work. Quotations are effective in some situations but must not be overused (e.g. to pad out your work). They can be valuable:

- when the original words express an idea in a distinctive way
- when the original is more concise than your summary could be
- when the original version is well known

All quotations should be introduced by a phrase which shows the source and also explains how this quotation fits into your argument:

Introductory phrase	Author	Reference verb	Quotation	Citation
This view is widely shared;	as Friedman	stated:	'Inflation is the one form of taxation that can be imposed without legislation'	(Friedman, 1974:93).

a)   Short quotations (1–2 lines) are shown by single quotation marks. Quotations inside quotations (nested quotations) use double quotation marks:

  As Kauffman remarked: 'his concept of "internal space" requires close analysis'.

b)   Longer quotations (3 or more lines) are either indented (given a wider margin) and/or are printed in smaller type. In this case quotations marks are not needed:

  Similarly, she says:

  One of the many things that people need to be able to do, if their life is to be worthy of human dignity, is to have access to the legal system on terms of equality with other people . . . .The due process rights . . . are also fundamental opportunities to act and be treated as a fully equal citizen.

  (Nussbaum, 2011a, p. 28)

c)   Page numbers should be given after the date.

d)   Care must be taken to ensure that quotations are the exact words of the original. If it is necessary to delete some words which are irrelevant, use dots (. . .) to show where the missing section was:

  'Few inventions . . . have been as significant as the mobile phone'.

e)   It may be necessary to insert a word or phrase into the quotation to clarify a point. This can be done by using square brackets []:

  ' . . . modern ideas [of freedom] differ radically from those of the ancient world. . .'

f) If you want to point out a mistake in the original use [*sic*]:

He claimed that 'the company was to [sic] big to fail'.

g) If a writer has published more than one book or article in a year, it is necessary to add a/b/c to the date:

(*Nussbaum, 2011a, p. 28*)

6 Practice

■ Read the following text from an article called 'Dealing with transition' in the journal *Education Review* (Autumn 2016, pp. 45–7) by A. Kelman.

Students entering Higher Education (HE, i.e. degree-level study) often find the transition from school to university difficult to manage. This can be especially true of the demands of essay writing, a skill required in the majority of subjects. A study by McEwan (2015) explored the reasons for difficulties at this stage by comparing the expectations of staff and students towards writing essays. He found significant differences between the two and suggested ways in which the differences could be reduced.

It often takes time for new students to adjust to the learning culture of HE, and much depends on their previous academic experience. Teaching staff at degree-level expect students to study independently and not to need regular supervision, although recently universities have begun to provide more support for first-year students to help them adjust to these expectations.

■ Compare the following:

a) **Summary**
    Kelman (2016) maintains that the transition from school to university study is particularly hard in terms of writing essays. She refers to McEwan's research on the mismatch between student and teacher expectations, and highlights the need to give students time to adapt to a new academic culture.

b) **Quotation**
    Kelman discusses McEwan's research on the gap between the expectations of staff and students with regard to essay writing at first-year university level:

It often takes time for new students to adjust to the learning culture of HE, and much depends on their previous academic experience. Teaching staff at degree-level expect students to study independently and not to need regular supervision.

(Kelman, 2016:45)

c) Summary and quotation

Kelman (2016) points out that one area of serious concern for first-year university students is writing essays. She looks at the study done by McEwan on the differences between teachers' and students' perceptions of essay writing, which highlighted one distinct difficulty: 'Teaching staff at degree-level expect students to study independently and not to need regular supervision'. (Kelman, 2016:45).

■ Read the next part of the same text, also from p. 45.

> McEwan argues that student success at university level is partly dependent on narrowing the difference between student and staff expectations. This is particularly important now that the student body includes an increasing proportion of international students, who may take longer to adapt to the university culture. The same is also true of the increasingly diverse university staff, who often come from very different academic cultures.
>
> The two most significant findings of the study concerned plagiarism and essay focus. In both cases there was a substantial difference between staff and student opinion. While all the students claimed to understand the meaning of plagiarism, a majority of teachers (over 60%) felt that they didn't. Similarly, nearly all the students claimed to focus on answering the question in the essay title, but only one-fifth of the teachers thought that they did.

a) ■ Write a summary of the main point, including a citation.

b) ■ Introduce a quotation to show the key point, referring to the source.

c) ■ Combine the summary and the quotation, again acknowledging the source.

7 Abbreviations in citations

In-text citations use the following abbreviations derived from Latin and printed in italics:

et al.:   used when three or more authors are given. The full list of names is given in the reference list:

> *Many Americans fail to vote* (Hobolt *et al.*, 2006:137).

ibid.:   taken from the same source (i.e. the same page) as the previous citation:

> *Older Americans are more likely to vote than the young (ibid.).*

op cit.:   taken from the same source as previously, but a different page.

Note that journal articles increasingly tend to use full citations at each occurrence, but students should still use abbreviations in their work.

▶ **See Unit 4.2 Abbreviations**

8 Secondary references

It is quite common to find a reference to an original source in the text you are reading.
For instance, in the text by Kelman in Section 6 on page 59 she says:

> *A study by McEwan (2015) explored the reasons for difficulties at this stage by comparing the expectations of staff and students towards writing essays.*

You may wish to use this information from the original (i.e. McEwan) in your writing, even if you have not read the whole work. This is known as a secondary reference. If it is not possible to locate the original, you can refer to it thus:

> *McEwan (2015),* **cited in Kelman (2016:45)**, *compared the expectations of . . .*

You must ensure that you include the work you have read (i.e. Kelman) in the list of references.

9 Organising the list of references

> There are many software systems available (e.g. RefWorks or Endnote) which automate the making of a list of references. Using one of them not only saves time but may also help to produce a more accurate result. Some are free and others require payment, but if you search your library website you may find one which you can access without charge.

At the end of an essay or report there must be a list of all the sources cited in the piece of writing. In the Harvard system, illustrated here, the list is organised alphabetically by the family name of the author. You should be clear about the difference between first names and family names. On title pages the normal format is first name, then family name:

> *Sheila Burford, Juan Gonzalez*

But in citations, only the family name is usually used:

Burford (2001), Gonzalez (1997)

In reference lists, use the family name and the initial(s):

Burford, S., Gonzalez, J.

If you are not sure which name is the family name, ask a classmate from that cultural background.

■ **Study the reference list on page 63 from an essay about transition from school to university and answer the following questions.**

a)   Find an example of:

   i)   a book by one author

   _____

   ii)   a journal article by nine authors

   _____

   iii) a chapter in an edited book

   _____

   iv)   a conference paper

   _____

   v)   a journal article by one author

   _____

   vi)   a book by two authors

   _____

b)   What are the differences between the format of references for books and journal articles?

   Books:_____

   Journal articles:_____

c)   When are italics used?

d)   How are capital letters used in titles?

e)   How is a source with no given author listed?

f)   Write citations for summaries of the first five sources in the list of references.

   i)   _____

   ii)   _____

   iii) _____

   iv)   _____

   v)   _____

REFERENCES

Bryman, A. (2004). *Social Research Methods*. 2nd ed. Oxford: Oxford University Press.

Carroll, J. (2007). *A Handbook for Deterring Plagiarism in Higher Education*. 2nd ed. Oxford: Oxford Centre for Staff and Learning Development.

Cook, A. and Leckey, J. (1999). 'Do expectations meet reality? A survey of changes in first-year student opinion.' *Journal of Further and Higher Education*, 23(2), pp. 157–171.

Crisp, G., Palmer, E., Turnbull, D., Nettelbeck, T., Ward, L., LeCouteur, A., Sarris, A., Strelan, P. and Schneider, L. (2009). 'First year student expectations: results from a university-wide student survey.' *Journal of University Teaching and Learning Practice*, 6(1), pp. 11–26.

Killen, R. (1994). 'Differences between students' and lecturers' perceptions of factors influencing students' academic success at university.' *Higher Education Research and Development*, 13(2), pp. 199–211.

Leese, M. (2010). 'Bridging the gap: supporting student transitions into higher education.' *Journal of Further and Higher Education*, 34(2), pp. 239–251.

Lowe, H. and Cook, A. (2003). 'Mind the gap: are students prepared for HE?' *Journal of Further and Higher Education*, 27(1), pp. 53–76.

Moore, D. and McCabe, G. (2006). *Introduction to the Practice of Statistics*. 5th ed. New York: W. H. Freeman and Company.

Ryan, J. and Carroll, J. (2005). 'Canaries in the coalmine: international students in Western universities.' In J. Carroll and J. Ryan (Eds). *Teaching International Students – Improving Learning for All*. Abingdon: Routledge.

Tinto, V. (1987). *Leaving College: Rethinking the Causes and Cures of Student Attrition*. Chicago: University of Chicago Press.

The Times. 'Coping with transition from sixth form to university.' p. 4, 26 September 2016

White, P. (2013). Embracing Diversity. 7th Annual Learning and Teaching Conference, 9th January 2013, [online]. Available from: www.shef.ac.uk/lets/cpd/conf/2013/res/preso [Accessed on 10th July 2014].

Combining Sources

For most assignments, students are expected to read a range of sources that often contain conflicting views on a topic. In some cases the contrast between the various views may be the focus of the task. This unit explains how writers can present and organise a range of contrasting sources.

1 Referring to sources

In the early stages of an essay it is common to refer to the views of other writers on the subject in order to show that you are familiar with their work and that your work will take their research into account. In a longer essay or thesis, this may form a section headed 'Literature review'.

■ **Read the following example from a study of student transition to university and answer the questions that follow.**

The expectations which students have of higher education are influenced by their prior educational experiences (Ramsden, 1992, p. 82; Tinto, 2005; Cook and Rushton, 2008). These experiences form a basis for the academic expectations which students have relating to learning and teaching (Dalglish and Chan, 2005), assessment (Ramsden, 1992, p. 84), academic support (Yorke, 2000; Crisp *et al.*, 2009), and academic interactions with staff (Crisp *et al.*, 2009).

(Source: McEwan, M. (2015) *Understanding student transition to university*)

a) How many sources are mentioned here?

b) Which writers examine expectations of learning and teaching?

c) What was the subject of Yorke's study?

d) Which writer looked at expectations of assessment?

e) Why do you think page numbers are given for Ramsden?

■ **Read another paragraph from the same study and answer the following questions.**

Academically, a diverse body of international university entrants have even greater diversity in pre-arrival expectations and prior educational experiences when compared to those of home students (e.g. Dalglish and Chan, 2005; Crisp *et al.*, 2009; White, 2013) resulting in a period of transition which can be more challenging with greater requirements for academic adjustment (Ramsey, Barker and Jones, 1999). For example, international students often need to make significant cultural (Ryan and Carroll, 2005) and linguistic (Wu and Hammond, 2011) adjustments and this takes time; perhaps many months or even years (Carroll, 2014).

f) What is the main subject of the paragraph?

g) Summarise the different points made by each of the five sets of sources cited.

Example:

i)   Dalglish and Chan, 2005; Crisp *et al.*, 2009; White, 2013

International students have wider variety of expectations compared to home students

ii) Ramsey, Barker and Jones, 1999

iii) Ryan and Carroll, 2005

iv) Wu and Hammond, 2011

v)   Carroll, 2014

▶ **See Unit 5.2 Literature Reviews and Book Reviews**

2 Taking a critical approach

It is important to compare a range of views to show that you are familiar with different or conflicting views on a topic. This is because most subjects worth studying are the subject of debate. The following texts, 2.1 and 2.2, reflect different views on the topic of climate change.

■   Read them both and then study the extract from an essay (2.3) which contrasts the two sources. Answer the questions which follow.

2.1 WHY THE EARTH IS HEATING UP

Most scientists now agree that global temperatures have risen over the last century, and that this trend is reflected in such phenomena as the melting of sea ice and the retreat of glaciers. There is a near-consensus that over the period the level of carbon dioxide (CO_2) in the earth's atmosphere has also risen, mainly as a result of burning fossil fuels such as coal and oil. The common view is that the first change is the result of the second; in other words a warmer climate has been caused by the CO_2, which has the effect of causing the heat from the sun's rays to be trapped inside the atmosphere; the so-called 'greenhouse effect'. If these theories are accepted it can be expected that temperatures will continue to increase in future as carbon dioxide levels rise, and since this will have harmful effects on agriculture and other human activities, efforts should be made to reduce the burning of fossil fuels.

(Source: Lombardo, 2009)

2.2 DOUBTS ABOUT GLOBAL WARMING

The conventional view that global warming is caused by a rise in carbon dioxide levels has been criticised on a number of grounds. Some critics claim that the recent period of warming is part of a natural cycle of temperature fluctuations which have been recorded over the past few thousand years. They point out that Europe experienced a warm period about 800 years ago which was unrelated to CO_2 levels. Other critics question the reliability of the basic temperature data, and maintain that the apparent rise in temperatures is caused by the growth of cities, regarded as 'heat islands'. In addition some claim that the warming is caused by a reduction in cloud cover, allowing more sunlight to reach the earth's surface. This effect, they believe, is the result of solar activity or sunspots, which are known to fluctuate on an 11-year cycle. As a result of these doubts, sceptics argue that there is no need to attempt to reduce the industrial activity that causes carbon dioxide to be produced.

(Source: Wong, 2011)

2.3 HOW STRONG IS THE EVIDENCE FOR GLOBAL WARMING?

Lombardo (2009) puts forward the view that the significant rise in the earth's temperature over the past century is the product of increased levels of atmospheric CO_2 caused by greater use of fossil fuels. He maintains that this position is now generally agreed, and that steps should be taken to reduce future warming by restricting the output of greenhouse gases such as carbon dioxide. However, Wong (2011) presents a range of counter-arguments. She mentions evidence of historical climate change which cannot have been caused by rising levels of CO_2, and also discusses the difficulty of obtaining reliable data on temperature changes, as well as other claims that solar activity may affect the amount of cloud cover and hence temperature levels. Such uncertainty, she considers, raises doubts about the value of cutting CO_2 production.

a) ■ Study the following example of an extract from 2.3 and the original text. Find two more examples from 2.3 and match them with the original texts.

Summary (2.3)	Original
. . . the significant rise in the earth's temperature over the past century is the product of increased levels of atmospheric CO_2 caused by greater use of fossil fuels.	(2.1) There is a near-consensus that over the period the level of carbon dioxide (CO_2) in the earth's atmosphere has also risen, mainly as a result of burning fossil fuels.

b)   Which verbs are used to introduce the summaries?

c)   Which word marks the point where the writer switches from summarising Lombardo to Wong?

d)   What other words or phrases could be used at this point?

3 Combining three sources

■   Read the third text on climate change below and then complete paragraph 2.3 on page 67 'How strong is the evidence for global warming?' by summarising Lahav's comments.

THE SCEPTICAL CASE

Debate on the issues around climate change have intensified recently, since while most scientists agree that global temperatures are rising as a result of ever-higher levels of carbon dioxide in the earth's atmosphere, a minority continue to argue that the rise is insignificant, short-term or unrelated to CO_2 levels. The controversy clearly has important political and economic implications, since international agreement is needed to control the output of greenhouse gases. Climate sceptics insist that computer models are unable to handle the complexity of the world's weather systems, and so should not be used as a basis for making major decisions. Their view is that because the science of global warming is uncertain, the money that would be spent, for example, on building wind farms could be better spent on improving health and education in the developing world.

(Source: Lahav, 2010)

---

4 Practice

The following three texts reflect different approaches to the topic of globalisation.

■   Read them all and then complete the paragraph from an essay entitled: 'Globalisation mainly benefits multinational companies rather than ordinary people – discuss', using all three sources, in about 100 words.

4.1 THE BENEFITS OF GLOBALISATION

It has been argued that globalisation is not a new phenomenon, but has its roots in the age of colonial development in the seventeenth and eighteenth centuries. However, its modern use can be dated to 1983, when Levitt's article 'The Globalisation of Markets' was published. Among the many definitions of the process that have been suggested, perhaps the simplest is that globalisation is the relatively free movement of services, goods, people and ideas world-wide. An indication of the positive effect of the process is that cross-border world trade, as a percentage of global GDP, was 15% in 1990 but is expected to reach 30% by 2020. Among the forces driving globalisation in the last two decades have been market liberalisation, cheap communication via the internet and telephony, and the growth of the so-called BRIC (Brazil, Russia, India and China) economies.

(Source: Costa, L. 2008)

4.2 GLOBALISATION AND ITS DRAWBACKS

Considerable hostility to the forces of globalisation has emerged in both the developed and developing worlds. In the former, there is anxiety about the outsourcing of manufacturing and service jobs to countries which offer cheaper labour, while developing countries claim that only a minority have benefited from the increase in world trade. They point out that per-capita income in the 20 poorest countries has hardly changed in the past 40 years, while in the richest 20 it has tripled. The markets of Western nations are still closed to agricultural products from developing countries, and while there is free movement of goods and capital, migration of people from poor countries to rich ones is tightly controlled.

(Source: Lin, Y. 2012)

4.3 MULTINATIONALS AND GLOBALISATION

Multinational companies have undoubtedly benefited from the relaxation of the import tariff regimes which previously protected local firms, allowing them to operate more freely in markets such as India which have recently liberalised. These corporations have evolved two distinct approaches to the challenge of globalisation.

Some, e.g. Gillette, have continued to manufacture their products in a few large plants with strict control to ensure uniform quality worldwide, while others, for instance Coca-Cola, vary the product to suit local tastes and tend to make their goods on the spot. They claim that an understanding of regional differences is essential for competing with national rivals. In either case, these giant companies are often able to minimise their tax liabilities by establishing headquarters in low-tax countries.

(Source: Brokaw, P. 2014)

Globalisation mainly benefits multinational companies rather than ordinary people – discuss.

There is good evidence that globalisation has resulted in a considerable increase in world trade over the past 20–30 years...

UNIT

1.10

Organising Paragraphs

Paragraphs are the basic building blocks of academic writing. Well-structured paragraphs help the reader understand the topic more easily by dividing up the argument into convenient sections. This unit looks at:

- the components of paragraphs
- the way the components are linked together
- the linkage between paragraphs in the overall text

1 Paragraph structure

■ Read the following paragraph and answer the questions.

> Spanish is one of the world's leading languages. It is spoken by over 500 million people, mainly in Spain and Central and South America, as a first or second language. This is a result of the growth of the Spanish colonies in Central and South America from the sixteenth century. Increasingly, Spanish is also widely used in North America, where Spanish language newspapers and radio stations are common. Spanish is a Romance language which evolved from Latin, but which also contains many words from Arabic, due to the historical Moorish presence in the Iberian peninsula.

a) What is the topic of this paragraph?

b) How are the sentences in the paragraph linked together?

The paragraph can be analysed thus:

1 Topic sentence	Spanish is one of the world's leading languages.
2 Supporting information	**It** is spoken by over 500 million people, mainly in Spain and Central and South America, as a first or second language.
3 Reason	**This** is a result of the growth of the Spanish colonies in Central and South America from the sixteenth century.
4 Extra information 1	**Increasingly,** Spanish is also widely used in North America, where Spanish language newspapers and radio stations are common.
5 Extra information 2	Spanish is a Romance language which evolved from Latin, **but** which also contains many words from Arabic, due to the historical Moorish presence in the Iberian peninsula.

This example shows that:

i)   A paragraph is a group of sentences which deal with a single topic. Dividing up the text into paragraphs helps both writer and reader to follow the argument more clearly.

ii)   The length of paragraphs varies significantly according to text type, but should normally be no less than four or five sentences.

iii) Usually (but not always) the first sentence introduces the topic. Other sentences may give definitions, examples, extra information, reasons, restatements and summaries.

iv)   The parts of the paragraph are linked together by the reference words, conjunctions and adverbs shown in bold in the table. They guide the reader through the arguments presented.

▶   **See Unit 3.1 Cohesion**

2 Practice A

■   **The sentences in the following paragraph on the topic of home ownership have been mixed up. Use the table to put them in the right order.**

i)   The reasons for this variation appear to be more cultural and historical than economic, since high rates are found in both rich and poorer countries.

ii)   There appears to be no conclusive link between national prosperity and the number of home owners.

iii) Both the US and Britain have similar rates of about 65%.

iv) The rate of home ownership varies widely across the developed world.

v) Germany, for instance, has one of the lowest rates, at 52%, while in Spain it is much higher, 78%.

Topic sentence	
Example 1	
Example 2	
Reason	
Summary	

3 Practice B

■ Read the next paragraph from the same essay and answer the questions that follow.

> Despite this, many countries encourage the growth of home ownership. Ireland and Spain, for instance, allow mortgage payers to offset payments against income tax. It is widely believed that owning your own home has social as well as economic benefits. Compared to renters, home owners are thought to be more stable members of the community who contribute more to local affairs. In addition, neighbourhoods of owner occupiers are considered to have less crime and better schools. But above all, home ownership encourages saving and allows families to build wealth.

a) Analyse the paragraph using the table, giving the function of each sentence

Topic sentence	Despite this, many countries encourage the growth of home ownership.

b) Underline the words and phrases used to link the sentences together.

c) Which phrase is used to link this paragraph to the one before?

4 Introducing paragraphs and linking them together

The paragraph in Practice B begins with a phrase which links it to the previous paragraph in order to maintain continuity of argument:

> *Despite this* (i.e. the lack of a conclusive link)

In order to begin a new topic you may use phrases such as:

> *Turning to the issue of child labour . . .*
>
> *Rates of infection must also be examined . . . .*
>
> *Inflation is another area for consideration . . .*

Paragraphs can also be introduced with adverbs:

> *Traditionally, few examples were . . .*
>
> *Finally, the performance of . . .*
>
> *Currently, there is little evidence of . . .*
>
> *Originally, most families were . . .*

▶   **See Units 4.4 Academic Vocabulary: Adverbs and Verbs and 4.5 Conjunctions**

5 Practice C

■   **Use the following notes to write two paragraphs on the subject of 'Trams'. Use conjunctions and other suitable phrases to introduce and link the paragraphs together.**

- Trams (streetcars in the US) first developed in late 19th century
- Provided cheap and convenient mass transport in many cities
- Rail-based systems expensive to maintain
- Fixed tracks meant system was inflexible
- During 1950s and 1960s many European and Asian cities closed tram systems
- Today trams becoming popular again
- Some cities (e.g. Paris and Manchester) building new systems
- Trams less polluting than cars and cheaper to operate
- Problems remain with construction costs and traffic congestion blocking tracks
- Expense of building modern tramways means that they remain controversial

6 Practice D

■   **Use the information in the following table and graph to write a paragraph on 'UK rainfall in 2016'.**

Jan	Feb	Mar	Apr	May	June	July	Aug	Sep	Oct	Nov	Dec	Overall
159	145	94	121	90	143	110	97	98	44	95	71	105

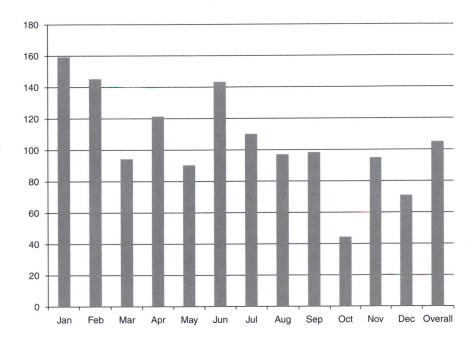

Figure 1 UK rainfall anomalies 2016 (percent of average monthly rainfall 1960–1989)

Source: The Met Office

Introductions and Conclusions

An effective introduction explains the purpose, scope and methodology of the paper to the reader. The conclusion should provide a clear answer to any questions asked in the title, as well as summarising the main points under discussion. With course-work, it may be better to write the introduction after writing the main body.

1 Introduction components

Introductions are usually no more than about 10% of the total length of an assignment. Therefore in a 2,000-word essay the introduction would be approximately 200 words.

▶ See Unit 1.5 From Understanding Essay Titles to Planning

a) ■ What components are normally found in an essay introduction? Choose from the following list.

Components		Y/N
i)	A definition of any unfamiliar terms in the title	
ii)	Your personal opinions on the subject of the essay	
iii)	Mention of some sources you have read on the topic	
iv)	A provocative idea or question to interest the reader	
v)	A suitable quotation from a famous authority	
vi)	Your aim or purpose in writing	
vii)	The method you adopt to answer the question	

viii) Some background or context of the topic	
ix) Any limitations you set yourself	
x) An outline of the main body	

b) ■ **Read the following extracts from introductions to articles and decide which of the components listed above (i – x) they are examples of.**

A)   In the past 20 years the ability of trial juries to assess complex or lengthy cases has been widely debated.

B)   The rest of the paper is organised as follows. The second section explains why corporate governance is important for economic prosperity. The third section presents the model specification and describes the data and variables used in our empirical analysis. The fourth section reports and discusses the empirical results. The fifth section concludes.

C)   We attempted to test our hypothesis by comparing the reactions of a random sample of postgraduates with a group of first-year students.

D)   There is no clear empirical evidence sustaining a 'managerial myopia' argument. Pugh *et al.* (1992) find evidence that supports such a theory, but Meulbrook *et al.* (1990), Mahoney *et al.* (1997), Garvey and Hanka (1999) and a study by the Office of the Chief Economist of the Securities and Exchange Commission (1985) find no evidence.

E)   'Social cohesion' is usually defined in reference to common aims and objectives, social order, social solidarity and the sense of place attachment.

F)   This study will focus on mergers in the media business between 2000 and 2010, since with more recent examples an accurate assessment of the consequences cannot yet be made.

G)   The purpose of this paper is to investigate changes in the incidence of extreme warm and cold temperatures over the globe since 1870.

2 Introduction structure

There is no standard pattern for an introduction, since much depends on the type of research you are conducting and the length of your work, but this is a common structure:

a) Definition of key terms, if needed

b) Relevant background information

c) Review of work by other writers on the topic

d) Purpose or aim of the paper

e) Your research methods

f) Any limitations you imposed

g) An outline of your paper

■ **Study the introduction to an essay entitled 'Evaluate the experience of e-learning for students in higher education'.**

There are a range of definitions of this term, but in this paper 'e-learning' refers to any type of learning situation where content is delivered via the internet. Learning is one of the most vital components of the contemporary knowledge-based economy. With the development of computing power and technology the internet has become an essential medium for knowledge transfer. Various researchers (Webb and Kirstin, 2003; Honig *et al.*, 2006) have evaluated e-learning in a healthcare and business context, but little attention so far has been paid to the reactions of students in higher education (HE) to this method of teaching. The purpose of this study was to examine students' experience of e-learning in an HE context.

A range of studies was first reviewed and then a survey of 200 students was conducted to assess their experience of e-learning. Clearly a study of this type is inevitably restricted by various constraints, notably the size of the student sample, which was limited to students of Pharmacy and Agriculture. The paper is structured as follows. The first section presents an analysis of the relevant research, focusing on the current limited knowledge regarding the student experience. The second part presents the methodology of the survey and an analysis of the findings, and the final section considers the implications of the results for the delivery of e-learning programmes.

■ **Underline the following sections (a-g) of the introduction above:**

a) Definition
Certain words or phrases in the title may need clarifying because they are not widely understood or are used in a special sense.

b) Context
It is useful to remind the reader of the wider context of your work. This may also show the value of the study you have carried out.

c) Reference to other researchers
While a longer article may have a separate literature review, in a shorter essay it is still important to show familiarity with researchers who have studied this topic previously. This may also reveal a gap in research which justifies your work.

d) Aim
The aim of your research must be clearly stated so the reader knows what you are trying to do.

e) Method
The method demonstrates the process that you undertook to achieve the given aim.

f) Limitations
You cannot deal with every aspect of this topic in an essay, so you must make clear the boundaries of your study.

g) Outline
Understanding the structure of your work will help the reader to follow your argument.

▶   **See Unit 2.4 Definitions**

3 Opening sentences

It can be difficult to start writing an essay, but especially in exams, hesitation will waste valuable time. The first few sentences should be general but not vague in order to help the reader focus on the topic. They often have the following pattern:

Time phrase	Topic	Development
Currently,	the control of water resources	has emerged as a potential cause of international friction.
Since 2008	electric vehicles	have become a serious commercial proposition.
Before 1950	antibiotic drugs	were not widely available.

It is important to avoid opening sentences which are over-general and vague.
    Compare:

Nowadays there is a lot of competition among different news providers.   ✗

In the last 20 years newspapers have faced strong competition from the internet for   ✓
news and entertainment.

■   **Working quickly, write introductory sentences for three of the following titles.**

a)   How important is it for companies to have women as senior managers?

b)   Are there any technological solutions to global warming?

c)   What can be done to reduce infant mortality in developing countries?

d)   Compare the urbanisation process in two contrasting countries.

▶   **See Unit 2.6 Generalisations**

4 Conclusions

Conclusions tend to be shorter and more varied in format than introductions. Some articles may have a 'summary' or 'concluding remarks'. But student papers should generally have a final section which summarises the arguments and makes it clear to the reader that the original question has been answered.

■   **Which of the following are generally acceptable in conclusions?**

a)   A statement showing how your aim has been achieved.

b)   A discussion of the implications of your research.

c)   Some new information on the topic not mentioned before.

d)   A short review of the main points of your study.

e)   Some suggestions for further research.

f)   The limitations of your study.

g)   Comparison with the results of similar studies.

h)   A quotation which appears to sum up your work.

■   **Match the following extracts from conclusions with the preceding acceptable features of conclusions. Example: a = vi**

i)   As always, this investigation has a number of limitations to be considered in evaluating its findings.

ii)   These results suggest that the risk of flooding on this coast has increased significantly and is likely to worsen.

iii) Several hurdles that we encountered provide a point of departure for subsequent studies.

iv) Our review of 13 studies of strikes in public transport demonstrates that the effect of a strike on public transport ridership varies and may either be temporary or permanent.

v)   These results of the Colombia study reported here are consistent with other similar studies conducted in other countries (Baron and Norman, 1992).

vi) This study has clearly illustrated the drawbacks to family ownership of retail businesses.

5 Conclusion structure

Although there is no fixed pattern, a common structure for an essay conclusion is:

a) Summary of main findings or results

b) Link back to the original question to show it has been answered

c) Reference of the limitations of your work (e.g. geographical)

d) Suggestions for future possible related research

e) Comments on the implications of your research

6 Practice

■ The following sentences form the conclusion to the essay titled 'Evaluate the experience of e-learning for students in higher education', whose introduction was given on page 78. The sentences have been mixed up. Put them into a logical order (1–5).

a) This finding was clear, despite the agreed convenience of e-learning.

b) Given the constraints of the small and limited sample, there is clearly room for further research in this field, in particular to explore whether certain disciplines are more suited to this mode of learning than others.

c) However, our survey of nearly 200 students found a strong preference for traditional classroom teaching.

d) But in general it would appear that e-learning is unlikely to be acceptable as a primary teaching method in higher education.

e) This study found that little relevant research on the HE student experience of e-learning has been conducted, and the research that has been reported indicates a mixed reaction to it.

UNIT 1.12

Rewriting and Proofreading

In exams, you have no time for rewriting, but for coursework it is important to take time to revise your work to improve its clarity and logical development. In both situations, proofreading is essential to avoid the small errors which may make parts of your work inaccurate or difficult to understand.

1 Rewriting

Although it is tempting to think that the first draft of an essay is good enough, it almost certainly can be improved. After completing your first draft you should leave it for a day and then reread it, asking yourself the following questions:

a)   Does this fully answer the question(s) in the title?

b)   Do the different sections of the paper have the right weight (i.e. is it well balanced)?

c)   Does the argument or discussion develop clearly and logically?

d)   Have I forgotten any important points which would support the development?

e)   Is the essay the required length, not too short or too long?

2 Practice A

As part of a module on Qualitative Research Methods, you have written the first draft of a 1,000-word paper titled 'What would be an acceptable number of interviews to carry out for a Master's dissertation?'

■   **Study the following introduction to this paper and decide how it could be improved, listing your suggestions in the table.**

An interview can be defined as a conversation with a definite structure and objective. It goes beyond an everyday conversation with no particular purpose. There are many possible interview situations, but all involve an interviewer and an interviewee. It is normal for the former to ask the latter direct questions and record the answers. The questions may be prepared in advance or they may occur as the interview develops. The recording is often done on paper, but may also be done by audio or video recording. Interviews can take place anywhere, in a street, café, office, bar, restaurant, and so on. It is hard to say how many interviews can be carried out in one day. I personally think that two is the maximum because it can get very tiring. A lot depends on the subject being researched.

	Suggestions for improvement
a)	
b)	
c)	
d)	
e)	

■ See Answers p. 276 for suggestions

With these points in mind, the introduction could be rewritten as follows:

Organising an interview involves a series of steps (Davies, 2007), including recruiting interviewees, finding a suitable venue and writing appropriate guidelines. However, depending on the research subject, a more flexible approach can be adopted, resulting in a less structured interview (Cooper and Schindler, 2008). For a Master's dissertation, interviews must contain data relevant to the research topic which the interviewer can later process. As King states: 'Gathering a large volume of cases does not guarantee the credibility of a study' (King, 2004:16). Most writers agree that two one-hour interviews per day are effectively the maximum for one interviewer, given the time needed for preparation and subsequent processing. Moreover, if audio or video recording is used there is more content to be analysed, for instance in terms of facial expression. The analysis of one interview can take up to three days' work. In order to answer the question, clearly much depends on the research topic and the time the researcher has available.

3 Practice B

■ **Read the next paragraph on 'Possible ethical issues raised by interview-based research'. Decide how it could be improved and rewrite it.**

> Any organisation that allows researchers to interview its employees runs a big risk. The interviewees may complain about the boss or about other workers. Another danger for the researcher is that employees may feel obliged to give positive answers to questions instead of their honest opinions. This is because they are afraid of their bosses finding out what they really think. Also the reputation of the organisation may suffer. I believe that researchers should make sure that this does not happen. They must make it clear why they are doing the research and keep identities secret by using false names. If this is not done, there's a good chance that the validity of the whole research project will be in danger.

4 Proofreading

After you have rewritten your work, the final stage is to proofread it. This means checking your work for small errors which may make it more difficult for the reader to understand exactly what you want to say. If a sentence has only one error:

> *She has no enough interpersonal skills to handle different relationships.*

it is not difficult to understand, but if there are multiple errors, even though they are all quite minor, the effect is very confusing:

> *A american senate once say: 'Truth is frist casualty off war'.*

Clearly, you should aim to make your meaning as clear as possible. Note that computer spell-checks will not always help you, since they may ignore a word which is spelt correctly but which is not the word you meant to use:

> *Tow factors need to be considered.*

5 Practice C

■ **The following are examples of the ten most common types of error in student writing. In each sentence underline the error and correct it.**

i) **Factual**: Corruption is a problem in many countries such as Africa.

ii) **Word ending**: She was young and innocence. *nt*

iii) **Punctuation**: What is the optimum size for a research team. *?*

iv) **Tense**: Since 2005 there were three major earthquakes in the region.
have been

v) **Vocabulary**: Flexibility is vital to the successfulness of a company operating in China. *s*

vi **Spelling**: Pervious experience can sometimes be a disadvantage.

vii) **Singular/plural**: It is one of the largest company in Asia.

viii) **Style**: Finally, the essay will conclude with a conclusion.

ix) **Missing word**: This is an idea established by David Ricardo in nineteenth century. *the*

x) **Word order**: Three skills are for needed success in the academic world.

6 Practice D

■ The following sentences each contain one type of error. Match each to one of the error types (i-x) above and correct the error.

a) Products such as Tiger biscuits are well known to kids. *children*

b) Both companies focus on mass marketing to promote its line of products. *their lines*

c) Failure to find the right coffee may lead to torment for consumers.

d) They found that different researchers had differently effects on the research. *viii*

e) This was after the single European market was established in 1873. *iv*

f) Experienced researchers can most likely come over these problems. *overcome*

g) The Arts Faculty has it's own library. *its*

h) She selected Budapest in Hungry for setting up the research centre.

i) Companies from the rest of world are eager to do business in India. *the*

j) From 2008 to 2012 there are few cases of cholera. *where*

7 Practice E

■ Underline the errors in the following paragraph and correct them.

BICYCLES

Bicycle is one of most efficient machine ever designed. Cyclists can travel for times faster than walkers when using less enorgy to do so. Various people invented early versions of the bicycle, but the first modle with pedals which was successful mass-produced was make by a frenchman, Ernest Michaux, on 1861. Later aditions included pneumatic tyres and gears. Today hundreds of million of bicycles are in use over all world.

Progress
Check 1

These exercises will help you assess your understanding of Part 1 – The Writing Process.

1   *Complete the following description of the process of essay writing by adding one suitable word to each gap.*

The first stage of essay writing is to read and understand the a) _____, and then to prepare a b) _____ of work for the time available. Then the topic should be brainstormed and a draft c) _____ prepared. Next, possible d) _____ have to be carefully evaluated and the most relevant selected, after which you can start e) _____ notes, using paraphrasing and summarising f) _____. When you have collected enough material to answer the question the first g) _____ of the main body can written from the notes, taking care to avoid any h) _____. Subsequently, you can write the first draft of the introduction and i) _____, ensuring that a logical approach to the title is developed. After this, the whole draft must be j) _____ reread and revised for both clarity and accuracy. The penultimate stage is to prepare final lists of k) _____, appendices and other items such as graphs and maps. Finally, the whole text should be thoroughly l) _____ before handing in the assignment on time.

2   *Decide if the following statements are true or false.*

a)   Academic writing aims to be accurate and impersonal.

b)   A case study looks at the views of other writers on the same topic.

c)   Academic journals are usually peer-reviewed.

d)   Students should read every page of the books on their reading lists.

e)   When searching library catalogues it is better to use very specific terms.

f)   Abstracts generally have a four-part structure.

g)   Plagiarism often means copying another writer's words without acknowledgement.

h)   An essay introduction should explain the purpose of the paper.

i)   Introductions are normally about 25% of the essay's length.

j)   Note-making should always include the source of the notes.

k)   Paraphrasing means to change both vocabulary and structure but keeping the meaning.

l)   Reference verbs always use the past tense.

m) Paragraphs always begin with a topic sentence.

n)   A good summary often includes several examples.

o)   Conclusions often mention the constraints on the paper (e.g. length).

p)   Most essays can be improved by rewriting.

q)   Proofreading means just checking for spelling mistakes.

r)   An essay conclusion should make it clear that the question has been answered.

s)   Websites are often less reliable sources than books.

t)   The best kind of outline is a mind map.

3   *Read the following book extract and write a summary of about 100 words, including a quotation, with citations. Then write a full reference for the text.*

A group of scientists working at Oxford University have been researching the behaviour of crows. Their work shows that the birds appear to be able to make simple tools, a skill which was thought to be unique to man and other primates. In an experiment a piece of meat was placed in a glass tube which was too long for the crow to reach with its beak. The bird was given a length of garden wire, 9 cms. long and 0.8 mm. thick, to extract the meat, but it soon discovered that this was not possible if the wire was straight. The bird then held one end of the wire with its feet while it used its beak to bend the other end, making a kind of hook. This could then be used for pulling the meat out of the tube, which in most cases was done within two minutes.

It has been known for some time that chimpanzees use simple tools like sticks to reach food, but it was never thought that crows could show similar levels of intelligence. Eight years ago, however, biologists in the forests of New Caledonia watched crows using sticks to reach insects inside trees. The Oxford experiment was designed to see if the same kind of bird could modify this ability to make a tool out of a material not found in their native forests (i.e. wire). According to Professor Kacelnik, one of the scientists involved, the research demonstrates that crows have an understanding of the physical properties of materials and the ability to adapt them for their own uses.

(Source: Frank Grummitt, *What Makes Us Human?* (2010) Roseberry Press, Dublin, p. 15)

Elements of Writing

Part 2 explains and practises the essential skills needed for writing academic papers. Many essays, for instance, require definitions to be made, causes and effects to be studied and examples to be given. Organised alphabetically, these skills range from presenting argument and discussion to displaying visual information.

Argument and Discussion

On most courses, students are expected to study the conflicting views on a topic and engage with them, which means analysing and critiquing them, if appropriate. This unit demonstrates ways of showing your familiarity with all sides of a debate and presenting your own conclusions in a suitably academic manner.

1 Discussion vocabulary

Essay titles commonly ask students to 'discuss' a topic:

Children will learn a foreign language more effectively if it is integrated with another subject – discuss.

This requires an evaluation of both the benefits and disadvantages of the topic, with a section of the essay, sometimes headed 'Discussion', in which a summary of these is made. The following vocabulary can be used:

+	–
benefit	drawback
advantage	disadvantage
a positive aspect	a negative feature
pro (informal)	con (informal)
plus (informal)	minus (informal)
one major advantage is. . .	a serious drawback is. . .
another significant benefit is. . .	. . . was a considerable disadvantage

One **serious drawback** to integrating content and language is the heavy demand it places on the teacher.

A **significant benefit** of teaching a subject through a foreign language is the increased motivation to master the language.

■   Write a paragraph of about 100 words on the benefits and drawbacks of studying in another country.

2 Organisation

The discussion can be organised in two ways; either by grouping the benefits in one section and the disadvantages in another (vertical), or by examining the subject from different viewpoints (horizontal). For example, the following essay title can be structured in the two ways as shown:

Prisons do little to reform criminals and their use should be limited – discuss.

a) Vertical

Drawbacks
Prisons are expensive; may be 'universities of crime'; most prisoners reoffend after leaving; many prisoners have mental health problems which are untreated.

Benefits
Prisons isolate dangerous criminals from society; act as a deterrent to criminal activity; may provide education or treatment (e.g. for drug addiction); provide punishment for wrong-doing.

Discussion
Numbers of prisoners are rising in many countries, which suggests that the system is failing. Evidence that short sentences are of little value. But prisons will always be necessary for some violent criminals and as a deterrent.

b) Horizontal

Economic
High costs of keeping prisoners secure. Compare with other forms of punishment.

Ethical
Do prisons reform criminals? What rights should prisoners have? Cases of wrongful imprisonment.

Social
Effect on families of prisoners, especially female prisoners with children. But also necessary to consider the victims of crime, especially violent crime, and provide punishment for wrong-doing.

Discussion
Numbers of prisoners are rising in many countries, which suggests that the system is failing. Evidence that short sentences are of little value, while cost of prison system is rising. But prisons will always be necessary for some violent criminals and as a deterrent.

■   What are the advantages of each format (i.e. vertical and horizontal)?

3 Practice A

You have to write an essay titled:

> *Working from home can be positive for many companies and their employees – discuss.*

■ Brainstorm the positive and negative aspects in the following box and then write an outline using one of the structures (vertical or horizontal) given on page 92.

+ Positive	– Negative
No time wasted commuting to work	

4 The language of discussion

In discussion, avoid personal phrases such as *in my opinion* or *actually, I think. . . .*
Use impersonal phrases instead, such as:

It is generally accepted that	*working from home saves commuting time.*
It is widely agreed that	*email and the internet reduce reliance on an office.*
Most people	*appear to need face-to-face contact with colleagues.*
It is probable that	*more companies will encourage working from home.*
The evidence suggests that	*certain people are better at self-management.*

These phrases suggest a minority viewpoint:

It can be argued that	*home-working encourages time-wasting.*
One view is that	*home-workers become isolated.*

When you are supporting your opinions with reference to sources, use phrases such as:

According to Emerson (2003)	*few companies have developed clear policies.*
Poledna (2007) claims that	*most employees benefit from flexible arrangements.*

5 Counter-arguments

Counter-arguments are ideas which are opposite to your ideas. In an academic discussion, you must show that you are familiar with all the various opinions and positions on the topic and provide reasons to support your own position. It is usual to deal with the counter-arguments first, before giving your view.

- What is the writer's position in the following example on the topic of prisons (2 on page 92)?

> It is claimed that prisons are needed to isolate dangerous criminals from society, and to provide punishment for wrong-doing. But while this may be true in a minority of cases, more commonly prisons act as 'universities of crime', which serve to reinforce criminal behaviour. The majority of prisoners are not dangerous and could be dealt with more effectively by other means.

- Study the following example and write two more sentences using ideas on the topic of home-working from page 93.

Counter-argument	Your position
Some people believe that home-workers become isolated,	*but this can be avoided by holding weekly meetings for all departmental staff.*

6 Providing evidence

Normally your conclusions on a topic follow an assessment of the evidence. You must show that you have examined the relevant sources, since only then can you give a balanced judgement.

- Study the following text, which discusses the idea that young people today who have grown up with computing and the internet are different from previous generations. Then answer the following questions.

DO 'DIGITAL NATIVES' EXIST?

Various writers have argued that people born around the end of the twentieth century (1990–2005) and who have been using computers all their lives have different abilities and needs to other people. Palfrey and Gasser (2008) refer to them as the 'net generation' and argue that activities such as putting videos on You Tube are more natural for them than writing essays. Similarly, Prensky (2001a) claims that the educational system needs to be revised to cater for the preferences of these so-called 'digital natives'.

But other researchers doubt that these claims can apply to a whole generation. Bennett, Maton and Kervin (2008) argue that these young people comprise a whole range of abilities and that many of them only have a limited understanding of digital tools. They insist that the so-called 'digital native' theory is a myth and that it would be a mistake to reorganise the educational system and abandon traditional means of assess-ment and enquiry such as essay writing to cater for their supposed requirements.

Clearly there are some young people who are very proficient in online technologies, and many more who regularly use social media in their daily lives, but taking a global perspective, millions still grow up and are educated in a traditional manner. Teaching methods are constantly being revised, but there is no clear evidence of a need to radically change them.

a)   How many sources are cited to support the 'digital native' theory?

b)   What do these writers suggest changing?

c)   Why do their critics disagree with them?

d)   What is the opinion of the writer of this text?

e)   What is your opinion of this subject?

7 Practice B

■   Write three paragraphs on the topic: 'Should young children (under 10) be allowed to use social media (e.g. Facebook)?' Add to the following ideas and make your position clear.

Pros

•   Social media allow children to keep in touch with friends and family

•   Using these sites teaches them computer skills

•   It is safer for children than playing outside or on the street

•   _____

(Source: Dobrowsky, 2012)

Cons

•   These children are too young to understand the dangers of the virtual world

•   Too much screen time diminishes real-life experience

•   Young children should be physically active, not looking at a computer

•   Can become addictive and lead to sleep loss

•   _____

(Source: Campbell and Childs, 2014)

▶   **See Unit 2.7 Problems and Solutions**

Cause and Effect

Academic work frequently involves explaining a link between a cause, such as a price rise, and an effect or result, such as a fall in demand. Alternatively, research may begin with a result, such as the French Revolution, and discuss possible causes. This unit demonstrates and practises two methods of describing the link, with the focus either on the cause or on the effect.

1 The language of cause and effect

A writer may choose to emphasise either the cause or the effect. In both cases, either a verb or a conjunction can be used to show the link.

a) **Focus on causes**

   With verbs

The poor harvest	*caused*	*higher prices*
	led to	
	resulted in	
	produced	

   With conjunctions

Because of	*the poor harvest*	*prices rose*
Due to		
Owing to		
As a result of		

b) **Focus on effects**

With verbs (note use of passives)

*The **higher prices***	*were caused by*	*the poor harvest*
	were produced by	
	resulted from	

With conjunctions

*There were **price rises***	*due to*	*the poor harvest*
	because of	
	as a result of	

Compare the following:

Because children **were vaccinated** diseases declined.   (because + verb)

Because of the **vaccination** diseases declined.   (because of + noun)

As/since children **were vaccinated** diseases declined.   (conjunction + verb)

Owing to/due to the **vaccination** diseases declined.   (conjunction + noun)

Note the position of the conjunctions in the following:

*The teacher was ill, **therefore/hence/so/consequently** the class was cancelled.*

▶ **See Units 3.4 Passive and Active and 4.5 Conjunctions**

2 Practice A

■ Match the causes with their likely effects and write two sentences linking each together, one emphasising the cause and the other the effect.

Causes	Effects
The cold winter of 2015	stores closing on the high street
Higher rates of literacy	more tourists arriving
Construction of the airport	a new government formed
Last year's national election	greater demand for secondary education
Installing speed cameras on main roads	**increased demand for electricity**
Opening a new hospital in 2012	a fall in the number of fatal accidents
More people shopping on the internet	reduced infant mortality

Example:

i) *Owing to the cold winter of 2015 there was increased demand for electricity.*

ii) *The increased demand for electricity was due to the cold winter of 2015.*

a) _____

_____

b) _____

_____

c) _____

_____

d) _____

_____

e) _____

_____

f) _____

_____

3 Practice B

■ Complete the following sentences with likely effects.

a)   Increasing use of email for messages _____

b)   The violent storms last week _____

c)   The new vaccine for tuberculosis (TB) _____

d)   Building a high-speed railway line _____

e)   The invention of the jet engine _____

■ Complete these sentences with possible causes.

f)   The serious motorway accident _____

g)   The high price of bread _____

h)   The increase in obesity _____

i)   Earthquakes _____

j)   The rising prison population _____

4 Practice C

■ Use conjunctions to complete the following text.

Why do women live longer?

In most countries today women, on average, tend to have a longer life expectancy than men. In France, for instance, men can expect to live to 79, while
for women the figure is 85. There is no clear explanation for the difference,
although various theories have attempted to explain it. Biologists have claimed
that women live longer a) _____ they need to bring up children.
Others argue that men take more risks, b) _____ they die earlier.
Another explanation for the discrepancy is c) _____ women have
healthier lifestyles (e.g. they smoke and drink less).

But now some British scientists believe that women live longer than men
d) _____ T cells, a vital part of the immune system that
protects the body from diseases. The team from Imperial College think that
the difference may be e) _____ women having better immune
systems. Having studied a large group of men and women they found that the
body produces fewer T cells as it gets older, f) _____ the ageing
process. However, they admit that g) _____ the complexity of the
topic this may not be the only factor, and so another research project may be
needed.

5 Practice D

a) ■ Study the following flow chart, which shows some of the possible effects of a
       higher oil price. Complete the paragraph describing this sequence.

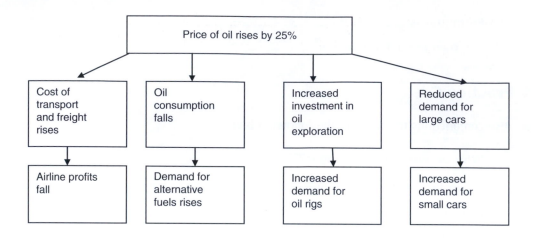

An increase of 25% in the price of oil would have numerous
results. First, it would lead to . . .

b) ■ Imagine that the government in your country passed a law making cigarettes
illegal. Draw a flow chart showing possible effects and write a paragraph
describing them.

c) ■ Choose a situation in your own subject. Draw a flow chart showing some probable
effects, and write a paragraph to describe them.

Comparison

It is often necessary to make comparisons in academic writing. The comparison might be the subject of the essay or might provide evidence for the argument. In all cases it is important to explain clearly what is being compared and to make the comparison as accurate as possible. This unit deals with different forms of comparison and practises their use.

1 Comparison structures

a)   Some studies are based on a comparison:

> *The purpose of this study is to compare Chinese and American consumers on their propensity to use self-service technology in a retail setting.*

In other cases, a comparison provides useful context:

> *The first attempt to decode the human genome took 10 years; now it can be done in less than a week.*

b)   The two basic comparative forms are:

i)   *France is **larger** than Switzerland.*

*The students were **happier** after the exam.*

(-er is added to one-syllable adjectives and two-syllable adjectives ending in -y, which changes into an 'i')

ii)   *Learning Chinese is **more difficult** than learning English.*

*Washington is **less crowded** than New York.*

(more/less . . . are used with other adjectives of two or more syllables)

c) These comparisons can be modified by the use of adverbs such as:

slightly, marginally (for small amounts)

considerably, significantly, substantially (for large amounts)

> France is **substantially larger** than Switzerland.
>
> Switzerland is **slightly smaller** than Holland.
>
> Winters in Poland are **significantly colder** than in Portugal.

d) Similarity or near-similarity can be noted by the use of *as* _____ *as* or *the same as:*

> The population of France is **approximately the same as** the population of Britain.
>
> Summers in Tokyo are **as wet as** in Singapore.

This form can be used for quantitative comparison:

> Britain is **half as large as** France.
>
> The journey by plane is **five times as fast as** by train.

▶   **See Unit 3.3 Numbers**

2 Practice A

■   **Study the table, which shows the price of quality residential property in various cities. Complete the following comparisons and write two more.**

€ per sq. m.	City
28,000	London
16,500	New York
16,200	Moscow
16,000	Paris
15,850	Tokyo
13,500	Rome
11,850	Singapore
11,000	Sydney

a) Residential property in London is twice as expensive _____ in Rome.

b) Property in Moscow is _____ cheaper than in New York.

c)   Tokyo property is nearly as expensive as property in _____

d)   Singapore has significantly cheaper property _____ New York.

e)   London is the _____ expensive of the eight cities, while Sydney is the cheapest.

f)   _____

g)   _____

3 Forms of comparison

■ Compare these three structures:

Parisian property is more expensive than Roman (property).

Property in Paris is more expensive than in Rome.

The price of property in Paris is higher than in Rome.

Note that high/low are used for comparing abstract ideas (e.g. rates):

*The birth rate was **higher** 20 years ago.*

More/less must be used with *than + comparison*:

*This module is **more difficult than** the last one.*

*Divorce is **less common** in Turkey **than** in Germany.*

4 Using superlatives (e.g. the largest/smallest)

When using superlatives, take care to define the group (i.e. 'the cheapest car' has no meaning):

*The cheapest car **in the Ford range/in the US.***

The most/the least are followed by an adjective:

*The **most interesting** example is the position of Ireland.*

The most/the fewest are used in relation to numbers:

*The **fewest** students studied biogenetics* (i.e. the lowest number).

5 Practice B

■ Study the table, which shows the income of the top ten clubs in European football. Then read the comparisons. Each sentence contains one error. Find and correct it.

Income of top ten European football clubs (2017)

Club	Revenue $m
Manchester United	703
Real Madrid	694
FC Barcelona	675
Bayern Munich	570
Manchester City	558
Arsenal	524
Chelsea	505
Liverpool	471
Juventus	415
Tottenham Hotspur	310

(Source: Deloitte)

a)   Manchester United had the highest income.

b)   Bayern Munich's income was almost twice much as Tottenham's.

c)   FC Barcelona earned marginally more than Juventus.

d)   Juventus had less revenue Liverpool.

e)   Arsenal's income was substantially less than Manchester City's.

f)   Arsenal earned approximately same as Chelsea.

6 Practice C

■ Study the following table and complete the gaps in the paragraph (one word per gap).

Marriage and divorce rates (per 1,000 population)

Country	Marriage rate	Divorce rate
Egypt	10.6	1.5
United States	8.4	4.7
Iran	8.4	0.8
Turkey	8.3	0.6
Japan	6.2	1.9

Russia	5.2	2.9
Spain	5.2	0.8
United Kingdom	5.2	3.1
South Africa	4.0	0.9

(Source: UN)

The table compares marriage and divorce rates (per thousand population) in a variety of countries. The marriage a) _____ ranges from 10.6 per thousand in Egypt to 4.0 in South Africa, while the rate of divorce b) _____ even more, from 4.7 in the US to only 0.9 in South Africa. The marriage rate in the US is the c) _____ as in Iran, which has a d) _____ higher rate e) _____ Spain. In countries such as Iran and Turkey only 10% of marriages appear to end in divorce, but in Britain and the US the number is f) _____ half. It seems possible that the g) _____ marriage rate in the US may be partly due to second marriages.

7 Practice D

■ Study the following data about London. Then make notes about a city you know well and write a comparison of the two cities in 150–200 words.

	London
Location	Port city, on River Thames, not far from coast
History	A town has been on this site for about 2,000 years
Status	National capital
Population	Over 7 million
Employment	Government offices, banking, finance, retail, entertainment
Culture	240 museums, 250 theatres
Public transport	London had the world's first underground railway. This now has 275 stations on 12 lines. Plus red double-decker buses
Climate	Cool wet winters, warm wet summers. Summer average approximately 17° C
Housing	Mainly brick terraced houses, also modern flats
Tallest building	The Shard (310 m)

Definitions

Definitions are usually found in introductions (see Unit 1.11). They are not needed in every paper, but if the title includes an unfamiliar phrase, or if the writer wants to use a term in a special way, it is important to make clear to the reader exactly what is meant in this context. This unit presents ways of writing both simple and complex definitions.

1 Simple definitions

Basic definitions, as found in a dictionary, are formed by giving a category and the application:

Word	Category	Application
An agenda	is a set of issues	to be discussed in a meeting.
A Master's degree	is an academic award	for postgraduate students, given on successful completion of a dissertation.
A grant	is a sum of money	given for a specific purpose.
A seminar	is an academic class	meeting with a tutor for study.

2 Category words

These are useful for making definitions.

■ Match the examples on the left with the categories on the right. Then complete a suitable definition.

Example:

Reinforced concrete is a building material consisting of cement, aggregates and steel rods, used in structures such as bridges.

Example	Category word
Reinforced concrete	Disease
Lizard	Cereal
Chain saw	Organisation
Malaria	Tool
Autocracy	Visual art
Weaving	Political system
Oats	**Building material**
Limited company	Penalty
Parking fine	Reptile
Sculpture	Process

■ Complete the following definitions by inserting a suitable category word or phrase from the box (There are more words than gaps).

fabric	theory	behaviour	organisation	process
instrument	organs	period	root vegetables	profession

a) A barometer is a scientific _____ designed to measure atmospheric pressure.

b) Kidneys are _____ that separate waste fluid from the blood.

c) A multinational company is a business _____ that operates in many countries.

d) Linen is a _____ made from flax.

e) Bullying is a pattern of antisocial _____ found in many schools.

f) Recycling is a _____ in which materials are used again.

g) A recession is a _____ of reduced economic activity.

h) Carrots are _____ widely grown in temperate climates.

■ Write definitions for the following:

i) A lecture is ———————————————————————— .

j) Tuberculosis (TB) is ———————————————————— .

k) The Red Cross is ————————————————————— .

l) An idiom is —————————————————————————— .

■ **Write two definitions from your own subject area:**

———————————————————————————————————————

———————————————————————————————————————

3 Complex definitions

It can be difficult to explain terms that you may feel are generally used and understood. For instance, what exactly is an 'urban area' or a 'non-governmental organisation'? This is the reason why it can be useful to make clear what you understand by such a phrase.

■ **Study the following examples and underline the terms being defined.**

a) The definition for a failed project ranges from abandoned projects to projects that do not meet their full potential or simply have schedule overrun problems.

b) Development is a socio-economic-technological process having the main objective of raising the standards of living of the people.

c) Bowlby (1982) suggested that attachment is an organised system whose goal is to make individuals feel safe and secure.

d) . . . the non-linear effect called 'self-brightening' in which large-amplitude waves decay more slowly than small-amplitude ones. . .

e) Globalisation, in an economic sense, describes the opening up of national economies to global markets and global capital, the freer movement and diffusion of goods, services, finance, people, knowledge and technology around the world.

These examples illustrate the variety of methods used in giving definitions.

■ **Which of the preceding example(s)**

i) quotes a definition from another writer?

ii) gives a variety of relevant situations?

iii) explains a process?

iv) uses category words?

4 Practice

■ Study the following titles, underline the terms that are worth defining and write definitions for three of them.

Example:

Title: <u>Higher education</u> should be free and open to all – discuss.

Definition: *Higher education usually means university-level study for first or higher degrees, normally at the age of 18 or above.*

a)   Capital punishment has no place in the modern legal system – discuss.

b)   How can the management of an entrepreneurial business retain its entrepreneurial culture as it matures?

c)   E-books are likely to replace printed books in the next 20 years. Do you agree?

d)   As urban areas continue to expand worldwide, will agriculture be able to feed the growing population of cities?

e)   Given the medical dangers of obesity, what is the best way of reducing its incidence?

UNIT 2.5

Examples

Examples are used in academic writing for support and illustration. Suitable examples can strengthen the argument, and they can also help the reader to understand a point. This unit demonstrates the different ways in which examples can be introduced and practises their use.

1 Using examples

Generalisations are commonly used to introduce a topic:

Many plants and animals are threatened by global warming.

But if the reader is given an example for illustration, the idea becomes more concrete:

Many plants and animals are threatened by global warming. **Polar bears, for example, are suffering from the lack of Arctic ice.**

Without examples, writing can seem too theoretical:

The overuse of antibiotics has had serious negative consequences.

But an example makes the idea easier to understand:

The overuse of antibiotics has had serious negative consequences. **Hospital-acquired infections such as MRSA have become more difficult to treat and this has resulted in many deaths.**

The example may also support the point the writer is making:

The past decade has seen International Relations enthusiastically embrace popular culture as a classroom resource. **George Orwell's '1984' has long had traction as a metaphor for a meta-regional dystopia . . .**

▶ **See Unit 2.6 Generalisations**

2 Phrases to introduce examples

a)   **for instance, for example**, **e.g.** (abbreviation of 'for example' in Latin)

   Some car manufacturers, for instance Kia, now offer seven-year guarantees.

b)   **such as**

   Extreme weather events such as hurricanes are becoming more frequent.

c)   **particularly, especially** (to give a focus)

   Certain Master's courses, especially American ones, take two years.

d)   **a case in point** (for single examples)

   A few diseases have been successfully eradicated. A case in point is smallpox.

■ Add a suitable example to each sentence and introduce it with one of the preceding phrases.

   Example:
      A number of sports have become very profitable due to the sale of television rights.
      *A number of sports, **for instance motor racing**, have become very profitable due to the sale of television rights.*

a)   Some twentieth-century inventions affected the lives of most people.

b)   Lately many countries have introduced fees for university courses.

c)   Various companies have built their reputations on the strength of one product.

d)   In recent years more women have become political leaders.

e)   Certain countries are frequently affected by earthquakes.

f)   Many musical instruments use strings to make music.

g)   Ship canals facilitate world trade.

h)   Politicians have discussed a range of possible alternative punishments to prison.

3 Practice A

■ Read the following text and add suitable example phrases from the box where appropriate.

such as Diet Coke

including eggs, butter, salt, sugar, fats and smoked meats

for example, bread or rice

(e.g. swimming, running or cycling)

in other words, a food may be condemned by one scientist but approved by another

such as fruit and meat

EATING FOR HEALTH

A hundred years ago most people's diets consisted of a few staple items that were cheap and also filling. Today many people are able to afford more variety and regularly eat more expensive foods. But along with the wider choice has come anxiety about the possible threats to health contained in certain foods. In recent years a broad range of products has been considered a risk to health. This has left many people confused, as much of the 'research' behind these claims is contradictory. One beneficiary of this process is the health food industry, a booming sector which promotes food and drink products to health-conscious young people. In fact, many doctors argue that instead of focusing exclusively on what they eat or drink, people's health would be improved by doing more exercise.

4 Practice B

■ Read the following text and then insert suitable examples where needed to illustrate the points.

A NEW PERSPECTIVE

Students who go to study abroad often experience a type of culture shock when they arrive in the new country. Of course, there are always different things to learn about in a fresh town or city. But in addition, customs which they took for granted in their own society may not be followed in the host country. Even everyday patterns of life may be different. When these are added to the inevitable differences which occur between every country, students may at first feel confused. They can experience rapid changes of mood or even want to return home. However, most soon make new friends and, in a relatively short period, are able to adjust to their new environment. They may even find that they prefer some aspects of their new surroundings and forget that they are not at home for a while!

5 Restatement

Another small group of phrases is used when there is only one 'example'. (Brackets may also be used for this purpose). This is a kind of restatement to clarify the meaning:

*The world's leading gold producer, **namely**, South Africa, has been faced with a number of technical difficulties.*

---

in other words   namely   that is (to say)   i.e.   viz. (very formal)

■ Add a suitable phrase from the box below to the following sentences to make them clearer.

a)   The company's overheads doubled last year.

b)   The Roman Empire was a period of autocratic rule.

c)   The Indian capital has a thriving commercial centre.

d)   Survival rates for the most common type of cancer are improving.

e)   Voting rates in most democracies are in decline.

---

that is to say, fewer people are voting

in other words the fixed costs

namely, New Delhi,

(27 BCE – 476 CE)

i.e. breast cancer

Generalisations

Generalisations are often used to introduce a topic. They can be powerful statements because they are simple and easy to understand. But they must be used with care, to avoid being inaccurate or too simplistic. This unit explains how to generalise clearly and effectively.

1 Using generalisations

a) Generalisations are often used to give a simple introduction to a topic. Compare:

> *The majority of smokers in Britain are women.*

with

> *56.2% of all UK smokers are women, and 43.8% are men.*

Although the second sentence is more accurate, the first is easier to understand and remember. The writer must decide when accuracy is necessary and when a generalisation will be acceptable.

b) You must avoid using generalisations which cannot be supported by evidence or research or are unclear:

> *Cats are more intelligent than dogs.*

> *Young children learn second languages easily.*

> *Smoking causes lung cancer.*

Such statements are dangerous because there may well be exceptions. Instead, it is better to use cautious phrases such as:

> *Cats **may be/tend to be** more intelligent than dogs.*

*Young children **often** learn second languages easily.*

*Smoking **can** cause lung cancer.*

■ Decide which of the following are valid generalisations:

a) It rains a lot in England.

b) Earthquakes are often difficult to predict.

c) There appears to be a link between poverty and disease.

d) Women work harder than men.

e) Travel by air is usually faster than train travel.

▶ See Unit 3.7.6 Style: The use of caution

2 Structure

Generalisations can be made in two ways:

a) Most commonly using the plural:

Computers have transformed the way we live.

b) Using the singular + definite article (more formal):

The computer has transformed the way we live.

3 Practice A

■ Write generalisations on the following topics:

Example:
fresh fruit/health – *Eating fresh fruit is important for health.*

a) regular rainfall/good crop yields   *helps to grow up*

b) honest judges/respect for the law

c) adequate sleep/academic success

d) industrial growth/pollution   *provoke hight*

e) cold weather/demand for gas

f) job satisfaction/interesting work   *int. work could more as j's*

g) regular training/sporting success   *is the base of success*

h) creativity and skill/great art   *not every time*

gorauty a the great art

4 Practice B

■ Study the table and write five generalisations using the information.

Results of a college survey on where students prefer to study.

	Undergraduates (%)		Graduates (%)	
	Male	**Female**	**Male**	**Female**
Library	20	17	47	32
Own room in silence	21	27	26	38
Own room with music	25	13	12	14
Own room in bed	15	24	6	10
Outdoors	6	9	4	2
Other	13	10	5	4

(Source: Author)

5 Building on generalisations

Generalisations can be used in various ways when presenting the results of research or developing a thesis.

■ Read the following text and note the generalisations in italics. Answer the questions that follow.

WHAT WOMEN WANT

What we look for in choosing a mate seems to vary from place to place. A recent study (Jones and DeBruine, 2010) explores the idea that female preferences in a mate might vary according to the society in which she lives. In their research, nearly 5,000 women in 30 countries were shown the same pictures of male faces and asked to state which they found more attractive. In countries where disease is common, women chose men with more masculine features, while in countries such as America with more advanced health care and lower levels of disease, more effeminate-looking men were preferred. The researchers conclude that *in healthier societies women are more interested in men who may form long-term relationships and help with child-rearing, while in places where child mortality rates are high they choose strongly featured men who seem more likely to produce healthy children.*

a)   What is the function of the first generalisation?

b)   What is the basis of the concluding generalisations?

c)   What is the purpose of the concluding generalisations?

6 Practice C

Most essays move from the general to the specific, as a generalisation has to be supported and developed. For example, an essay with the title 'The impact of globalisation on the Chinese economy' might develop in this way:

Generalisation	Support	Development > Specific
Since the mid-twentieth century there has been a remarkable increase in international trade.	*The reasons for this are a combination of international agreements such as GATT, better transport and improved communications.*	*China has played a significant part in this process, with its international trade growing by 16 times in just 20 years, while its GDP increased by nearly 10% per year.*

■ Choose a title from the following list (or select one from your own subject) and then write a generalisation and develop it in the same way.

a)   Does tourism always have a negative effect on the host country?

b)   Should governments use taxation to promote public health?

c)   Is it more important to protect forests or to grow food?

d)   Is it better for the state to spend money on primary or university education?

Generalisation	Support	Development > Specific

▶   See Unit 1.11 Introductions and Conclusions

Problems and Solutions

Writing tasks frequently ask students to examine a problem and evaluate a range of solutions. This unit explains ways in which this kind of text can be organised. Note that some of the language is similar to that practised in Unit 2.1 Argument and Discussion.

1 Paragraph structure

■ Study the organisation of the following paragraph:

How can road congestion be reduced?

Currently, roads are often congested, which is expensive in terms of delays to the movement of people and freight. It is commonly suggested that building more roads, or widening existing ones, would ease the traffic jams. But not only is the cost of such work high, but the construction process adds to the congestion, while the resulting extra road space may encourage more traffic, so it is only a short-term answer. Therefore constructing more roads is unlikely to solve the problem and other remedies, such as road pricing or greater provision of public transport, should be examined.

Problem: Currently, roads are often congested, which is expensive in terms of delays to the movement of people and freight.

Solution A: It is commonly suggested that building more roads, or widening existing ones, would ease the traffic jams.

Arguments against solution A: But not only is the cost of such work high, but the construction process adds to the congestion, while the resulting extra road space may encourage extra traffic, so it is only a short-term answer.

Conclusion in favour of solutions B and C: . . . other remedies, such as road pricing or greater provision of public transport, should be examined.

2 Alternative structure

The same ideas could be reordered to arrive at a different conclusion:

How can road congestion be reduced?

Currently, roads are often congested, which is expensive in terms of delays to the movement of people and freight. It is commonly suggested that building more roads, or widening existing ones, would ease the traffic jams. This remedy is criticised for being expensive and liable to lead to more road use, which may be partly true, yet the alternatives are equally problematic. Road pricing has many practical difficulties, while people are often reluctant to use public transport. There is little alternative to a road building programme except increasing road chaos.

Problem: Currently, roads are often congested, which is expensive in terms of delays to the movement of people and freight.

Solution A: It is commonly suggested that building more roads, or widening existing ones, would ease the traffic jams.

Arguments against solution A: This remedy is criticised for being expensive and liable to lead to more road use, which may be partly true . . .

Solutions B and C and arguments against: . . . yet the alternatives are equally problematic. Road pricing has many practical difficulties, while people are often reluctant to use public transport.

Conclusion in favour of solution A: There is little alternative to a road building programme except increasing road chaos.

3 Vocabulary

The following words can be used as synonyms for ***problem*** and ***solution***.

*three main **difficulties** have arisen . . .*
*the main **challenge** faced by nurses . . .*
*one of the **concerns** during the recession . . .*
*the new process created two **questions** . . .*
*the team faced three main **issues** . . .*
*our principal **worry/dilemma** was . . .*

*the best **remedy** for this may be . . .*
*two **answers** have been put forward . . .*
*another **suggestion** is . . .*
*Matheson's **proposal** was finally accepted.*
*this was **rectified/solved** by . . .*
*another **avenue** worth exploring is . . .*

4 Practice A

■ Read the following text and then rewrite it to reach a different conclusion.

The housing dilemma

In many expanding urban areas there is a serious housing shortage caused by people moving from the country to seek urban opportunities. There are various possible answers to this problem, but each has its drawbacks. The traditional response is to build family houses with gardens, which offer privacy and space but require a lot of land. Building these is slow and the growth of suburbs creates longer journeys to work. Another solution is to construct tall blocks of flats, which will accommodate more people at high density quite cheaply. However, families may find them noisy and cramped. A third option is to build prefabricated three-storey houses which can be erected more quickly and cheaply than traditional houses, and can be designed to achieve a higher density of population. For many cities these may be the best solution, avoiding the growth of both extensive suburbs and high-rise blocks.

5 Practice B

■ Use the following points to write a paragraph on university expansion.

Topic: University expansion

Problem: Demand for university places is growing, leading to overcrowding in lectures and seminars

Solution A: Increase fees to reduce demand

Argument against A: Unfair to poorer students

Solution B: Government pays to expand universities

Argument against B: Unfair to average taxpayer who would be subsidising the education of a minority who will earn high salaries

Conclusion: Government should subsidise poorer students

6 Practice C

■ Think of a similar problem in your subject area. Complete the form and write a paragraph which leads to a conclusion.

Topic: _____

Problem: _____

_____

Solution A: _____

_____

Argument against A: _____

_____

Solution B: _____

_____

Argument for/against B: _____

_____

(Solution C): _____

_____

Conclusion: _____

_____

Visual Information

In many subjects it is essential to support your writing with statistical data. Visual devices such as graphs and tables are a convenient way of displaying large quantities of information in a form that is easy to understand. This unit explains and practises the language connected with these devices.

1 Types of visuals

Some of the main types of visual devices used in academic texts are presented in the following table. Note that they are often combined (e.g. a bar chart with a line graph).

■ Complete the table to show the main use (a-i) and the example (A-I) of each type.

Types	Use	Example
1 Diagram		
2 Table		
3 Map		
4 Pie chart		
5 Flow chart		
6 Line graph		
7 Bar chart		
8 Plan		
9 Scatter graph/plot		

Use:

a) location – small scale

b) location – large scale

c) changes in time

d) sequence of process

e) comparison

f) proportion

g) structure

h) statistical display

i) relation between two sets of variables

A Cinema ticket sales

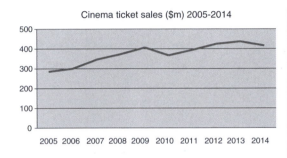

Cinema ticket sales ($m) 2005-2014

B Average life expectancy – both sexes (2015, in years)

Japan	83.7
France	82.4
United States	79.3
United Arab Emirates	77.1
India	68.3
South Africa	62.9
Afghanistan	60.5
Nigeria	54.5
Angola	52.4

C Electricity output from coal (2015)

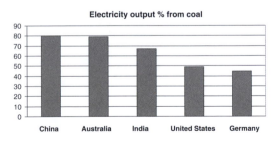

Electricity output % from coal

D Origins of international students

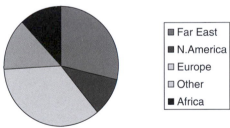

- ■ Far East
- ■ N.America
- ☐ Europe
- ☐ Other
- ■ Africa

E Planning an essay

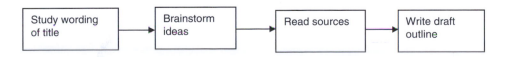

Study wording of title → Brainstorm ideas → Read sources → Write draft outline

F The human ear

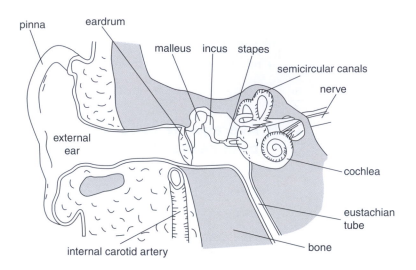

G Layout of the language centre

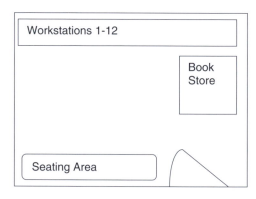

H The regions of Italy

I Height versus armspan

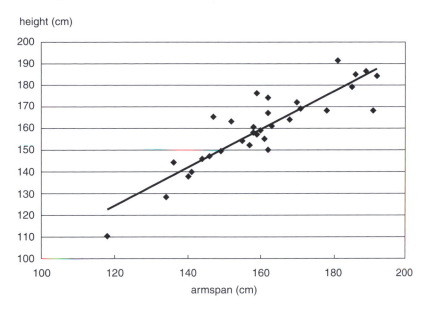

height (cm)

armspan (cm)

2 The language of change

(past tenses in brackets)

Verb ↗	Adverb	Verb ↘	Adjective + noun
grow (grew)	slightly	drop (dropped)	a slight drop
rise (rose)	gradually	fall (fell)	a gradual fall
increase (increased)	steadily	decrease (decreased)	a sharp decrease
climb (climbed)	sharply	decline (declined)	a steady decline
also: a peak, to peak, a plateau, to level off, a trough			

Average temperatures **rose steadily** *until 2012 and then* **dropped slightly.**

There was a **sharp decrease** *in sales during the summer and then a* **gradual rise.**

■ Study the following graph and the description.

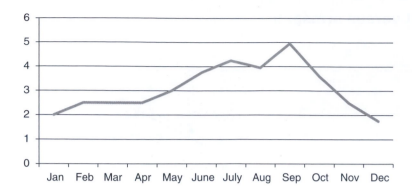

Figure 1 Inflation (%) January – December 2016

The graph (Fig. 1) shows that the rate of inflation was 2% in January and then **rose** to 2.5% in February. After that it **levelled off** until April and then **increased steadily** to over 4% in July. Inflation **fell slightly** in August but then **climbed** to a **peak** of 5% in September. From there it **dropped sharply** to below 2% in December.

3 Describing visuals

Although visuals do largely speak for themselves, it is common to help the reader interpret them by briefly commenting on their main features.

The graph	shows	the changes in the price of oil since 1990.
The map	illustrates	the main sources of copper in Africa.
The diagram	displays	the organisation of both companies.

a) ■ Read the following descriptions of the next chart. Which is better, and why?

   i) The chart (Fig. 2) shows the quantity of tea consumed by the world's leading tea-consuming nations. India and China together consume more than half the world's tea production, with India alone consuming about one-third. Other significant tea consumers are Turkey, Russia and Britain. 'Others' includes the United States, Iran and Egypt.

   ii) The chart (Fig. 2) shows that 31% of the world's tea is consumed by India, 23% by China and 8% by Turkey. The fourth-largest consumers are Russia, Japan and Britain, with 7% each, while Pakistan consumes 5%. Other countries account for the remaining 12%.

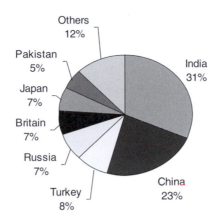

Figure 2 World tea consumption

(Source: The Tea Council)

b) ■ **Complete the description of the following bar chart.**

The bar chart (Fig. 3) shows population a) _____ in a variety of countries around the world. It b) _____ the extreme contrast c) _____ crowded nations such as South Korea (475 people per sq. km.) and much d) _____ countries such as Canada (three people per sq. km.). Apparently, climate plays a major e) _____ in determining population density, f) _____ the least crowded nations g) _____ to have extreme climates (e.g. cold in Russia and Canada or dry in Algeria).

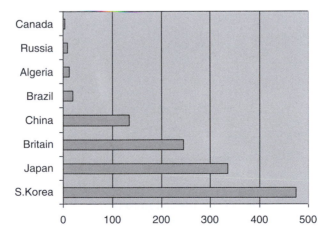

Figure 3 Population density (people per square kilometre)

(Source: OECD)

4 Labelling

- When referring to visual information in the text, the word 'figure' is used for almost everything (such as maps, charts and graphs) except tables (see examples above).
- Figures and tables should be numbered and given a title. Titles of tables are written above, while titles of figures are written below the data.
- As with other data, sources must be given for all visual information.
- If you are writing a lengthy work such as a dissertation you will need to provide lists of tables and figures, showing numbers, titles and page numbers after the contents page.

5 Practice A

■ Complete the description of the following table (one word per gap).

Table 1 Projected population changes in various European countries 2015–2050 (millions).

Country	Population 2015 (millions)	Projected population 2050	Change (%)
France	62	67	+ 5
Germany	82	71	− 11
Italy	60	57	− 3
Poland	38	32	− 6
Portugal	10.7	10	− 0.7
Russia	140	116	− 24
Spain	45	51	+ 6
UK	62	72	+ 11

(Source: UN)

The table a) _____ the projected population changes in various European countries b) _____ 2015 and 2050. It can be seen that in a c) _____ the population is expected to fall, in some cases (e.g. Germany and Russia) quite d) _____. However, the populations of France, e) _____ and the UK are predicted to f) _____, in the case of the latter by more g) _____ 10%.

6 Practice B

■ Write a paragraph commenting on the main features of the following chart.

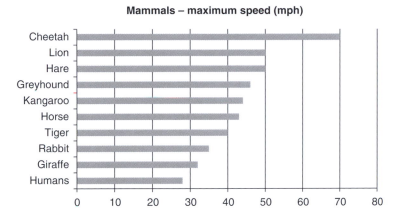

Progress Check 2

These exercises will help you assess your understanding of Part 2 – Elements of Writing.

1   *Give two synonyms for 'benefit'.*

2   *What is the difference between vertical and horizontal formats for discussion essays?*

3   *What is a counter-argument?*

4   *Write sentences giving possible causes for the following effects:*

   a) A rise in unemployment

   b) A railway accident

   c) A power cut

5   *Write three sentences comparing Australia with New Zealand using the following data.*

	Australia	New Zealand
Area (square kilometres)	7.6 m	270,000
Population	21.5 m	4.3 m
GDP per head	$50,750	$32,370

6   *Write definitions for:*

   a) A semester

   b) A hammer

   c) A midwife

7   *Insert suitable examples into each sentence.*

   a) Certain capital cities are smaller than the commercial centres of their country.

   b) Many varieties of fruit contain vital vitamins.

c) A few kinds of mammals live in the sea.

d) Most planets in our solar system have moons.

8 *In the following, underline any generalisations you find unsafe.*

In the past century, photography has gone from being an exclusive hobby to something accessible to everyone. This is largely due to the invention of the digital camera. In the last 20 years this has made it simple to take colour photographs cheaply and to modify pictures easily by using editing programmes. So now that everyone has a smartphone, with its built-in camera, photography has become democratic and high-quality photographs can be produced by anybody.

9 *Complete each sentence with synonyms for 'problem' or 'solution'.*

a) The main _____ facing the engineers was the extreme cold.

b) The only _____ was to repeat the experiment.

c) Sherlock Holmes found an unusual _____ to the mystery of the Missing Mask.

d) The safe disposal of nuclear waste is a _____ without an easy _____

10 *Write a paragraph commenting on the data in the following table.*

Table 2 Student survey of library facilities: % students rating facilities as good.

Library facilities	Undergraduates (%)	Postgraduates (%)
Opening hours	72	63
Staff helpfulness	94	81
Ease of using electronic catalogue	65	87
Availability of working space	80	76
Café area	91	95
Availability of short-loan stock	43	35
Quality of main book stock	69	54

(Source: Author)

Language Issues

PART 3

Part 3 deals with the language issues that international students find most challenging when writing in English. For example, proper use of definite articles, correct use of punctuation and effective use of a suitable academic style can be problematic for any student. The units in this part, arranged alphabetically, can also be studied on a remedial basis when a problem arises.

UNIT

3.1

Cohesion

> Cohesion means joining a text together with reference words (he, she, theirs, the former) and conjunctions (but, then) so that the whole text is clear and readable. This unit practises the use of reference words, while conjunctions are examined in Unit 4.5.

1 Reference words

Reference words are used to avoid repetition:

> **Leonardo da Vinci** (1452–1519) was a fifteenth-century Italian genius who produced only a handful of **finished artworks**. However, **they** include the **Mona Lisa** and The Last Supper, **the former** perhaps the most famous painting in the world. Although **he** is remembered mainly as an artist, **he** was also an innovative engineer, scientist and anatomist. **His designs** include tanks and flying machines, and although few of **these** were built in **his** lifetime, **he** is still remembered as the man who saw **their** possibility.

Here the reference words function as follows:

Leonardo da Vinci	finished artworks	Mona Lisa	designs
He/His	they	the former	these/their

Examples of reference words and phrases:

Pronouns	he/she/it/they
Possessive pronouns	his/her/hers/its/their/theirs
Object pronouns	her/him/them
Demonstrative pronouns	this/that/these/those
Other phrases	the former/the latter/the first/the second/the last

2 Practice A

■ Read the following paragraph and complete the table.

BUSINESS SHORT LIFE

La Ferrera (2016), a researcher at the University of Leipzig, has researched the life cycle of new business start-ups in Britain and Germany. She found that they have an average life of only 3.4 years and considers this is due to two main reasons: one economic and the other social. The former appears to be a lack of initial working capital, the latter a failure to carry out sufficient market research. La Ferrera considers that together these factors account for approximately 70% of business failures. Her conclusion is that the failure to do market research is the more serious disadvantage, as this affects the whole design of the new enterprise.

Reference	Reference word/phrase
La Ferrera	*She*
new business start-ups	
average life of only 3.4 years	
one economic	
the other social	
the former. . ., the latter. . . . . . sufficient market research	
the failure to do market research	

3 Preventing confusion

To avoid confusing the reader, it is important to use reference words only when the reference is clear and unambiguous. For example:

> *Pablo Picasso moved to Paris in 1904 and worked with Georges Braque from 1908 to 1909.* ***He*** *became interested in the analysis of form, which led to cubism.*

In this case, it is not clear which person (Picasso or Braque) 'he' refers to. So to avoid this, write:

> *Pablo Picasso moved to Paris in 1904 and worked with Georges Braque from 1908 to 1909.* ***Picasso*** *became interested in the analysis of form, which led to cubism.*

4 Practice B

■ In the following paragraph, insert suitable reference words in the gaps.

Famous for?

When Andy Warhol died at the age of 58 in 1987, few people guessed that
a) _____*he*_____ would soon become one of the most valuable artists in
the world. In 2007, total sales of b) _____*his*_____ work at auction reached
$428 million dollars. When, a year later, c) _____*his*_____ painting 'Eight
Elvises' sold for over $100 million, d) _____*it* (this)_____ was one of the
highest prices ever paid for a work of art. In e) _____*his*_____ working life,
f) _____*he*_____ made about 10,000 artworks, and dealers believe that
g) _____*these*_____ will continue to be popular with collectors in future.
h) _____*This*_____ is because of Warhol's huge reputation as a super-cool
trendsetter and innovator. i) _____*He*_____ is also remembered for
j) _____*his*_____ remark: 'In the future everyone will be famous for
15 minutes', which seems to forecast today's celebrity culture.

5 Implied language

In various written forms, certain words may be omitted for convenience. For instance, in emails the subject (noun or pronoun) is frequently left out:

   (I) Hope to see you on Friday.

   (We are) Looking forward to reading your article.

In other cases, nouns may be implied in order to avoid repetition:

   Various metals are used to make alloys with nickel. One such (metal) is chromium.

   Oil (production) and gas production have fallen since 2015.

   It is hoped to select suitable candidates from the 10,000 (candidates) who apply each year.

In places, a whole phrase might be implied:

   They are hoping to reach that goal soon. By 2025 they probably will. (reach that goal)

Implied language is frequently found in comparisons:

   The price of land in rural areas is much less than (the price of land) in cities.

Until you are a very confident writer, it is better not to omit such words or phrases, but it is useful to understand why it is done.

6 Practice C

■ Read the following paragraphs and replace the words in bold with reference words.

Velcro

Velcro is a fabric fastener used with clothes and shoes. **Velcro** was invented by a Swiss engineer called George de Mestral. **Mestral's** idea was derived from studying the tiny hooks found on some plant seeds. **The tiny hooks** cling to animals and help disperse the seeds. Velcro has two sides, one of which is covered in small hooks and the other in loops. When **the hooks and loops** are pressed together they form a strong bond.

Mestral spent eight years perfecting **Mestral's** invention, which **Mestral** called 'Velcro' from the French words 'velour' and 'crochet'. **The invention** was patented in 1955, and today over 60 million metres of Velcro are sold annually.

7 Practice D

■ Use the following information to write a paragraph about the invention of nylon, paying careful attention to the use of reference words.

Nylon

Inventor:	Wallace Carothers
Company:	DuPont Corporation (US)
Carothers' position:	Director of research centre
Carothers' background:	Chemistry student, specialising in polymers (molecules composed of long chains of atoms)
Properties:	Strong but fine synthetic fibre
Patented:	1935
Mass produced:	1939
Applications:	Stockings, toothbrushes, parachutes, fishing lines, surgical thread

UNIT
3.2

Definite Articles

Students often find the rules for using articles ('a', 'an' and 'the') in English confusing. This unit focuses on the definite article, 'the', and provides guidelines, examples and practice.

1 Use of articles

Unless they are uncountable, all nouns need an article when used in the singular. The article can be either **a/an** or **the**. Compare:

a)   *Research is an important activity in universities.*

b)   ***The*** *research begun by Dr Mathews was continued by Professor Brankovic.*

c)   ***An*** *interesting piece of research was conducted among 200 patients in the clinic.*

In a) research, which is usually uncountable, is being used in a general sense.

In b) a specific piece of research is identified, started by Dr Mathews.

In c) the research is mentioned for the first time, and the word 'piece' is used to 'count' the research.

▶   **See Unit 3.6 Singular or Plural? – Uncountable nouns**

2 Using definite articles

The rules for using **the** (the definite article) are quite complex.

■ **Decide why it is used, or not used, in the following examples.**

  a) The world's fastest animal is the cheetah.

  b) The US was founded in the eighteenth century.

  c) The government increased taxation in the 1990s.

  d) The French Revolution was partly caused by bad harvests.

  e) The *New Scientist* is published every week.

  f) The south is characterised by poverty and emigration.

  g) Pablo Picasso, the Spanish artist, was born in Malaga.

  h) The River Seine runs through the middle of Paris.

  i) The United Nations was founded in 1945.

  j) The euro was introduced in 2002.

In general, **the** is used with:

i) superlatives (*fastest*)

ii) time periods (*eighteenth century/1990s*)

iii) unique things (*government, world*)

iv) specified things (*French Revolution*)

vi) regular publications (*New Scientist*)

vii) regions and rivers (*south/River Seine*)

viii) very well-known people and things (*Spanish artist*)

ix) institutions and bodies (*United Nations*)

x) positions (*middle*)

xi) currencies (*euro*)

It is **not** used with:

xii) things in general (bad harvests)

xiii) names of countries (except for the UK, the US and a few others)

xiv) abstract nouns (e.g. poverty, love)

xv) companies/things named after people/places (e.g. Sainsbury's, Heathrow Airport)

Note the alternate forms:

> ***The*** *deserts of Australia are expanding.*

> *Australian deserts/Australia's deserts are expanding.*

3 Practice A

It can be difficult to decide if a noun phrase is specific or not. Compare:

Climate change *is a serious threat for many people.*	(not specific)
The ***Russian climate*** *is characterised by long, cold winters.*	(specific)
Mobile phones *are vital tools for many businesses.*	(not specific)
The ***mobile phone*** *she bought was a Samsung.*	(specific)

■ **In the following sentences, decide if the words and phrases in bold are specific or not and whether 'the' should be added.**

Example:

_____ **inflation** was a serious problem for _____ **Brazilian government**.

Inflation was a serious problem for **the** Brazilian government.

a) _____ **engineering** is the main industry in _____ **northern region**.

b) _____ **insurance firms** have made record profits in _____ **last decade**.

c) _____ **global warming** is partly caused by _____ **fossil fuels**.

d) _____ **mayor** has been arrested on suspicion of _____ **corruption**.

e) _____ **moons of Jupiter** were discovered in _____ **eighteenth century**.

f) _____ **tourism** is _____ **world's** biggest industry.

g) _____ **forests of Scandinavia** produce most of _____ **Britain's** paper.

h) _____ **Thai currency** is _____ **baht**.

i) _____ **computer crime** has grown by 200% in _____ **last five years**.

j) _____ **main causes** of _____ **Industrial Revolution** are still debated.

k) Three percent of _____ **working population** are employed in _____ **call centres**.

l) _____ **latest forecast** predicts _____ **warmer winters** in the next decade.

m) Research on _____ **energy saving** is being conducted in _____ **Physics Faculty**.

n) _____ **best definition** is often _____ **simplest**.

o) During _____ **last recession** there was a sharp increase in _____ **child poverty**.

4 Practice B

Note the difference in meaning between:

A government minister   (one of several/many)

The Minister of Health   (the only one)

■ Complete the following text by inserting a/the (or nothing) in each gap. (Note that in some cases more than one answer is possible).

A Northern model?

Norway is a) _____ global leader in b) _____ use of electric cars: in 2016 nearly 30% of vehicle sales were battery-powered or hybrid models. In c) _____ past five years sales have increased sharply due to d) _____ development of better batteries, so now e) _____ country's five million people are f) _____ world's largest electric car market. g) _____ Transport Minister talks of ending sales of cars powered by h) _____ fossil fuels by 2025. i) _____ government is subsidising j) _____ installation of charging points on main roads and shopping centres. In addition, drivers of k) _____ zero-emission vehicles pay no sales tax or parking fees and may use bus lanes in cities. But this pattern may not be l) _____ model for other countries: Norway has m) _____ surplus of cheap electricity thanks to n) _____ hydropower, and it taxes petrol and diesel fuel heavily.

Numbers

Students are often required to write clearly and accurately about statistical data. This unit explains and practises the language of numbers and percentages. Presenting data in charts and tables is dealt with in Unit 2.8 Visual Information.

1 The language of numbers

a) In introductions, numbers are often used to give an accurate summary of a situation:

   Approximately 1,800 children between the ages of five and 12 years were selected.

   The earth's atmosphere appears to be gaining 3.3 billion metric tons of carbon annually.

   Five winters in the twentieth century were more than 2.4° C colder than average.

The words **figures** and **numbers** are both used to talk about statistical data in a general sense:

   *The **figures/numbers** in the report need to be read critically.*

But **number** is used more widely:

   *She forgot her mobile phone **number.***

   *Thirteen is an unlucky **number** in some cultures.*

Digits are individual numbers.

   *4,539 is a four-**digit** number.*

Both **fractions** (½) and **decimals** (0.975) may be used.

b) There is no final 's' on hundred/thousand/million used with whole numbers:

   *Six **million** people live there.*

but:

Thousands of people were forced to move from the flooded valley.

When discussing money, put the currency symbol first: *$440 m* (440 million US dollars).

Rates are normally expressed as percentages (e.g. *the literacy rate is 75%*) but may also be per thousand (e.g. *the Austrian birth rate is 8.7*).

It is normal to write whole numbers as words from one to ten and as digits above ten:

There were 16 students in the class, but only eight came to the lecture.

2 Percentages

These are commonly used for expressing rates of change:

Since 2008 the number of prisoners has risen by 22%.

■ Complete the following sentences using the data in the next table.

a)   Between 2014 and 2015, the number of students increased by _____ %.

b)   The number increased by _____ % the following year.

c)   Between 2014 and 2017 there was a _____ % increase.

Students studying Law and Politics 2014–2017

2014	2015	2016	2017
200	300	600	1000

3 Simplification

Although the accurate use of numbers is vital, too many statistics can make texts difficult to read. If the exact number is not important, words such as *various, dozens* or *scores* may be used instead:

The snow storm closed 47 schools.

*The snow storm closed **dozens** of schools.*

a couple   2

few   a small number, less than expected

a few   approximately 3–6 depending on context

several	approximately 3–4
various	approximately 4–6
dozens of	approximately 30–60
scores of	approximately 60–100

■ Rewrite the following sentences using one of the words or phrases in the preceding list.

Example:

> **Only three** people attended the meeting.
> **Few** people attended the meeting.

a) 77 students applied for the scholarship.

b) Since 1975, 53 primary schools have been rebuilt.

c) The students thought of four good topics for their project.

d) Five names were suggested but rejected for the new chocolate bar.

e) Last year 49 books were published on biogenetics.

4 Further numerical phrases

The expressions listed here can also be used to present and simplify statistical information. For example:

> *The course fees rose from $1,200 to $2,500 in two years.*

could be written:

> *The course fees **doubled** in two years.*

If appropriate, *roughly/approximately* can be added:

> *The course fees **roughly doubled** in two years.*

one in three	*One in three engineering students is from China.*
twice/three times as many	*Twice as many women as men study business law.*
a five/tenfold increase	*There was a fivefold increase in the price of oil.*
to double/halve	*The rate of infection halved after 2001.*
the highest/lowest	*The lowest rate of home ownership was in Germany.*

a quarter/fifth	*A fifth of all employees leave every year.*
the majority/minority	*The majority of births are in hospital.*
on average, the average	*On average, each judge hears two cases per day.*
a small/large proportion	*The website generates a large proportion of their sales.*

NB: 5–20%   =   a small minority
     21–39%   =   a minority
     40–49%   =   a substantial/significant minority
     51–55%   =   a small majority
     56–79%   =   a majority
     80% +   =   a large majority

■ **Rewrite each sentence in a simpler way, using a suitable expression from the preceding list.**

a) In 1973, a litre of petrol cost 12p, while the price is now £1.20.

_____

b) Out of 18 students in the group, 12 were women.

_____

c) The new high-speed train reduced the journey time to Madrid from seven hours to three hours, 20 minutes.

_____

d) The number of students applying for the Psychology course has risen from 350 last year to 525 this year.

_____

e) More than 80% of students in Britain complete their first degree course; in Italy the figure is just 35%.

_____

f) Tap water costs 0.07p per litre, while bottled water costs, on average, 50p per litre.

_____

g) The rate of unemployment in Europe ranges from 23% in Greece to 3% in Norway.

_____

h) 57 percent of the members supported the suggestion, but of these, 83% had some doubts.

_____

5 Practice

■ Study the data in the following table and write sentences using suitable numerical phrases.

Selected Olympic Games 1896–2012

Year	Host	Sports	Events	Athletes	% Women
1896	Athens	9	43	241	0.0 %
1924	Paris	17	126	3,089	4.4 %
1964	Tokyo	19	163	5,151	13.2 %
1992	Barcelona	32	257	9,356	28.9 %
2008	Beijing	28	302	10,942	42.4%
2012	London	28	302	10,700	45%

Source: IOC

a) *At the Paris Olympics in 1924 a small minority of athletes were female.*

b) _____

c) _____

d) _____

e) _____

f) _____

Passive and Active

The passive voice is more common in academic writing than in other genres, making it more impersonal and formal, but the passive should not be overused. This unit explains where it is appropriate to use the passive and provides practice in developing a balanced style.

1 Active and passive

The passive is used when the writer wants to focus on the result, not on the cause or agent:

> *Jupiter's moons were discovered in 1610.* (passive)

> *Galileo discovered Jupiter's moons in 1610.* (active)

In the first sentence, the emphasis is on the moons, in the second on Galileo. So the passive is often used in written English when the cause or agent (a person or thing) is less important or unknown.

> *Aluminium **was** first **produced** in the nineteenth century. (by someone)*

> *The colony **was abandoned** in the 1630s. (for some unknown reason)*

The cause of the action can be shown by adding 'by. . .':

> *The city was flooded **by a severe hurricane**.*

The passive is also used in written work to provide a more impersonal style:

> *The findings **were evaluated**. (not 'I evaluated the findings')*

▶ **See Unit 3.7 Style**

2 Structure

All passive structures have two parts:

Form of the verb to be	Past participle
is	constructed
was	developed
will be	reorganised

■ **Change the following sentences into the passive to make them more impersonal.**

   a) We collected the data and compared the two groups.

   b) I interviewed 120 people in three social classes.

   c) They checked the results and found several errors.

   d) We will make an analysis of the findings.

   e) He asked four doctors to give their opinion.

   f) She wrote the report and distributed ten copies.

3 Use of the passive

The passive tends to be commonly employed in certain situations:

a) Describing a process

   Urea can **be made** *cheaply by mixing ammonia and carbon dioxide.*

   What causes this antibody to **be produced** *is unclear.*

   Printed skin might eventually **be employed** *for grafts.*

b) Describing a piece of research

   The results **were adjusted** *to allow for the variation.*

   It **was found** *that the smallest were the most effective.*

   The process **was discovered** *in the 2000s.*

   One study **was conducted** *in America and* **published** *in 2011.*

In both of these situations the use of the passive puts the emphasis on the action and not on the people involved.

■ Change the following sentences from active to passive.

    a) The researchers exposed the vaccines to temperatures below the limit.

    b) Some historians believe that the Atacama desert was too dry for animal life.

    c) Dr Weber suggests that foreign competition can damage them.

    d) They researched the life cycles of three main bee species.

    e) She argued that prisons had a negative effect on the inmates.

4 Adverbs with passives

Adverbs are frequently inserted into the passive structure to add information:

*Emigration was **largely** banned until 1991.*

*The vaccine was **accidentally** frozen.*

■ Underline the passive forms in the following paragraph and add suitable adverbs to each from the box.

MARS MANIA

In the past it <u>was **commonly** believed</u> that creatures lived on Mars. Due to the similarity of size with Earth, the planet was thought to have a climate that would permit life. It was discovered that Mars had four seasons, although they were longer than their equivalents on Earth. In the late nineteenth century, straight lines seen on the surface of Mars were considered to be canals, built by Martian engineers. An invasion of Earth by superior beings from Mars was described by H.G. Wells in his novel *War of the Worlds*. Even today it is claimed that primitive life exists on the planet.

~~commonly~~ **graphically occasionally generally ridiculously additionally**

▶ See Unit 4.4 Academic Vocabulary: Adverbs and Verbs

5 Practice

Overuse of the passive can make a text seem very formal. A balanced style mixes both active and passive.

■   **Read the following and change some of the passive forms into active.**

MAKING BREAD

Bread is traditionally made from wheat flour, salt, water and yeast. The whole-meal or white flour is mixed with a little salt and yeast, and then lukewarm water is gradually added. Other ingredients such as chopped nuts or seeds may be included. Then the dough is mixed until a soft ball is formed, which can be kneaded by hand. In the kneading process the dough is vigorously pounded and reshaped so that all the ingredients are fully combined. After being thoroughly kneaded the dough is left for a few hours to rise. When this is finished the dough is again worked by hand to shape it into loaves or rolls. After two more hours the loaves will have risen again, due to the action of the yeast. They are baked in a hot oven for about half an hour and then allowed to cool.

Punctuation

Accurate punctuation and the correct use of capital letters help the reader to understand exactly what the writer means. While some aspects of punctuation, such as the use of commas, can be a matter of individual style, correct punctuation in areas such as quotation is vital.

1 Capital letters

It is difficult to give precise rules about the use of capital letters in modern English, where nowadays there is a tendency to use them less than before. However, they should always be used in the following cases:

a) The first word in a sentence   *In the beginning . . .*

b) Days and months   *Friday 21st July*

c) Nationality words   *Indonesia and the Indonesians*

d) Languages   *Most Swiss speak French and German*

e) Names of people/places   *Dr Martin Lee from Sydney, Australia*

f) Book titles (main words only)   *Power and the State*

g) Historical periods   *The Bronze Age, the Great Depression*

h) Names of organisations   *Sheffield Hallam University*

i) The first person pronoun   *By Monday I had finished the book*

NB: Seasons are not capitalised (*The course began in autumn*)

2 Full stops (.) [*US: period*]

These are used to show the end of a sentence:

The first chapter provides a clear introduction to the topic.

They are also used with certain abbreviations formed from the first part of a word:

govt./Jan./p.397

But do not use full stops with acronyms such as:

BBC/UN/VIP

▶   **See Unit 4.2 Abbreviations**

3 Commas (,)

These are one of the commonest punctuation marks, but also one of the hardest to provide guidance for, because comma use is partly a matter of individual style. It may be useful to think of commas as providing a brief pause for readers, to give them a chance to make sense of a chunk of text. Overuse can slow down the reader, but equally the lack of commas can be confusing. Some instances of necessary comma usage are:

a)   after introductory words or phrases:

However, more cases should be considered before reaching a conclusion.

b)   around examples or comments (these are phrases that can be left out without loss of meaning):

Certain crops, for instance wheat, are susceptible to diseases.

Nationalism, it is widely recognised, has a positive and a negative side.

c)   before some conjunctions:

Three hundred people were interviewed, and most of these expressed approval.

d)   in lists of three or more items:

Tomatoes, beans, cabbages and potatoes were all genetically modified in turn.

e)   finishing direct speech:

'Don't forget the deadline', the teacher told them.

f)   to show contrasting elements:

It was well written, but badly spelt.

g)   with a group of adjectives:

It was a long, rambling, humorous and controversial book.

4 Apostrophes (')

These can be one of the most confusing features of English punctuation. They are mainly used in two situations:

a) to show contractions   *He's the leading authority on Hegel.*

   NB: contractions are not common in academic English. It is usually better to write the full form:

   He is the leading authority on Hegel.

b) with possessives   *The professor's secretary* (singular)
   Students' marks (plural words ending in 's')
   Dickens's novels (names ending in 's')

   Women's rights (for irregular plurals)

   NB: **It's** is the contraction of **it is**   *It's possible the course will be cancelled.*

   The third person singular possessive form is **its**   *'Civilization and its Discontents' (Freud)*

   There is no need to use the apostrophe with generic plurals: *1980s, HGVs*

5 Semicolons (;)

Semicolons are used to show the link between two connected clauses, when a comma would be too weak and a full stop too strong:

Seven people applied for the post; six were shortlisted and then interviewed.

Nobody questioned the results; they were quite conclusive.

Semicolons are also used to divide up items in a list when they have a complex structure, as in a multiple citation:

(Maitland, 2006; Rosenor, 1997; New Scientist, 2006b; University of Michigan, 2000).

6 Colons (:)

Colons have three main uses:

a) to introduce explanations   *The meeting was postponed: the Dean was ill.*

b) to start a list   *Three aspects were identified: financial, social and ethical.*

c) to introduce a quotation   *As the Duchess of Windsor said: 'You can never be too rich or too thin'.*

7 Quotations marks/inverted commas (" "/' ')

a) Single quotation marks are used to show quotations from other writers:

Goodwin's (1977) analysis of habit indicates that, in general, 'It will be more difficult to reverse a trend than to accentuate it'.

b) they are also used to emphasise a word or phrase:

The word 'factory' was first used in the seventeenth century.

The Swedish 'third way' or the welfare state is a possible model.

c) to show direct speech:

'Can anyone find the answer?' asked the lecturer.

d) longer quotations are usually indented (i.e. have a wider margin) and/or are set in smaller type:

More recently, she has stated the point even more directly:

> *Government, I hold, should not give people an option to be treated with respect and non-humiliation . . . . Government should treat all people respectfully and should refuse to humiliate them (Nussbaum, 2011b, p. 26).*

e) Double quotation marks are used to show quotations inside quotations (nested quotations):

As Kauffman remarked: 'His concept of "internal space" requires close analysis'.

NB: American English uses double quotation marks to show standard quotations.

▶ **See Written British and American English – A Short Guide**

f) In references, quotation marks are used for the names of articles and chapters, but book or journal titles normally use italics:

Russell, T. (1995) 'A future for coffee?' *Journal of Applied Marketing* 6, 14–17.

▶ **See Unit 1.8 References and Quotations**

8 Others

Hyphens (-) are used with certain words, such as compound nouns, and in some structures:

It is a well-researched, thought-provoking book.

Her three-year-old daughter is learning to read.

But note that the use of hyphens is generally declining (e.g. 'proofreading' rather than 'proof-reading').

Exclamation marks (!) and question marks (?):

'Well!' he shouted, 'Who would believe it?'

Brackets or parentheses () can be used to give additional detail without interfering with the flow of the main idea:

Relatively few people (10–15%) were literate in sixteenth-century Russia.

9 Practice A

■ Punctuate the following sentences and make any other changes needed.

a) the study was carried out by christine zhen-wei qiang of the national university of singapore

b) professor rowans new book the end of privacy 2017 is published in new york

c) as keynes said its better to be roughly right than precisely wrong

d) banks such as hsbc and barclays were in penny pinching mode in the 1990s

e) as Matheson 1954 wrote it was the germ that was the villain

f) thousands of new words such as app enter the english language each year

g) the bbcs world service is broadcast in 33 languages including somali and vietnamese

h) she scored 56% on the main course the previous semester she had achieved 67%

10 Practice B

■ Punctuate the following text and make any changes needed.

studying will play a vital part in your life as an oxford student but you will also find an enormous amount to do in oxford in your spare time oxford is the youngest city in england and wales and has two universities oxford university and oxford brookes 35% of people who live here are aged 15–29 and 27% 40,000 of a total population of 150,000 are university students if you ever feel like a change of scene the bus to london takes around 90 minutes and runs 24 hours a day there are now two railway stations the central oxford station and the recently opened oxford parkway oxford is a youthful and cosmopolitan city with plenty to see and do there are dozens of historic and iconic buildings including the bodleian libraries ashmolean museum sheldonian theatre the cathedral and the colleges in the city centre you will find lots of shops cafés restaurants theatres cinemas pubs and clubs there are plenty of green spaces too riverside walks englands oldest botanic garden the university parks and college gardens

UNIT 3.6 Singular or Plural?

> The choice of singular or plural can be confusing in various situations, such as in the use of countable and uncountable nouns. This unit illustrates the main areas of difficulty and provides practice with these.

1 Five difficult areas

The main problem areas with singular/plural for international students are shown here.

a) Nouns should agree with verbs, and pronouns with nouns:

  *There **are** many **arguments** in favour.*

  ***Those problems** are unique.*

b) Uncountable nouns and irregular plurals usually have no final 's':

  *Most students receive free **tuition**.*

  *The main export is tropical **fruit**.*

c) General statements normally use the plural:

  *State **universities** have lower **fees**.*

d) 'Each/every' are followed by singular noun and verb forms:

  *Every **student gets** financial support.*

e) Two linked nouns should agree:

  *Both the **similarities** and **differences** are important.*

■ **Find the mistakes in the following sentences and decide what type (a – e above) they are.**

i)   The proposal has both advantages and disadvantage.   ( )

ii)   A majority of children in Thailand is vaccinated against measles.   ( )

iii) There are few young people in rural area.   ( )

iv)   Many places are experiencing an increase in crimes.   ( )

v)   Each companies have their own policies.   ( )

2 Group phrases

■   Study the following 'group' phrases.

singular + plural	plural + singular	plural + uncountable
half the universities	two types of institution	three areas of enquiry
a range of businesses	various kinds of course	several fields of research
one of the elements	many varieties of response	different rates of progress

Note that if a verb has more than one subject it must be plural, even if the preceding noun is singular:

*Scores of students, some teachers and the president **are** at the meeting.*

*Their valuable suggestions and hard work **were** vital.*

Certain 'group' nouns (e.g. team/army/government) can be followed by either a singular or plural verb:

*The team **was** defeated three times last month.* (collectively)

*The team **were** travelling by train and bus.* (separately)

It is not always clear, in sentences with two nouns, which one the verb agrees with. Compare these:

*The quality of candidates **was** improving.*

*The majority of candidates **were** French.*

In the first case the verb should agree with 'quality', in the second with 'candidates'.

3 Uncountable nouns

a)   Most nouns in English are countable, but the following are generally uncountable (i.e. they are not usually used with numbers or the plural 's').

accommodation	information	scenery
advice	knowledge	staff
chaos	money	traffic
commerce	news	travel
data	permission	trouble
education	progress	vocabulary
equipment	research	weather
furniture	rubbish	work

Many of these can be 'counted' by using an extra noun:

*A **piece** of advice*

*Three **patterns** of behaviour*

*An **item** of equipment*

*Six **members** of staff*

b) Another group of uncountable nouns consists of materials:

wood/rubber/iron/coffee/paper/water/oil/stone

*Little **wood** is used in the construction of motor vehicles.*

*How much **paper** is needed to produce these magazines?*

But many of these nouns can be used as countable nouns with a rather different meaning:

*How many daily **papers** are published in Delhi?*

*Most **woods** are home to a wide variety of birds.*

c) The most difficult group can be used either as countable or uncountable nouns, often with quite different meanings:

*She developed **an interest** in genetics.*   (countable)

*The bank is paying 4% **interest**.*   (uncountable)

(further examples: business/capital/experience)

Other nouns with a similar pattern are used for general concepts (e.g. love/fear/hope):

*Most people feel that **life** is too short.*   (uncountable – in general)

*Nearly twenty **lives** were lost in the mining accident.*   (countable – in particular)

▶   **See Unit 4.3 Academic Vocabulary: Nouns and Adjectives**

4 Practice A

■ Choose the correct alternative in these sentences.

a) <u>Little/few</u> news about the accident was released.

b) He established three successful <u>businesses/business</u> in 2015.

c) Substantial <u>experiences/experience</u> of report writing <u>are/is</u> required.

d) It is often claimed that <u>travel broadens/travels broaden</u> the mind.

e) The college was built of grey <u>stones/stone.</u>

f) How <u>much advice/many advices</u> were they given before coming to Australia?

g) She had <u>little interest/few interests</u> outside her work.

h) The insurance policy excludes the effects of civil <u>war/wars.</u>

i) <u>Irons were/Iron was</u> first powered by electricity in the twentieth century.

j) They studied the <u>work/works</u> of three groups of employees over two years.

5 Practice B

■ Read the text and choose the correct alternatives.

TRAVEL TROUBLE

As the volume of <u>traffic/traffics</u> has grown, <u>travel/travels</u> to <u>work/works</u> has become slower for many college <u>staffs/staff</u>. <u>Research/researches</u> on commuting time in five <u>capitals/capital</u> shows that on average drivers spend 125 minutes in their <u>vehicles/vehicle</u> each <u>day/days</u>. This means that they are spending more than 10% of their waking <u>life/lives</u> driving, and also consuming huge quantities of <u>petrol/petrols</u> in traffic <u>jams/jam</u>. Another negative <u>factor/factors</u> is the <u>stress/stresses</u> caused by commuting, so the best <u>advices/advice</u> to drivers <u>are/is</u> to relax by listening to classical <u>music/musics</u>.

Style

There is no one correct style of academic writing, but in general it should attempt to be accurate, impersonal and objective. For example, personal pronouns like 'I' and idioms (i.e. informal language) are used less often than in other kinds of writing. Students should study examples of writing in their own subject area, and then aim to develop their own 'voice'. This unit gives guidelines for an appropriate style and provides practice.

1 Developing an academic style

■ Study this paragraph and underline any examples of poor style.

In the last few years there's been lots of discussion about trains. Trains are often run by the state. The state pays for new lines and new equipment. This is because they do an important job moving people around. What's more, developing the railways costs lots of money, which only governments can find. But in some countries like England the railways have been privatised, so as to offer more choice to passengers. The problem is that the private trains still need money from the government to keep running. That's the only way to get everyone to work in big cities. So either way I think that there's no easy answer to the problem.

Some of the problems with the style of this paragraph can be analysed as follows:

Poor style	Reason
In the last few years	Vague – how many years?
there's been	Avoid contractions
lots of discussion, lots of money	Avoid 'lots of'

trains	Imprecise vocabulary – use 'railways'
Trains are often run by the state. The state pays for new lines and new equipment.	Repetition, and sentences too short
do an important job	Too informal
What's more	Too idiomatic
like England	Avoid 'like', use 'such as' England is not correct, use 'Britain' or 'the UK'
The only way . . . either way	Repetition
That's the only way	Caution needed – 'that's the best method'
to get everyone to work	Avoid 'get' phrases
So either way I think	Too personal

The paragraph could be rewritten in a more suitable style:

> In the past two decades there has been considerable debate about the owner-ship of national railway networks. In many countries these are operated by the state, partly because the provision of mass transit is seen as a public service, but also because railway systems demand large-scale capital investment which is often beyond the reach of the private sector. However, there has been a trend towards railway privatisation, as for example in Britain and Germany, since in these countries it was thought useful to introduce some competition into the industry. Yet even these systems still often require public money to subsidise passenger services, which are essential to allow millions of people to travel safely to work each day. Neither the public nor the private model seems to pro-vide a fully satisfactory answer to the issue.

2 Guidelines

There are no rules for academic style which apply to all situations and all academic disciplines. The following guidelines should help you develop a style of your own.

a) Do not use idiomatic or colloquial vocabulary: *kids, boss*. Instead use standard English: *children, manager*.

b) Use vocabulary accurately. There is a difference between *rule* and *law*, and *weather* and *climate*, for example, which you are expected to know if you study these subjects.

c) Be as precise as possible when dealing with facts or figures. Avoid phrases such as *about a hundred* or *hundreds of years ago*. If it is necessary to estimate numbers, use *approximately* rather than *about*.

d)   Conclusions should use tentative language. Avoid absolute statements such as *unemploy-ment causes crime*. Instead use cautious phrases: *unemployment may cause crime* or *tends to cause crime.*

e)   Avoid adverbs that show your personal attitude: *luckily, remarkably, surprisingly.*

f)   Do not contract auxiliary verb forms: *don't, can't.* Use the full form: do not, cannot.

g)   Avoid complicated expressions of gender. Instead of writing:

   each candidate has his or her presentation prepared

write: *all candidates have their presentations prepared*

Try not to use sexist language such as *chairman* or *policeman*. Use *chairperson* or *police officer.*

h)   Avoid the following:

   *   *like* for introducing examples. Use *such as* or *for instance.*
   *   *thing* and combinations *nothing* or *something.* Use *factor, issue* or *topic.*
   *   *lots of.* Use *a significant/considerable number.*
   *   *little/big.* Use *small/large.*
   *   'get' phrases such as *get better/worse.* Use *improve* and *deteriorate.*
   *   *good/bad* are simplistic. Use *positive/negative* (e.g. *the changes had several positive aspects*)

i)   Do not use rhetorical question forms such as *Why did war break out in 1914?* Instead use statements: *There were three reasons for the outbreak of war . . .*

j)   Avoid numbering sections of your text, except in reports and long essays. Use conjunctions and signposting expressions to introduce new sections (*Turning to the question of detecting cancer . . .*).

▶   **See Unit 1.10 Organising Paragraphs**

k)   When writing lists, avoid using *etc.* or *and so on.* Insert *and* before the last item:
   The main products were pharmaceuticals, electronic goods and confectionery.

l)   Avoid using two-word verbs such as *go on* or *bring up* if there is a suitable synonym (e.g. *continue* or *raise*).

▶   **See Unit 4.4 Academic Vocabulary: Adverbs and Verbs**

3 Practice A

■   **In the following sentences, underline examples of poor style and rewrite them in a more suitable way.**

a) Another thing to think about is the chance of crime getting worse.

_____

b) Regrettably these days lots of people don't have jobs.

_____

c) Sometime soon they will find a vaccine for malaria.

_____

d) Luckily the firemen soon got the fire under control.

_____

e) You can't always trust the numbers in that report.

_____

f) Sadly, the bad inflation led to poverty, social unrest and so on.

_____

g) He was over the moon when he won the prize.

_____

h) I think we should pay students to study.

_____

i) Years ago they allowed women to vote.

_____

j) What were the main causes of the Russian Revolution?

_____

4 Avoiding repetition and redundancy

Instead of repeating the same word in a short text:

*Most family businesses employ fewer than ten people. These **businesses** . . .*

Try to make the text more interesting by using synonyms:

*Most family businesses employ fewer than ten people. These **firms** . . .*

▶ **See Unit 4.8 Synonyms**

Redundancy (i.e. repeating an idea or including an irrelevant point) suggests that the writer is not fully in control of the material. It gives the impression that either he does not properly understand the language or is trying to 'pad' the essay by repeating the same point. Avoid statements such as:

Homelessness is a global problem in the whole world.

Good writing aims for economy and precision:

> *Homelessness is a global problem.*

■   **In the following text, remove all repetition and redundancy, rewriting where necessary.**

FAST FOOD

Currently these days, fast food is growing in popularity. Fast food is the kind of food that people can buy ready to eat or cook quickly. It's called fast food because it doesn't take long to make. This essay examines the advantages of fast food and the drawbacks of fast food. First above all, fast food is very convenient. Most of the people who work in offices are very busy, so that they do not have time to go to their homes for lunch. But the people who work in offices can eat in restaurants such as McDonald's, which are franchised in hundreds of countries, because they are very popular. In addition, the second benefit of fast food is its cheapness. It is produced in large quantities, and this high volume means that the companies can keep costs down. As a result fast food is usually less expensive than a meal in a conventional restaurant, so people can buy it regularly.

---

5 Varying sentence length

Short sentences are clear and easy to read:

> *Car scrappage schemes have been introduced in many countries.*

But too many short sentences are monotonous:

> *Car scrappage schemes have been introduced in many countries. They offer a subsidy to buyers of new cars. The buyers must scrap an old vehicle. The schemes are designed to stimulate the economy. They also increase fuel efficiency.*

Long sentences are more interesting but can be difficult to construct and read:

> *Car scrappage schemes, which offer a subsidy to buyers of new cars (who must scrap an old vehicle) have been introduced in many countries; the schemes are designed to stimulate the economy and also increase fuel efficiency.*

Effective writing normally uses a mixture of long and short sentences, often using a short sentence to introduce the topic:

> *Car scrappage schemes have been introduced in many countries. They offer a subsidy to buyers of new cars who must scrap an old vehicle. The schemes are designed to stimulate the economy and also increase fuel efficiency.*

■ Rewrite the following paragraph so that instead of six short sentences there are two long and two short sentences.

> Worldwide, enrolments in higher education are increasing. In developed countries over half of all young people enter college. Similar trends are seen in China and South America. This growth has put financial strain on state university systems. Many countries are requiring students and parents to contribute to the cost. This leads to a debate about whether students or society benefit from tertiary education.

■ The following sentence is too long. Divide it into shorter ones.

> China is one developing country (but not the only one) which has imposed fees on students since 1997, but the results have been surprising: enrolments, especially in the most expensive universities, have continued to rise steeply, growing 200 per cent overall between 1997 and 2011; it seems in this case that higher fees attract rather than discourage students, who see them as a sign of a good education and compete more fiercely for places, leading to the result that a place at a good college can cost $8,000 per year for fees and maintenance.

Until you feel confident in your writing, it is better to use shorter rather than longer sentences. This should make your meaning as clear as possible.

6 The use of caution

A cautious style is necessary in many areas of academic writing in order to avoid making statements that can be contradicted in some way:

> Demand for healthcare **usually** exceeds supply.

> **Most** students find writing exam essays difficult.

> Fertility rates **tend to** fall as societies get richer.

Areas where caution is particularly important include:

a) outlining a hypothesis which needs to be tested (e.g. in an introduction)

b) discussing the results of a study, which may not be conclusive

c) commenting on the work of other writers

d) making predictions (normally with **may** or **might**)

Caution is also needed to avoid making statements which are too simplistic:

> Crime is linked to poor education.

Such statements are rarely completely true. There is usually an exception which needs to be considered. Caution can be shown in several ways:

Crime **may** be linked to poor education.   (modal verb)

Crime is **frequently** linked to poor education.   (adverb)

Crime **tends to** be linked to poor education.   (verb)

■ Complete the following table with more examples of each.

Modals	Adverbs	Verb/phrase
may	frequently	tends to

▶ See Unit 2.6 Generalisations

7 Using modifiers

Another way to express caution is to use **quite**, **rather** or **fairly** before an adjective:

a **fairly** accurate summary

a **rather** inconvenient location

quite a significant discovery

NB: **quite** is often used before the article. It is mainly used positively, while **rather** tends to be used negatively.

■ Insert quite/rather/fairly in the following to emphasise caution.

a) The company's efforts to save energy were successful.

b) The survey was a comprehensive study of student opinion.

c) His second book had a hostile reception.

d) The first-year students were fascinated by her lectures.

e) The latest type of arthritis drug is expensive.

f) This mountain tiger has become rare.

g) The class found the essay topic challenging.

8 Practice B

■ Rewrite the following sentences in a more cautious way.

a) Private companies are more efficient than state-owned businesses.

b) Exploring space is a waste of valuable resources.

· c) Older students perform better at university than younger ones.

d) Word-of-mouth is the best kind of advertising.

♪ e) English pronunciation is confusing.

f) Some cancers are caused by psychological factors.

g) Global warming will cause the sea level to rise.

h) Most shopping will be done on the internet in ten years' time.

i) Online education is inferior to taught classes.

j) By 2025 driverless cars will be in common use.

Time Markers

When describing a sequence of events, it is important to make clear what happened when. Time markers such as 'ago' and 'since' are often used to explain the timing of events. But the application of some of these words is restricted to particular tenses. This unit explains these limitations and practises their application.

1 How time markers are used

■ Study the following:

She went on a training course **for** six weeks.	(with numbers, without start date)
The report must be finished **by** June 12th.	(on or before)
He has been president **since** 2007.	(with present perfect, must specify start date)
They are studying in Bristol **until** March.	(end of a period)
The library was opened two years **ago**.	(usually with past)
The hotel is closed **during** the winter.	(with noun)
Before writing he studied over 100 sources.	(often followed by – ing form; also **after**)
He applied in May and was accepted two months **later**.	(often used with numbers; also **earlier**)
She bought the car **while** working at Harvard.	(two things happening at the same time)

2 Practice A

■ Choose the best alternative in each case.

a) <u>Currently/Recently</u> she has been researching the life cycle of a Brazilian wasp.

b) He worked there <u>until/during</u> he retired.

c) Dr Hoffman has lived in Melbourne <u>since/for</u> sixteen years.

d) <u>Last month/In the last month</u> a new book was published on genetics.

e) Applications must be received <u>by/on</u> November 25th.

f) <u>Since/During</u> her arrival last May she has reorganised the department.

g) <u>During/For</u> the winter most farmers in the region find work in the towns.

h) <u>After/While</u> giving the lecture she answered all their questions.

3 Tenses

■ Compare the tenses used with the following time markers:

Last year there ***was*** an election in Spain.	(past – finished event)
While he ***was doing*** the experiment, he ***saw*** his mistake.	(past continuous + past)
In the last year there ***has been*** a decline in inflation.	(present perfect – unfinished)
Recently, there ***has been*** a sharp rise in internet use.	(present perfect – unfinished)
Currently, there ***is*** widespread concern about plagiarism.	(present – focus on now)

4 Practice B

■ Study the details of Napoleon's life and complete the biography.

1769	Born in Corsica
1784	Entered military school in Paris
1789	French revolution started
1793	Promoted to brigadier-general
1796	Appointed to command army of Italy; married Josephine
1799	Returned from Egypt and became First Consul of France

1807	France controlled most of continental Europe
1810	Divorced Josephine and married Marie-Louise, daughter of Austrian emperor
1812	Forced to retreat from Russia – thousands of soldiers killed
1814	Exiled to island of Elba
1815	Defeated at battle of Waterloo and exiled to island of St Helena
1821	Died in exile

Napoleon entered military school in 1784 at the age of 15, five years a) _____ the French Revolution began. Four years b) _____ he was promoted to brigadier-general, and c) _____ the age of 27 he became commander of the army in Italy, and also married Josephine. d) _____ returning from Egypt in 1799 he became the First Consul of France, and e) _____ 1807 France was in control of most of Europe. Three years f) _____ he divorced Josephine and married Marie-Louise, the Austrian emperor's daughter. But g) _____ his retreat from Russia thousands of his soldiers were killed, and two years h) _____ he was defeated at Waterloo. i) _____ the battle he was finally exiled to St Helena.

5 Practice C

■ Complete each gap in the following text with a suitable word.

Eating out

a) _____ the last few decades there has been a significant change in eating habits in the UK. b) _____ the early 1980s eating out in restaurants and cafés has increased steadily. There are several reasons for this trend.

Sixty years c) _____ most women were housewives and cooked for their families every day. But d) _____, with more women working outside the home, less time has been available for food preparation. e) _____, 75% of women aged 20–45 are at work, and f) _____ 2025 it is estimated that this will rise to 90%.

Another factor is the growth in disposable income, which has risen significantly g) _____ the late 1970s. With more money in their pockets, people are more likely to save the trouble of shopping and cooking by visiting their local restaurant. h) _____ the last decade there has also been an enormous increase in the variety of restaurants in the high street. Eating out has become more exciting and adventurous.

Progress Check 3

These exercises will help you assess your understanding of Part 3 – Language Issues.

1   *Rewrite the paragraph using reference words where suitable.*

   William Shakespeare was born in Stratford-upon-Avon in 1564, into a wealthy landowning family. When Shakespeare was only 18 he married Anne Hathaway, who was six years older than William. Anne subsequently had three children, but William and Anne's only son, Hamnet, died young. Apparently William spent most of his time in London after their marriage, where he acted and started to write plays. The plays were mainly comedies at first, and were very successful. In the early 1600s Shakespeare's work became darker, and this is when William wrote his most famous plays, such as *Hamlet and King Lear*. These famous plays have secured Shakespeare's worldwide reputation as a great dramatist and poet. William Shakespeare died in 1616 aged only 52, while Anne lived for another seven years.

2   *Complete the following text by inserting a/an/the (or nothing) in each gap. (Note that in some cases more than one answer is possible.)*

The origins of @

Giorgio Stabile, a professor of a) _____ history at La Sapienza University in Rome, has demonstrated that b) _____ @ sign, now used in email addresses, was actually invented 500 years ago. Professor Stabile has shown that c) _____ @, now d) _____ symbol of e) _____ internet, was first used by f) _____ Italian merchants during g) _____ sixteenth century.
   He claims that it originally represented h) _____ unit of volume, based on i) _____ large jars used to carry liquids in j) _____ ancient Mediterranean world. He has found k) _____ first example of its use in l) _____ letter written in 1546 by m) _____ merchant from Florence. n) _____ letter, which was sent to Rome, announces o) _____ arrival in Spain of p) _____ ships carrying gold from q) _____ South America.

3   *Rewrite the paragraph, simplifying the numerical expressions.*

250 international students were interviewed about their experience of study abroad. Of this total 51 were from China, 48 from India, 24 from Nigeria and the rest were from a variety of European countries. 196 students were satisfied with their courses, but the other 54 had concerns about the quantity of work required. Just 25 complained about the quality of teaching. 124 students said they found it easy to adapt to a different culture and way of life, but of the others 39 disliked the food, 26 found living too expensive and nine mentioned bad weather.

4   *The following text is in the active voice. Change it to the passive where appropriate.*

Our research aimed to find the best taxi business for campus use, so we compared the performance of six local taxi companies. We selected companies that had their offices within a kilometre of the campus. We timed the response of each company to requests made at the same time of day (7 p.m.). Response times varied from ten to 24 minutes. The passengers then asked each driver to take them to the railway station. They recorded the friendliness of the drivers and the length of time taken, as well as the fare the driver asked for. Overall we found that AZ Taxis had the fastest response and the cheapest fare, but not the most friendly driver.

5   *Punctuate the following text and make any spelling corrections or other changes needed.*

the school of biomedical sciences at borchester university is offering two undergraduate degree courses in neuroscience this year students can study either neuroscience with pharmacology or neuroscience with biochemistry there is also a masters course which runs for four years and involves a period of study abroad during november and december professor andreas fischer is course leader for neuroscience and enquiries should be sent to him via the website

6   *Choose the correct verb form in each sentence.*

a)   Several types of response was/were recorded.

b)   Three avenues of research were/was suggested.

c)   One of the groups was/were eliminated from the competition.

d)   Half the graduates were/was from Indonesia.

e)   The government was/were defeated at the election.

f)   The performance of the athletes were/was improved by his training method.

7   *Rewrite the following in a more suitable academic style.*

These days lots of people don't get enough exercise. Sadly, they sit on the sofa watching telly instead. That's why they get fat. Lots of research shows they'd be healthier if they went for a walk every day. I think they'd feel better too. You can't beat exercise in the fresh air.

8   *Study Dr Gonzalez's schedule. Then complete the sentences with time markers. Today is June 13th.*

June 8   Fly to Berlin for conference

June 9   Give lecture at conference

June 10   Train to Prague

June 11   Meet colleagues at Charles University, Prague

June 12   Fly home

a)   Dr Gonzalez went to Berlin five days _____

b)   He was in Berlin _____ two days.

c)   _____ his stay in Berlin he gave a lecture.

d)   _____ leaving Berlin he went to Prague.

e)   _____ staying in Prague he met colleagues at Charles University.

f)   _____ June 10th he had travelled 2,300 kilometres.

Vocabulary for Writing

PART 4

International students may be understandably concerned by the quantity and complexity of vocabulary required for reading academic texts. But developing an effective vocabulary in English involves more than learning lists of words. The units in Part 4, arranged alphabetically, provide a variety of approaches to improving students' understanding in this area, from learning abbreviations to recognising synonyms.

Approaches to Vocabulary

This unit examines some of the key difficulties students face when reading academic texts, such as processing new vocabulary, avoiding confusion with similar words, and recognising phrases from other languages. Some of the vocabulary needed to discuss language features is also practised.

1 Vocabulary issues

■ This paragraph illustrates some of the vocabulary difficulties students face when reading and writing academic texts. Read it carefully, paying particular attention to words in bold.

Going to extremes?

Muller (2012) **maintains** that the increased frequency of extreme weather events is linked to global warming, **in particular** to rising sea temperatures. **However**, McKenzie (2013) **insists** Muller has **a bee in his bonnet** on this topic, caused by using a **dysfunctional** model, and that there is no real evidence that **phenomena** such as flooding and hurricanes are becoming more common. He considers that the **key** issue is the growing population in areas vulnerable to events such as floods. Muller's **principal** concern is a rise in the temperature of the North Pacific Ocean of 0.5° C since 1968, which McKenzie regards as being within the normal range of historical **fluctuation**. But Javez (2009) and Simmonds (2011), *inter alia*, have argued for an international research programme under the **auspices** of **UNESCO** to monitor these events, given the threefold rise in the cost of insurance claims since 2000.

■ Study the following table, which shows where these vocabulary issues are dealt with more fully in Part 4.

Line	Item	Vocabulary issue	Unit
1	maintains	referring verbs for summarising ideas	4.4
3	insists		
2	in particular	conjunctions	4.5
	however		
3	a bee in his bonnet	idiom	4.1
4	dysfunctional	can be understood by the prefix	4.6
4	phenomena	approximate synonym for 'events'	4.8
6	key	metaphor	4.1
7	principal	often confused with 'principle'	4.1
9	fluctuation	formal or technical vocabulary	4.1
10	auspices		
9	*inter alia*	phrase from another language	4.1
10	UNESCO	abbreviation	4.2

2 Dealing with new vocabulary

Students will meet two vocabulary areas when reading: subject-specific and general academic. For example, in the text on page 179 students of Environmental Studies may know 'fluctuation' but not understand 'auspices'. Instead of trying to learn all the new vocabulary you encounter, you should screen it to select which words are worth learning. It can be a mistake to attempt to learn too many new words: for most students, subject-specific language will have priority. This can be seen as a process:

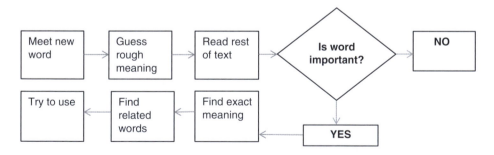

When you have selected a word or phrase to learn, make a note of its part of speech and any useful related words, along with its meaning:

fluctuation (noun) – variation

to fluctuate (verb) – to vary

You should also check the register of the word or phrase. Most vocabulary you read in academic work will be standard English, but 'under the auspices' (meaning 'with the authority of'), for instance, is rather formal, while 'a bee in his bonnet' is idiomatic. It is generally better to use standard English in your own written work.

3 Language features

The following words (all nouns) are used to describe common features of language.

■ **Discuss the words in the list with a partner. Try to think of an example sentence for each.**

Ambiguity	*Where more than one interpretation is possible; lack of clarity*
Anecdote	*A story told to illustrate a situation or idea*
Cliché	*An overused idea or phrase; lacking in freshness*
Euphemism	*A word or phrase used to avoid naming something unpleasant directly*
Idiom	*A phrase used in colloquial speech, the meaning of which is not obvious*
Metaphor	*A word used to refer to something but that literally means something else*
Paradox	*An idea that seems wrong but yet may be true*
Proverb	*A traditional statement or rhyme containing advice or a moral*
Saying	*An often-repeated comment that seems to contain some truth*
Simile	*A comparison of two things, using 'like' or 'as'*
Slogan	*A frequently repeated phrase used in advertising or politics*
Statement	*A rather formal comment on a situation*
Synopsis	*A summary of something*

4 Practice

■ **Working with a partner, study the following sentences and decide which of the features listed above list is illustrated by each one.**

a) The President said she regretted the loss of life in the typhoon and sympathised with the survivors. (*statement*)

b) At the beginning of the lecture Professor Chang told them about an accident she had seen that morning. (_____)

c) There's no such thing as a free lunch, he warned them. (_____)

d) The author of the report passed away on November 21st. (_____)

e) He told the class that their law course was a voyage over an uncharted ocean. (_____)

f) She said that the older she got, the less she seemed to know. (_____)

g) After the price rise, sales fell like a stone. (_____)

h) It is said that the early bird catches the worm. (_____)

i) Their teacher explained that the novel consisted of two parts; the first historical, the second contemporary. (*synopsis*)

j) He was over the moon when he won the scholarship. (_____)

k) 'Finger lickin' good' has sold millions of chicken meals. (_____)

l) His feelings towards his old school were a mixture of love and hate. (_____)

m) Paris is the capital of romance; the city for lovers. (_____)

5 Confusing pairs

Certain common words can cause confusion because they have similar but distinct spellings and meanings:

*The drought **affected** the wheat harvest in Australia.*

*An immediate **effect** of the price rise was a fall in demand.*

'Affect' and 'effect' are two different words. 'Affect' is a verb, while 'effect' is commonly used as a noun.

■ **Study the differences between other similar confusing pairs (most common form of use in brackets).**

accept (verb)/except (prep)

*It is difficult to **accept** their findings.*
*The report is finished **except** for the conclusion.*

compliment (noun/verb)/complement (verb)

*Her colleagues **complimented** her on her presentation.*
*His latest book **complements** his previous research on South African politics.*

economic (adj)/economical (adj)

*Inflation was one **economic** result of the war.*
*Sharing a car to go to work was an **economical** move.*

its (possessive pronoun)/it's (subject pronoun + verb)

*The car's advanced design was **its** most distinct feature.*
***It's** widely agreed that carbon emissions are rising.*

led (verb – past tense of lead)/lead (noun)

> His research **led** him to question the orthodox opinion.
>
> **Lead** (Pb) is a valuable mineral.

lose (verb)/loose (adj)

> No general ever plans to **lose** a battle.
>
> He stressed the **loose** connection between religion and psychology.

principal (adj/noun)/principle (noun)

> Zurich is the **principal** city of Switzerland.
>
> All economists recognise the **principle** of supply and demand.

rise (verb – past tense rose)/raise (verb – past tense raised)

> The population of Sydney **rose** by 35% in the last century.
>
> The university **raised** its fees by 10% last year.

site (noun)/sight (noun)

> The **site** of the battle is now covered by an airport.
>
> His **sight** began to weaken when he was in his eighties.

tend to (verb)/trend (noun)

> Young children **tend to** enjoy making a noise.
>
> In many countries there is a **trend** towards smaller families.

■ Choose the correct word in each sentence.

a) The company was founded on the <u>principals/principles</u> of quality and value.

b) Millions of people are attempting to <u>lose/loose</u> weight.

c) Sunspots have been known to <u>affect/effect</u> radio communication.

d) Professor Poledna received their <u>compliments/complements</u> politely.

e) The ancient symbol depicted a snake eating <u>it's/its</u> tail.

f) Both social and <u>economical/economic</u> criteria need to be examined.

g) It took many years for some of Einstein's theories to be <u>accepted/excepted</u>.

6 Words and phrases from other languages

When reading academic texts, you may meet words and phrases from other languages, usually Latin, German or French. They are generally used because there is no exact English equivalent, and they are often printed in italics:

He argued for the *de facto* independence of the states.

You are not expected to use these phrases in your own writing, but it is useful to understand them when you read. They can be found in a dictionary, and some of the more common ones are listed here:

Latin

ad hoc	unplanned
de facto	as it really is
de jure	according to law
inter alia	among others
in vitro	studies conducted on isolated organs (in Biology)
pro rata	proportional

French

à propos de	on the subject of
ancien régime	old ruling system
coup d'état	military takeover
déjà vu	sensation of having seen something before
fait accompli	accomplished fact
raison d'être	reason for living

German

Bildungsroman	a story of growing-up
Mitteleuropa	central Europe
Realpolitik	political reality
Schadenfreude	pleasure from another's misfortune
Zeitgeist	spirit of the times

UNIT

4.2

Abbreviations

Abbreviations are an important and expanding feature of contemporary English, widely used for convenience and space-saving. Students need to be familiar with both general and academic abbreviations.

1 Types of abbreviation

Abbreviations take the form of shortened words, acronyms, or a set of letters, as shown here.

a) **Shortened words** are often used without the writer being aware of the original form. 'Bus' comes from 'omnibus', which is hardly used in modern English, and 'disco' is more common than 'discothèque', while 'refrigerator' is still better in written English than the informal 'fridge'. Yet 'lab' for 'laboratory', 'memo' for 'memorandum' and 'vet' for 'veterinary surgeon' are quite acceptable.

b) **Acronyms** are made up of the initial letters of a name or phrase (e.g. AIDS = Acquired Immune Deficiency Syndrome). They are pronounced as words. In some cases, users have forgotten that these are acronyms and they are treated as ordinary words (e.g. 'radar' comes from 'radio detection and ranging').

c) **Other abbreviations** are read as sets of individual letters. They include names of countries, organisations and companies (US/BBC/IBM), and also abbreviations which are only found in written English (e.g. PTO means 'please turn over'). Note that in many cases abbreviations are widely used without most users knowing what the individual letters stand for (e.g. DNA, DVD).

2 Common abbreviations

There are thousands of abbreviations in standard English, but these are some of the most frequently used in an academic context.

AGM	annual general meeting
ASAP	as soon as possible
BA	Bachelor of Arts
BCE	before the common era (previously BC)
BSc	Bachelor of Sciences
CAD	computer-aided design
CE	common era (previously AD)
CV	curriculum vitae
DIY	do-it-yourself
ETA	estimated time of arrival (for journeys)
EU	European Union
FE	further education (non-university study above 16/18)
GM	genetically modified
GNP	gross national product
HE	higher education (university study above 18)
HR(M)	human resource (management)
ICT	information and communications technology
IMF	International Monetary Fund
LLB	Bachelor of Laws
MA	Master of Arts
MSc	Master of Science
PG	Postgraduate
PGCE	Postgraduate Certificate of Education
PhD	Doctor of Philosophy
PLC	public limited company
PR	public relations
UCAS	Universities and Colleges Admissions Service (UK)
UG	undergraduate
UN	United Nations
URL	uniform resource locator (website address)
VC	Vice-Chancellor
WTO	World Trade Organisation

However, writers often employ more specialised, subject-specific abbreviations:

*Starting from the **resource-based view** (RBV) of the firm, it is argued that...*

*The **Technology Readiness Index** (TRI) was introduced by Parasuraman (2000).*

Note that the first time a phrase is used it must be written in full with the abbreviation appearing after it in brackets, but on subsequent occasions the abbreviation can be used alone.

3 Punctuation

There are many standard abbreviations which have a full stop after them to show that it is a shortened form of a word (e.g. Tues. = Tuesday). Other examples are govt. (government), co. (company) and Oct. (October). With acronyms and other abbreviations it is now normal to write the letters without full stops (e.g. BBC, ABS).

4 Duplicate abbreviations

Abbreviations can be confusing. PC, for example, may stand for 'personal computer' but also 'politically correct' or 'Police Constable'. It is useful to be aware of these potential confusions. A good dictionary should be used to understand more unusual abbreviations.

5 Abbreviations in writing

While all academic subjects have their own abbreviations, there are certain abbreviations common to most types of academic writing. They include:

anon.	anonymous (no author)
c.	*circa* (in dates – about)
cf.	compare
ed.	editor/edition
e.g.	for example
et al.	and others (used for giving names of multiple authors)
etc.	*et cetera* (and so on – do not use this in formal academic work)
Fig.	figure (for labelling charts and graphs)
ibid.	in the same place (to refer to source mentioned immediately before)
i.e.	that is
K	thousand
NB:	take careful note
nd.	no date (i.e. an undated source)
No.	number
op. cit.	in the source mentioned previously
p.a.	yearly (per annum)
pp.	pages
PS	postscript
re:	with reference to
sic	in quotations, used to show a mistake in the original
vs	versus

▶ See Units 1.8 References and Quotations and 3.5 Punctuation

6 Practice

■ Explain the abbreviations in the following sentences.

a) The failure rate among ICT projects in HE reaches 40% (Smith *et al.*, 2015).

b) GM technology is leading to advances in many fields (e.g. forestry).

c) The world's most populous country (i.e. China) joined the WTO in 2001.

d) NB: CVs must be submitted to HR by Sep. 30th.

e) The city seems to have been destroyed c. 2500 BCE.

f) The EU hopes to achieve a standard rate of VAT.

g) Her PhD thesis examined the threat of TB in SE Asia.

h) Fig. 4 – Spanish GNP 2008–2016.

i) The VC is meeting the PGCE students.

j) Director of PR required – salary approx. $75K.

k) Re: next month's AGM: the report is needed ASAP.

l) Dr Wang argued that the quality of MSc and MA research was falling.

Academic Vocabulary
Nouns and Adjectives

To read and write academic papers effectively, students need to be familiar with the rather formal vocabulary widely used in this area. This unit focuses on nouns and adjectives; Unit 4.4 looks at verbs and adverbs.

1 Introduction

The quantity and complexity of vocabulary needed to read academic texts often concern international students. But it is worth remembering that much of that vocabulary is specific to your subject area, for example, in the sentence:

> The **effectiveness** of this **malaria vaccine** has been a subject of **controversy**.

'Malaria vaccine' will be understood by medical students, while 'effectiveness' and 'controversy' are general academic vocabulary which all students need to understand. The focus of this unit is on the general vocabulary common to most disciplines.

2 Nouns

■ Study the following list of common academic nouns with examples of use. With a partner, discuss the meaning of each noun.

accuracy	*Repeating the experiment will improve the **accuracy** of the results.*
analysis	*His **analysis** of the alloy showed a high percentage of copper.*
approach	*Professor Han has brought a new **approach** to the study of genetics.*
assessment	*She failed the first module **assessment** but passed the final one.*
assumption	*He made the **assumption** that all the students spoke French.*
authority	*Dr James is our leading **authority** on marine law.*

category	Her work established two **categories** of local governance.
claim	Their **claim** that the island was first inhabited in 550 BCE is false.
controversy	Climate change is an issue that has caused much **controversy**.
correlation	They found a **correlation** between height and health.
deterrent	The harsh climate of the desert acted as a **deterrent** to exploration.
emphasis	Their teacher put an **emphasis** on practical research.
evidence	The X-ray provided **evidence** of his lung infection.
exception	The Tesla is an **exception** to the idea of slow, small electric cars.
extract	He read a short **extract** from his paper on Hegel to the class.
ideology	Military power was at the heart of Roman **ideology**.
implication	The **implication** of the report is that we need to do more research.
innovation	Steam power was a significant **innovation** in the eighteenth century.
intuition	**Intuition** has been described as 'a gut feeling'.
motivation	Money is often claimed to be the primary **motivation** for most workers.
perspective	Sigmund Freud's work opened a new **perspective** on human behaviour.
phenomenon	Earthquakes are an unusual **phenomenon** in Britain. (NB: Irregular plural – phenomena)
policy	The university has a zero-tolerance **policy** on plagiarism.
preference	Her **preference** was criminal law, but other fields were more profitable.
process	The drug trials involved a three-stage **process** that took two years.
proposal	The professor's **proposal** for more seminars was rejected.
provision	The library has increased its **provision** of computer terminals by 100%.
sequence	Writing is a **sequence** of reading, note-taking, planning and drafting.
strategy	Swimming every day was part of his **strategy** for getting fit.
substitute	To what extent can natural gas be a **substitute** for oil?
technique	She developed a new **technique** for collecting the beetles.
validity	Events confirmed the **validity** of his prediction.

■ Complete each sentence with a suitable noun.

a) The excavation found no _____ of human settlement before 1250 BCE.

b) The tutor asked the class for their _____ for next semester's topics.

c) Many great discoveries were based on _____ rather than logic.

d) Due to the rising birth rate _____ was made for more school places.

e) Few believed Galileo's _____ that the earth went round the sun.

f) Hurricanes and typhoons are both weather _____

g) The new _____ for making steel boosted production by 60%.

h) They looked for a _____ between birth month and longevity.

3 Nouns and adjectives

A simple way of expanding vocabulary is to learn related parts of speech. Many of the nouns in the list on pages 189–90 have a related adjective (e.g. accuracy/accurate).

■ **Write example sentences to show the meaning of the following related adjectives.**

accurate   *The arrival of railways created a demand for accurate*
analytical   *timekeeping.*
approachable
authoritative
controversial
emphatic
exceptional
ideological
innovative
intuitive
motivational
phenomenal
preferential
provisional
sequential
strategic
technical
valid

4 Confusing nouns and adjectives

It is easy to confuse the noun and adjective form of words such as 'possible' and 'possibility'.

■ **Compare these sentences:**

> The **efficiency** of the machine depends on the **precision** of its construction.
>
> **Precise** construction results in an **efficient** machine.

The first sentence uses the nouns 'efficiency' and 'precision'. The second uses the adjectives 'precise' and 'efficient'. Although the meaning is similar, the first sentence is more formal. Effective academic writing requires accurate use of both nouns and adjectives.

■ Complete the gaps in the following table.

Noun	Adjective	Noun	Adjective
approximation	approximate		particular
superiority		reason	
	strategic		synthetic
politics		economics/economy*	
	industrial		cultural
exterior		average	
	high		reliable
heat		strength	
	confident		true
width		probability	
	necessary		long
danger		relevance	

* Compare the three nouns:

> **Economics** is a demanding undergraduate degree course.   (academic subject)
>
> The Greek **economy** is heavily in debt.   (national economy, countable)
>
> **Economy** is needed to reduce the deficit.   (saving money, uncountable)

5 Practice A

■ Insert a suitable noun or adjective from the table into each sentence.

a)   The students were _____ their project would be successful.

b)   One of Tokyo's _____ is its excellent transport system.

c)   There is a strong _____ that fees will rise next year.

d) The students complained that the lecture was not _____ to their course.

e) The results are so surprising it will be _____ to repeat the experiment.

f) The _____ household size in Turkey is 4.1 people.

g) Regularly backing up computer files reduces the _____ of losing vital work.

h) Revising for exams is a tedious _____

i) These data appear to be _____ and should not be trusted.

j) The _____ date of the founding of Rome is 750 BCE.

k) The _____ consequences of the war were inflation and unemployment.

l) They attempted to make a _____ of all the different proposals.

6 Similar adjectives

Certain common adjectives have two forms with slightly different meanings:

>*High inflation is an **economic** problem.* (related to the economy)
>
>*It is more **economical** to travel by bus than train.* (saving money)
>
>*Martin Luther King made his **historic** speech in Washington.* (memorable or significant)
>
>*Cleopatra was a **historical** character, born in 69 BCE.* (real person in past)
>
>*The **electric** guitar was developed in the 1930s.* (worked by electricity)
>
>***Electrical** engineering was a popular course.* (relating to electricity)

7 Academic adjectives

The following adjectives are best understood and learnt as pairs of opposites:

absolute	*relative*
abstract	*concrete*
accurate	*inaccurate*
ambiguous	*unambiguous*
analytic	*synthetic*

effective	*ineffective*
exclusive	*inclusive*
logical	*illogical*
metaphorical	*literal*
precise	*vague* or *approximate* or *rough*
rational	*irrational*
reliable	*unreliable*
relevant	*irrelevant*
specific	*non-specific*
subjective	*objective*
theoretical	*practical* or *empirical* or *pragmatic*

*Inflation is an **abstract** concept.*

*The **metaphorical** use of the word 'key' is probably more common than its **literal** one.*

*The study of engineering is very **relevant** to architecture.*

*Her paper on women in education was criticised for being too **subjective**.*

*In Europe, **empirical** research began in the sixteenth century.*

8 Practice B

■ Complete each sentence with a suitable adjective from the list in 7).

a) The teacher complained that the quotes were _____ to the title.

b) His _____ approach led him to ignore some inconvenient facts.

c) _____ examples are needed to make the argument clear.

d) It is sufficient to give _____ figures for national populations.

e) Poverty is usually regarded as a _____ concept.

f) They approached the task in a _____ way by first analysing the title.

g) The students preferred examining case studies to _____ discussion.

h) The results were _____: the victims had definitely been poisoned.

9 Practice C

■ **Underline the adjective in each sentence and write the related noun in brackets.**

Example:

Several steel producers are <u>likely</u> *to shut down next year.* (*likelihood*)

a) The HR team have just completed a strategic review of pay. (_____)

b) Dr Lee adopted an analytical approach to the inquiry. (_____)

c) Nylon was one of the earliest synthetic fibres. (_____)

d) Her major contribution to the research was her study of antenatal care. (_____)

e) All advertising must respect cultural differences. (_____)

f) Some progress was made in the theoretical area. (_____)

g) A frequent complaint is that too much reading is expected. (_____)

h) We took a more critical approach to marketing theory. (_____)

i) The Department of Social Policy is offering three courses this year. (_____)

j) Finally, the practical implications of my findings will be examined. (_____)

Students wishing to develop their academic vocabulary should study the Academic Word List (AWL). This is a list of 570 items commonly found in academic texts across various disciplines created by Averil Coxhead.

See: https://canvas.bham.ac.uk/courses/12947/pages/vocabulary-and-the-academic-word-list for links to various websites on this subject.

Academic Vocabulary

Verbs and Adverbs

When reading a text, it is useful to identify and understand the main verb: this is often the key to understanding the whole sentence. This unit looks at the more formal verbs used in academic writing, the verbs of reference used to introduce summaries, and outlines the use of adverbs.

1 Understanding main verbs

■ Study the following sentence and underline the main verbs:

The author concludes that no reasonable alternative is currently available to replace constitutional democracy, even though he does not completely reject the possibility of creating a better political system in the future.

To follow the writer's meaning, the reader needs to be clear that 'conclude' and 'reject' are the main verbs in the two parts of the sentence.

Academic writing tends to use rather formal verbs to express the writer's meaning accurately:

*In the last decade the pace of change **accelerated**.*

*Could Darwin have **envisaged** the controversy his work would cause?*

In spoken English we are more likely to use 'speed up' and 'imagined'.

■ Study the following list and find a synonym in each case.

(Some of these verbs (e.g. 'hold') are used in academic writing with a special meaning).

Verb	Example of use	Synonym
to adapt	*the health system has been **adapted** from France*	*modified*
to arise	*a similar situation **arises** when we look at younger children*	
to conduct	*the largest study was **conducted** in Finland*	
to characterise	*developing countries are **characterised** by . . . .*	
to clarify	*the project was designed to **clarify** these contradictions*	
to concentrate on	*that study **concentrated on** older children*	
to be concerned with	*the programme is **concerned** primarily **with** . . .*	
to demonstrate	*further research has **demonstrated** that few factors . . .*	
to determine	*the water content was experimentally **determined***	
to discriminate	*a failure to **discriminate** between the two species*	
to establish	*the northern boundary was **established** first*	
to exhibit	*half of the patients **exhibited** signs of improvement*	
to focus on	*her work **focused on** female managers*	
to generate	*a question which has **generated** a range of responses*	
to hold	*Newton's Second Law, F=ma, **holds** everywhere*	
to identify	*three main areas have been **identified***	
to imply	*his absence **implies** a lack of interest*	
to interact	*understand how the two systems **interact***	
to interpret	*the result can be **interpreted** as a limited success*	
to manifest	*as **manifested** in antisocial behaviour*	
to overcome	*both difficulties were **overcome** in the first week*	
to propose	*they **propose** that social class is the main factor*	
to prove	*the use of solar power is **proving** successful*	
to recognise	*he is now **recognised** as a leading expert*	
to relate to	*the pattern was **related to** both social and physical factors*	
to supplement	*the diet was **supplemented** with calcium and iodine*	
to undergo	*the system **underwent** major changes in the 1980s*	
to yield	*both surveys **yielded** mixed results*	

2 Using verbs of reference

Referring verbs are used to summarise another writer's ideas:

> *Previn **argued** that global warming was mainly caused by the solar cycle.*

> *Bakewell (1992) **found** that most managers tended to use traditional terms.*

They may also be used to introduce a quotation.

> *As Scott **observed:** 'Comment is free, but facts are sacred'.*

Most of these verbs are followed by a noun clause beginning with 'that'.

a) The following mean that the writer is presenting a case:

> argue   claim   consider   hypothesise   suggest   believe   think   state

> *Melville (2007) **suggested** that eating raw eggs could be harmful.*

b) A second group describe a reaction to a previously stated position:

> accept   admit   agree with   deny   doubt

> *Handlesmith **doubts** Melville's suggestion that eating raw eggs could be harmful.*

c) Others include:

> assume   conclude   discover   explain   imply   indicate   maintain   presume   reveal   show

> *Patel (2013) **assumes** that inflation will remain low.*

3 Practice A

■ Write a sentence referring to what the following writers said (more than one verb may be suitable). Make sure you use the past tense.

Example:

> *Z: 'My research shows that biofuels are environmentally neutral'.*
> *Z **claimed/argued** that biofuels were environmentally neutral.*

a) A: 'I may have made a mistake in my calculations on energy loss'.

b) B: 'I did not say that women make better doctors than men'.

c) C: 'Small firms are more dynamic than large ones'.

d) D: 'I support C's views on small firms'.

e) E: 'I'm not sure, but most people probably work to earn money'.

f) F: 'After much research, I've found that allergies are becoming more common'.

g)   G: 'I think it unlikely that electric cars will replace conventional ones'.

h)   H: 'There may be a link between crime and sunspot activity'.

4 Further verbs of reference

A small group of verbs is followed by the pattern (**somebody/thing + for + noun/gerund**):

blame   censure   commend   condemn   criticise

*Lee (1998) **blamed** the media for creating uncertainty.*

NB: All except 'commend' have a negative meaning.

Another group is followed by (**somebody/thing + as + noun/gerund**):

assess   characterise   classify   define   describe

evaluate   identify   interpret   portray present

*Terry **interprets** rising oil prices as a result of the Asian recovery.*

▶   See Unit 1.8.3 References and Quotations – Reference verbs

5 Practice B

■   **Rewrite the following statements using verbs from the lists in (4).**

Example:

   K: 'Guttman's work is responsible for many of the current social problems'.
   K ***blamed*** *Guttman's work for many of the current social problems.*

a)   L: 'She was very careless about her research methods'.

b)   M: 'There are four main types of children in care'.

c)   N: 'That company has an excellent record for workplace safety'.   *commended*

d)   O: 'The noises whales make must be expressions of happiness'.   *interpreted*

e)   P: 'Wind power and biomass will be the leading green energy sources of the   *identif.* future'.   */presented*

f)   Q: 'Darwin was the most influential naturalist of the nineteenth century'.   *discribe /portrayes*

6 Using adverbs

In the following sentence, adverbs are used to give information about time (currently) and degree (completely).

*The author concludes that no reasonable alternative is **currently** available to replace constitutional democracy, even though he does not **completely** reject the possibility of creating a better political system in the future.*

1 Adverbs are used in academic writing in a variety of ways. Among the most important are:

a) to provide more detail, with verbs and adjectives:

> ***Reasonably*** *good data are available for only the first two years.*

> *Decomposition **eventually** ceases in modern landfills.*

b) individually, often at the beginning of sentences, to introduce new points or link sentences together:

> ***Currently***, *the Earth's atmosphere appears to be warming up.*

> ***Alternatively***, *the use of non-conventional renewable energies is worth exploring.*

NB: Adverbs used individually need to be employed with care. It is dangerous to overuse them, since they can be like the author commenting on the topic. As an academic writer aims to be objective, adverbs such as 'fortunately' or 'remarkably' may be unsuitable.

2 Adverbs linked to verbs and adjectives usually fall into three groups.

a) Time (when?)

> ***previously*** *published*

> ***retrospectively*** *examined*

b) Degree (how much?)

> *declined **considerably***

> *contribute **substantially***

c) Manner (in what way?)

> ***medically*** *complicated*

> ***remotely*** *located*

Further common examples include:

Time	Degree	Manner
recently	*clearly*	*(un)surprisingly*
increasingly	*particularly*	*factually*
originally	*broadly*	*politically*
presently	*highly*	*locally*
currently	*wholly*	*alternatively*
traditionally	*crucially*	*similarly*
continuously	*emphatically*	*psychologically*

▶ **See Unit 3.4.4 Passive and Active – adverbs with passives**

7 Practice C

■ Insert suitable adverbs from the preceding table into the gaps in the sentences.

a) Most houses do not have electricity. _____, then, there is little chance of improving living standards.

b) _____, the internet was mainly used for academic purposes.

c) Some courses are assessed purely by exams. _____, course-work may be employed.

d) _____, there has been growing concern about financing the health service.

e) Many birds use bright colours to attract a mate. _____, flowers advertise their position to fertilising insects.

f) _____, the development should be acceptable environmentally.

g) Despite some disagreement, the team were _____ united on the next step.

h) Although _____ correct, many details were missing from the report.

8 Practice D

■ Complete the text by inserting a suitable adverb from the box into each gap.

> **virtually conventionally basically originally recently illicitly significantly substantially**

_____, the earliest keys were made by the Egyptians from wood, and _____ improved by the Romans, who used metal. Today's keys are _____ the same: a piece of metal with teeth, _____ produced by cutting and stamping. But _____ a new technology, 3D printing, has made it possible to manufacture much more intricate designs which are _____ im-possible to copy _____. Although _____ more expensive, these hi-tech keys offer remarkable security.

Conjunctions

Conjunctions are words or phrases which join sections of text together. Effective reading and writing requires clarity about the specific meaning of conjunctions. This unit describes the different functions of conjunctions and practises their use. Other ways of linking sections of text are explained in Unit 3.1 Cohesion.

1 How conjunctions work

When reading a text, conjunctions are like signposts, helping the reader to follow the ideas.

■ Read the following paragraph and study the functions of the conjunctions (in bold).

BIOFUELS

Newly published research examines some important questions about the growing use of biofuels, **such as** ethanol made from maize. The production of these has increased sharply recently, **but** the replacement of food crops with fuel crops has been heavily criticised. **Although** initially seen as a more environmentally friendly type of fuel, the research shows that producing some biofuels, **for instance** biodiesel palm oil, is more polluting than using conventional oil. The ethanol produced from sugar cane, **however**, can have negative emissions, **in other words** taking carbon dioxide from the atmosphere, which is a beneficial process. **Consequently**, it can be seen that the situation is rather confused, **and** that biofuels are **neither** a magical solution to the energy problem, **nor** are they the environmental disaster sometimes suggested.

Note that some conjunctions link parts of sentences together:

> *The production of these has increased sharply recently,* **but** *the replacement of food crops with fuel crops has been heavily criticised.*

While others join a new sentence to the previous one:

> *. . . carbon dioxide from the atmosphere, which is a beneficial process.* **Consequently,** *it can be seen that the situation is rather confused . . .*

2 Types of conjunctions

Note the way conjunctions work in the following sentences:

> *Demand for food is increasing* **because** *the population is growing.*

> *Mechanisation has increased crop yields,* **yet** *production is still inadequate.*

In the first sentence 'because' introduces a reason, in the second 'yet' indicates opposition between the two parts of the sentence.

■ **Underline the conjunctions in the following sentences.**

    a) A few inventions, for instance television, have had a major impact on everyday life.

    b) Furthermore, many patients were treated in clinics and surgeries.

    c) The definition of 'special needs' is important since it is the cause of some disagreement.

    d) The technology allows consumers a choice, thus increasing their sense of satisfaction.

    e) Four hundred people were interviewed for the survey, then the results were analysed.

    f) However, another body of opinion associates globalisation with unfavourable outcomes.

■ **There are six main types of conjunction. Match each of the following types to one of the preceding sentences.**

    i) Addition   (b)
    ii) Result   (d)
    iii) Reason   (c)
    iv) Opposition   (f)
    v) Example   (a)
    vi) Time   (e)

■ **Read the paragraph on biofuels on page 202 and decide what the function of each conjunction is (i.e. types i – vi in this section).**

Conjunction	Type	Conjunction	Type
a) such as	example	f) however	opposition
b) but	opposition	g) in other word	example
c) although	" — "	h) and	addition
d) for istance	example	i) neither nor	opposition
e) consequently	result		

▶ See Unit 2.2 Cause and Effect

3 Common conjunctions

■ Working with a partner, complete the table with as many examples of conjunctions as possible.

Addition	Result	Reason	Opposition	Example	Time
and as well as also plus	consequently so this is why as a result	since because owing to due to	yet neither nor but although	such as for ex.. in other words for instance	then while meanwhile.

4 Practice A

■ Insert a suitable conjunction into each gap.

a) _____After_____ checking the equipment the experiment was repeated.

b) _____While_____ most people use the train, a minority walk or cycle.

c) Brick is a thermally efficient building material. It is, _____moreover_____, cheap.

d) Demand has increased for summer courses, _____so_____ extra ones are offered this year.

e) Many writers, _____for example_____ Chekhov, have been doctors.

f) _____ the increase in residence fees more students are moving out.

g) _____ teaching at the Sorbonne she was writing a novel.

h) _____ he was studying Italian he spent a semester in Bologna.

5 Practice B

■ Insert a suitable conjunction into each gap.

Geoengineering

Geoengineers believe that it may be possible to counteract the effects of global warming by large-scale engineering projects, a) _____ the 'solar umbrella' designed to reflect sunlight back into space. b) _____ no major schemes have yet been attempted, there is already controversy about the risks involved.

Two different approaches are suggested: c) _____ to block incoming sunlight, d) _____ alternatively to take carbon dioxide out of the atmosphere. One proposal, e) _____, consists of putting iron into the sea in order to encourage the growth of the tiny sea creatures which absorb carbon dioxide. f) _____ this second approach is unlikely to create major problems, blocking sunlight is potentially dangerous, g) _____ the risk of affecting rainfall patterns h) _____ even ocean currents. i) _____ bioengineers are anxious to establish clear guidelines before any large-scale experiments are carried out.

6 Confusing conjunctions

In a few cases conjunctions have two meanings:

> **While** there were risks with the drug, he thought they were minor. (opposition)
>
> **While** listening to the lecture, she was planning the essay. (time)
>
> He has been in Washington **since** Tuesday. (time)
>
> **Since** she couldn't read Russian she had the paper translated. (reason)

7 Conjunctions of opposition

In some ways these are the most important type of conjunction, and can be the most difficult to use accurately. Note the position of the conjunctions in the following examples:

> **Although/While** there are frequent strikes, the economy is strong.
>
> **In spite of/Despite** the frequent strikes, the economy is strong.

There are frequent strikes. **However/Nevertheless**, *the economy is strong.*

The economy is strong, **but/yet** *there are frequent strikes.*

■ Write two sentences in each case.

Example: The equipment was expensive/unreliable

The equipment was expensive but unreliable.

Although the equipment was expensive, it was unreliable.

a)   The government claimed that inflation was falling. The opposition said it was rising.

i)   _____

ii)   _____

b)   This department must reduce expenditure. It needs to install new computers.

i)   _____

ii)   _____

c)   Sales of the new car were poor. It was heavily advertised.

i)   _____

ii)   _____

8 Practice C

■ Finish the sentences in a suitable way.

a)   In contrast to America, where gun ownership is common,

b)   Despite leaving school at the age of 14,

c)   The majority displayed a positive attitude to the proposal, but

d)   While the tutor insisted that the essay was easy,

e)   Although the spring was cold and dry,

f)   He finished the project before the deadline, yet

g)   She prefers speaking French, nevertheless

h)   Since it was nearly dark

Prefixes and Suffixes

Prefixes and suffixes are the first and last parts of certain words. Understanding the meaning of prefixes and suffixes can help you work out the meaning of a word and is particularly useful when you meet specialist new vocabulary.

1 How prefixes and suffixes work

'Unsustainable' is an example of a word containing a prefix and suffix. Words like this are much easier to understand if you know how prefixes and suffixes affect word meaning.

Prefixes change or give the meaning.

Suffixes show the meaning or the word class (e.g. noun, verb).

Prefix	Meaning	STEM	Suffix	Word class/Meaning
un-	negative	**sustain**	**-able**	adjective/ability

*The rate of growth was **unsustainable** (i.e. could not be continued).*

■ **Find the meaning of the words in bold:**

Prefabrication of the flats speeded up the building process.

*He was **revitalised** by the holiday in the mountains.*

pre-	before	fabric	-ation	noun
re-	again	vital	-ise	verb

2 Prefixes

a) Negative prefixes: NON-, UN-, IN-, IM-, MIS-, DE- and DIS- often give adjectives and verbs a negative meaning: **non**sense, **un**clear, **in**capable, **im**possible, **mis**hear, **de**crease, **dis**agree.

   NB. There are a few exceptions (e.g. 'invaluable' means very useful).

b) A wide variety of prefixes define meaning (e.g. PRE- usually means 'before', hence **pre**fer, **pre**history and, of course, **pre**fix)!

Common prefixes of meaning

■ Find the meaning(s) of each prefix (NB: some prefixes have more than one meaning).

Prefix	Example	Example sentence	Meaning
anti	antidepressant	**Antidepressant** drugs are often overprescribed.	*against*
auto	automatically	Over-18s **automatically** have the right to vote.	
co	co-ordinator	The **co-ordinator** invited them to a meeting.	
ex	ex-president	The **ex-president** gave a speech on climate change.	
ex	exclusive	It is difficult to join such an **exclusive** club.	
fore	forecast	The long-term **forecast** is for higher inflation.	
inter	intervention	Early medical **intervention** saves lives.	
macro	macroeconomics	Keynes focused on **macroeconomics.**	
micro	microscope	She examined the tiny animals with a **microscope.**	
multi	multinational	Ford is a **multinational** motor company.	
non	nonfiction	They specialise in publishing **nonfiction**.	
over	oversleep	He missed the lecture because he **overslept**.	
poly	polyglot	She was a true **polyglot**, speaking five languages.	
post	postpone	The meeting is **postponed** until next Monday.	
pro	promote	Their website **promoted** the college's facilities.	
re	retrain	The firm **retrained** staff to use the new software.	
sub	subtitle	Chinese films often have **subtitles** in the West.	

tele	televise	Parliament was first **televised** in 1989.	
trans	transmitter	Early radio **transmitters** were short-range.	
under	undergraduate	Most **undergraduate** courses last three years.	
under	undercook	Eating **undercooked** meat can be dangerous.	

3 Practice A

Prefixes allow new words to be created (e.g. 'unfriend' [to delete a 'friend' from social media]).

■ **Suggest possible meanings for the recently developed words in bold.**

a) Criminal activity seems to be very common among the **underclass**.

b) Some passengers found the plane was **overbooked** and had to wait for the next flight.

c) The **microclimate** in this district allows early vegetables to be grown.

d) It is claimed that computers have created a **post-industrial** economy.

e) Most film stars have **ex-directory** phone numbers.

f) The class was **underwhelmed** by the quality of the lecture.

g) The couple decided to draw up a **prenuptial** agreement.

h) The company is looking for a **proactive** manager.

4 Suffixes

a) Some suffixes like –ION, –IVE or –LY help the reader find the word class (e.g. noun, adjective or adverb).

b) Other suffixes add to meaning (e.g. –FUL or –LESS LESS after an adjective has a positive or negative effect [thought**ful**/care**less**]).

Word class suffixes

Nouns   -ER often indicates a role: *teacher, gardener*
-EE can show a person who is the subject: *employee, trainee*
-ISM and -IST are often used with belief systems and their supporters: *socialism/socialist*
-NESS converts an adjective into a noun: *sad > sadness*
-ION changes a verb to a noun: *convert > conversion*

Adjectives   -IVE *effective, constructive*
-AL *commercial, agricultural*
-IOUS *precious, serious*

Verbs	-ISE/-IZE to form verbs from adjectives: *private > privatise* NB: In the US only –ize spelling is used, but both forms are accepted in the UK
Adverbs	-LY most (but not all) adverbs have this suffix: *happily*

Meaning suffixes

A few suffixes contribute to the meaning of the word:

* –ABLE has the meaning of 'ability': *a **watchable** film, **changeable** weather*
* –WARDS means 'in the direction of': *the ship sailed **northwards**, he walked **homewards***
* –FUL and LESS: ***hopeful** news, a **leaderless** team*

5 Practice B

■ Give the word class and suggest possible meanings for:

a) cancellation   f) unpredictable
b) coincidental   g) saleable
c) uncooperatively   h) interviewee
d) evolutionary   i) consumerism
e) protester   j) symbolically

6 Practice C

■ Study each sentence and find the meaning of the words underlined.

a) The film is an Anglo-Italian co-production made by a subsidiary company.

b) When the car crashed, she screamed involuntarily but was unharmed.

c) Using rechargeable batteries has undoubted benefits for the environment.

d) They rearranged the preschool tests.

e) The unavailability of the product is due to the exceptional weather.

f) The miscommunication led to a reorganisation of their software system.

g) Her incorrect pronunciation was laughable.

h) He was told to rewrite his unreadable essay.

▶ See Unit 4.3 Academic Vocabulary: Nouns and Adjectives

Prepositions

Prepositions are generally short words such as 'by' or 'at' which have a variety of uses. They are important because different prepositions can change the meaning of a sentence. This unit explains how they can be understood and learnt by linking them to nouns, adjectives and verbs. Students should consult a standard English grammar for a full list of prepositional combinations.

1 Using prepositions

Many international students find the use of prepositions confusing. This is because, although they are mainly short words, a different preposition can change the meaning of a sentence.

a) ■ Compare:

*Essays must be handed in **on** January 15th.*

*Essays must be handed in **by** January 15th.*

In the first sentence essays have to be submitted on the exact date, but in the second the date is the final deadline and essays can be submitted earlier.

b) ■ Study the use of prepositions in the following text (ignoring to + infinitives).

The **purpose of** this paper is to examine the **development of** the textile industry **in Catalonia in the period** 1780–1880. This clearly **contributed to** the region's industrialisation and was **valuable for** stimulating exports. **In conclusion**, the paper attempts to demonstrate the **relationship between** the **decline in** agricultural employment and the **supply of** cheap labour **in the factory context**.

c) ■ These are the main ways of using prepositions. Find examples of each in the text.

Noun + preposition	_____
Verb + preposition	_____
Adjective + preposition	_____
Preposition of place	_____
Preposition of time	_____
Phrase	_____

Note that prepositions linked to nouns, verbs and adjectives normally **follow** the word they are connected with, while prepositions of time and place generally come **before** the word.

2 Practice A

■ Study these further examples of prepositional use and decide on their type.

a) There are a number **of** limitations to be considered. . . (_noun +_)

b) The results would be applicable **to** all children. . . (_____)

c) . . . the data were gathered **from** a questionnaire (_____)

d) All the items were placed **within** their categories... (_____)

e) The results **of** the investigation are still pertinent. . . (_____)

f) The respondents had spent **on** average 4.9 years. . . (_____)

g) . . . most countries **in** sub-Saharan Africa. . . (_____)

h) . . . **within** a short spell of four years (_____)

3 Prepositions and nouns

■ Insert a suitable preposition with the nouns in the following sentences.

a) Evidence is presented in support _____ the value of women's work.

b) A small change _____ wind direction can lead to large temperature changes.

c) Many examples _____ tax evasion were found.

d) The answer _____ the problem was 0.585.

e) The head _____ the council has just resigned.

f) The second point is their impact _____ developing countries.

4 Prepositions in phrases

■ Complete the following phrases with the correct preposition.

a) _____ the whole

b) point _____ view

c) in respect _____

d) _____ spite of

e) in support _____

f) _____ the other hand

g) _____ order to

h) standard _____ living

5 Prepositions of place and time

Note the difference between 'among' and 'between':

Among 14 *students in the class, only two were from Africa.*   (large group)

He divided his time **between** *the offices in Barcelona and Madrid.* (limited number)

■ Complete the following sentences with suitable prepositions of place or time.

a) _____ the respondents, few had any experience of working abroad.

b) The illiteracy rate declined gradually _____ 1976 _____ 1985.

c) Most workers _____ the European Union retire before the age _____ 60.

d) Leonardo da Vinci was born _____ Florence _____ 1452.

e) Chocolate sales fall _____ summer and peak _____ Christmas.

f) _____ the surface, there is no difference _____ male and female responses.

g) The countries _____ the Mediterranean held a meeting _____ May 20th.

h) _____ 15 and 20 students study chemical engineering every year.

▶ See Unit 3.8 Time Markers

6 Practice B

■ Complete the following text with suitable prepositions.

This study attempts to answer the controversial question a) _____ whether

increased food supply b) _____ a country makes a significant contribution c) _____ reducing malnutrition d) _____ children. It uses data collected e) _____ 75 countries f) _____ 1995 and 2005. The findings are that there was a considerable improvement g) _____ the majority h) _____ countries, despite increases in population i) _____ the period. However, a clear distinction was found j) _____ the poorest countries (e.g. k) _____ South Asia), where the improvement was greatest, and the wealthier states such as those l) _____ North Africa. Other factors, notably the educational level m) _____ women, were also found to be critical n) _____ improving childhood nutrition.

7 Verbs and prepositions

The following verbs are generally used with these prepositions:

Verb + prep.	*Example*
add to	The bad weather **added to** the team's difficulties.
agree with	Yu (1997) **agrees with** Martin and Jenks (1989).
associate with	Monetarism is an economic policy **associated with** Mrs Thatcher.
believe in	The survey showed that 65% **believed in** life after death.
blame for	He **blamed** unfair questions **for** his poor exam results.
concentrate on (*also: focus on*)	She dropped all her hobbies to **concentrate on** her work.
consist of	Parliament **consists of** two Houses: the Commons and the Lords.
depend on (*also: rely on*)	The company **depends on** ICT for a rapid flow of sales data.
derive from	Modern computers **derive from** wartime decoding machines.
divide into	Trees are **divided into** two main types: conifers and deciduous trees.
invest in	Far more money needs to be **invested in** primary education.
learn from	All successful students **learn from** their mistakes.
pay for	Goods delivered in April must be **paid for** by June 30[th.]
point out	Goodson (2001) **points out** the dangers of generalisation.
specialise in	This department **specialises in** French poetry.

8 Practice C

■   Complete the following with suitable verbs and prepositions.

a)   The enquiry _____ the cause of the accident, not the consequences.

b)   Dr Cracknell _____ that there were only two weeks before the deadline.

c)   After graduating he _____ designing security software.

d)   Albert Einstein is commonly _____ the theory of relativity.

e)   A football pitch is _____ two halves.

f)   A series of strikes were _____ the decline in production during May.

g)   Millions of men died for the cause they _____

h)   She _____ French _____ her mother, who came from Rouen.

Synonyms

Synonyms are different words with a similar meaning, such as 'figures' and 'numbers'. A good writer uses synonyms to avoid repetition and thus provide more interest for the reader. Synonyms should also be used when paraphrasing or note-making to avoid plagiarism.

1 How synonyms work

■ Underline the synonyms in the following text and complete the table.

Royal Dutch Shell is the <u>largest</u> oil company in the world by revenue, with a significant share of the global hydrocarbon market. The <u>giant</u> firm employs over 100,000 people internationally, including over 8,000 employees in Britain. Shell produces about 13% of the UK's oil and gas.

Word/phrase	Synonym
largest	*giant*
oil	
company	
in the world	
people	
Britain	

a)   Synonyms are not always exactly the same in meaning, so that in the example on page 216 'employees' is more specific than 'people'. It is important not to change the register: 'firm' is a good synonym for 'company', but 'boss' is too informal to use for 'manager'.

b)   Many common words (e.g. culture, economy or industry) have no effective synonyms.

2 Common synonyms in academic writing

■   Match the academic synonyms in each list.

Nouns		Verbs	
area	advantage	accelerate	**take apart**
authority	part	alter	help
behaviour	argument	**analyse**	question
benefit	disadvantage	assist	change
category	tendency	attach	explain
component	**field**	challenge	evolve
controversy	source	clarify	examine
difficulty	emotion	concentrate on	establish
drawback	target	conduct	insist
expansion	explanation	confine	speed up
feeling	conduct	develop	join
framework	topic	evaluate	decrease
goal	possibility	found	demonstrate
interpretation	production	maintain	increase
issue	research	predict	reinforce
method	increase	prohibit	focus on
option	figures	raise	forecast
results	type	reduce	ban
statistics	structure	respond	carry out
study	system	retain	limit
trend	findings	show	keep
output	problem	strengthen	reply

NB: These pairs are commonly synonymous, but not in every situation.

3 Practice A

■   Find synonyms for the words and phrases underlined, rewriting the sentences where necessary.

a) Professor Hicks <u>questioned</u> the <u>findings</u> of the <u>research</u>.

b) The <u>statistics show</u> a steady <u>increase</u> in applications.

c) The institute's <u>prediction</u> has caused a major <u>controversy</u>.

d) Cost seems to be the <u>leading drawback</u> to that <u>system</u>.

e) They will <u>concentrate on</u> the first <u>option</u>.

f) After the lecture she tried to <u>clarify</u> her <u>concept</u>.

g) Three <u>issues</u> need to be <u>examined</u>.

h) The <u>framework</u> can be <u>retained</u>, but the <u>goal</u> needs to be <u>altered</u>.

i) OPEC, the oil producers' cartel, is to <u>cut production</u> to <u>raise</u> global prices.

j) The <u>trend</u> to smaller families has <u>speeded up</u> in the last decade.

4 Practice B

■ Identify the synonyms in this text by underlining them and linking them to the word they are substituting for.

Example: agency – organisation

The chairman of the UK's food standards **agency** has said that a national advertising campaign is necessary to raise low levels of personal hygiene. The **organisation** is planning a £3m publicity programme to improve British eating habits. A survey has shown that half the population do not wash before eating, and one in five fail to wash before preparing food. There are over six million cases of food poisoning in this country every year, and the advertising blitz aims to cut this by 20%. This reduction, the food body believes, could be achieved by regular hand washing prior to meals.

5 Practice C

■ In the following text, replace all the words or phrases in bold type with suitable synonyms.

Many motor manufacturers are currently introducing electric cars. Their aim is to **manufacture cars** which are cheaper to run and less polluting. But these **motor manufacturers** face several key difficulties. One **key difficulty** is the limited range of the battery, while another **difficulty** is its cost and weight. But the **motor manufacturers** predict that these **difficulties** will soon be overcome and **predict** that 10% of cars will be powered by electricity in five years' time. However, electrical **power** must be generated by something, and unless it is **generated** by renewables (e.g. wind or solar power) such **cars** may not be as 'green' as their makers claim.

▶ See Unit 1.7 Summarising and Paraphrasing

Progress Check 4

These exercises will help you assess your understanding of Part 4 – Vocabulary for Writing.

1   *Which of the following should be avoided in academic writing?*

    a) a cliché   b) a synopsis   c) a proverb   d) an idiom

2   *Choose the correct form in each sentence.*

    a) The Democratic Liberal Party may lose/loose the election.

    b) I finished the essay accept/except for the conclusion.

    c) The site/sight of the accident was guarded by police.

3   *Explain the following:*

    a) The IMF has revised its GDP forecast for next year.

    b) cf. *The Legend of Layla* (anon.) c. 550 BCE.

    c) His MSc dissertation was on the trials of GM strawberries.

4   *Give the opposite adjectives:*

    a) relative

    b) literal

    c) objective

    d) vague

    e) concrete

5   *Give the nouns related to these adjectives:*

    a) high

    b) synthetic

c) long

d) probable

e) relevant

6 *Rewrite the sentences using verbs of reference.*

a) X: I have found that eating spiders keeps you healthy.

b) Y: I don't agree with X's theory; it is based on poor research.

c) Z: I support Y's opinion of X's work.

---

rarely   particularly   traditionally   locally   increasingly   continuously   obviously

---

7 *Add a suitable adverb from the box above to each sentence.*

a) The site of London has been occupied _____ since Roman times.

b) As central government was weak, decisions were taken _____.

c) In the past, there was a high mortality rate among children, _____ the youngest.

d) Young adults are _____ delaying marriage until their late twenties.

e) _____, becoming a carpenter required a seven-year apprenticeship.

8 *Complete the paragraph with suitable conjunctions.*

a) _____ she was tired, she had to finish the essay that night, b) _____ the deadline was 9 a.m. next morning. c) _____ she made a cup of coffee d) _____ sat down to write. e) _____ she could not write a word, f) _____ she was feeling so hungry. g) _____ she remembered she had not eaten all day, h) _____ she had been on the train. i) _____ she cooked an omelette, ate it with some salad, j) _____ felt much better.

9 *State the word class of the following:*

a) saleable

b) salvation

c) privatise

d) attendee

e) agnosticism

10 *Link the words on the left to the meanings on the right, based on the prefixes.*

antidote	under the skin
correspondent	preliminary section of book
foreword	relation of one thing to another
polytechnic	institute where many scientific subjects are taught
proportion	assess worth of something too cheaply
subcutaneous	medicine to counter effects of poison
undervalue	person you write to regularly

11 *Find the correct prepositions to complete the text.*

a) _____ the eighteenth century, news travelled as fast as a horseman or sailing ship. It could take weeks b) _____ news c) _____ a battle d) _____ Europe to reach America. e) _____ the mid-nineteenth century railways had accelerated the distribution f) _____ newspapers, so that they reached distant provinces g) _____ hours, and then the telegraph allowed news to be sent h) _____ seconds. Today we can be overwhelmed i) _____ the volume j) _____ news k) _____ all over the world which we can continuously receive l) _____ our phones and laptops.

12 *Find synonyms for the underlined words, rewriting the sentence where necessary.*

a) Their research <u>methods</u> caused serious <u>argument</u>.

b) The <u>statistics demonstrate</u> the <u>benefits</u> of increased investment.

c) There is a <u>possibility</u> of <u>studying</u> the family records.

d) Her <u>findings reinforce</u> Jung's theory.

e) Her <u>area</u> of <u>research</u> was Catherine the Great.

f) They <u>conducted</u> a survey into the <u>behaviour</u> of international students.

Writing Models

The types of writing that students need to produce vary enormously according to both level (undergraduate, postgraduate) and subject. However, most will have to write case studies and literature reviews, often as part of longer papers, and many will write reports of some kind, while almost all need to write letters and emails during their course. Part 5 provides examples of these formats and also introduces the practice of writing in a group.

Case Studies

Both essays and reports may include case studies, which are detailed examples illustrating the topic under discussion. One case study may be the main subject of an essay, or several may be included to illustrate different situations.

1 Using case studies

A case study attempts to show exactly what happened in a particular situation. For example, if you are discussing methods of fighting malaria in rural areas, a case study might follow the real-life efforts of a medical team in a specific district of Indonesia over a period of months.

What are the advantages of including case studies?

Are there any disadvantages?

■ Match the topics on the left with the example case studies on the right.

Topics	Case studies
Methods of teaching dyslexic children	A programme to cut smoking among pregnant women in a Greek clinic
Improving crop yields in semi-deserts	Work and learning – how a Brazilian scheme encouraged convicts to stay out of jail
Reducing infant mortality	The Berlin experiment: increasing public participation in collecting and sorting waste
Building earthquake-resistant bridges	Using solar power to operate irrigation pumps in Ethiopia
Dealing with reoffending among prisoners	The lessons from Chile – how three structures withstood the 2010 earthquake
Improving recycling rates in large cities	An experimental approach to reading difficulties with children under eight in Singapore

2 Model case study

■ Read this example of a case study taken from a longer essay and answer the questions that follow.

Topic: Adapting international brands to local markets

Case Study: The experience of IKEA in China

Introduction

The Chinese economy has expanded at an annual rate of about 8% for the past 30 years. Parallel to this, the Chinese furniture industry has grown vigorously, with annual sales recently rising by over 20% a year. Legislation to privatise home ownership and rapidly rising income levels have created unprecedented growth in the home improvement market, and China is now the world's second-largest furniture market. This demand has boosted domestic production and also prompted international furniture manufacturers to enter this lucrative market.

IKEA, a Swedish furniture company, was one of the international companies which moved into China. It is a major furniture retailer operating in over 28 countries around the world and had annual sales of over 35 billion euros in 2016 (IKEA website). It entered the Chinese market in 1998 with its first store in Beijing and sees great potential in the country, having already expanded to ten stores and five distribution centres. Despite this successful growth, IKEA has found itself facing a number of challenges in terms of local differences in culture and business practices.

Marketing IKEA in China

Marketing management needs to be largely tailored to local contexts. IKEA has kept this notion in mind when designing marketing strategies and trying to appeal to local customers while maintaining profitability. The company attempts to find the best possible compromise between standardisation and adaptation to local markets. Its product policy pays careful attention to Chinese style and integrates the set of product attributes effectively (Armstrong and Kotler, 2006).

The store layouts reflect the floor plan of many Chinese apartments, and since many of these have balconies, the stores include a balcony section. In contrast with traditional Chinese furniture, which is dark with much carving, IKEA introduces a lighter and simpler style. However, efforts have been made to adapt its products to

Chinese taste. For instance, it has released a series of products just before each Chinese New Year. In 2008, the year of the rat, the series 'Fabler' was designed using the colour red, which is associated with good luck.

Changes were also made to some product ranges. In Sweden, people are used to sleeping in single beds or to putting two single beds together to form a double bed. However, this idea was not very well received by Chinese couples, due to the fact that sleeping in separate beds symbolises a poor relationship and is believed to bring bad luck. In addition, Chinese brand names should have positive connotations. The Chinese name of IKEA (Yi Jia) means 'comfortable home', which gives the company a useful advantage in the market.

An important feature of a retailer is the services it offers. The Shanghai store, for instance, has a children's playground and a large restaurant, which make it distinctive. However, Chinese consumers expect free delivery and installation, and although IKEA has reduced its charges for these, it still compares unfavourably with its competitors.

Price

When the company first entered China, its target market was couples with an income of 5–8,000 Rmb per month. Following steady price reductions, this has now been lowered to families with just over 3,000 Rmb. Various strategies have been adopted to achieve these reductions, the most effective being to source locally. Seventy percent of IKEA products sold in China are now made in the country (Song, 2005). Furthermore, IKEA replaced its thick annual catalogue with thinner brochures which now appear five times a year. These not only cut printing costs but also give greater flexibility to adjust prices.

Accessibility is also an important issue for the Chinese market. In most countries IKEA stores are sited near main roads, but as only 35% of likely customers own cars in China, easy access to public transport is vital (Miller, 2004).

Advertising plays an important role in the total promotional mix. IKEA uses advertising effectively, with adverts in the local newspapers to keep customers informed of special offers. All TV commercials are produced locally with Chinese characters. Public relations is also vital to building a good corporate image. In China, IKEA co-operates with the World Wide Fund for Nature (WWF) on forest projects. The company insists on using environmentally friendly and recyclable materials for the packaging of its products, as part of its efforts to build a good corporate image.

Discussion and conclusion

IKEA's product policy in China has been to successfully standardise products as much as possible but also customise as much as needed. But it has learned that service is also vital: free delivery and installation are the perceived rules in the local market which it needs to follow. It has further found that it is better to locate in a downtown area, easily accessible with public transport, when free delivery is not provided.

International companies which operate in China, such as IKEA, face more complicated marketing decisions than local companies. They must become culture-conscious and thoroughly research local requirements rather than simply introduce a standard model of business.

a) Give examples of problems the company has faced in this market.

b) What has IKEA done to adapt to the Chinese market?

c) What could be done to improve the case study?

UNIT
5.2

Literature Reviews and Book Reviews

Literature reviews are sections of a paper in which the writer summarises recently published work on the topic. They are standard in dissertations, but in most essays a summary of relevant and recent authorities may be included in the introduction.

Book reviews can be written by graduate students for academic journals in order to broaden their knowledge and achieve publication.

1 Literature reviews

Occasionally the whole focus of an essay may be a lengthy literature review, but in most student writing it will only form a relatively short section of the paper. Only a minority of essays have a separate section headed 'The Literature' or 'Literature Review'. But in all cases it is necessary to show that you are familiar with the main sources in order to provide your work with credibility and so that your writing can build on these sources.

A literature review is not simply a list of sources that you have studied. It can be used to show that there is a gap in the research that your work attempts to fill:

This article has a different standpoint from other studies, because it believes that the influence of the state on the market has structurally increased since the neo-liberal era.

This article focuses on information production, not information accessibility. That is the difference between this research and previous studies.

It is also common to use the literature section to clarify the varying positions held by other researchers:

> *The political competition literature comprises two main strands – voter monitoring and political survival.*

▶ **See Unit 1.9 Combining Sources**

2 Example literature review

■ Study the following example from a student essay on motivation theory. Answer the questions which follow.

CONTENT AND PROCESS THEORIES

The various theories of motivation are usually divided into content theories and process theories. The former attempt to 'develop an understanding of fundamental human needs' (Cooper *et al.*, 1992:20). Among the most significant are Maslow's hierarchy of needs theory, McClellan's achievement theory and Herzberg's two-factor theory. The process theories deal with the actual methods of motivating workers and include the work of Vroom, Locke and Adams.

Content theories

Maslow's hierarchy of needs theory was first published in 1943 and envisages a pyramid of needs on five levels, each of which has to be satisfied before moving up to the next level. The first level is physiological needs such as food and drink, followed by security, love, esteem and self-fulfilment (Rollinson, 2005:195–6). This theory was later revised by Alderfer, who reduced the needs to three: existence, relatedness and growth, and renamed it the ERG theory. In addition, he suggested that all three needs should be addressed simultaneously (Steers *et al.*, 2004:381). McClelland had a slightly different emphasis when he argued that individuals were primarily motivated by three principal needs: for achievement, affiliation and power (Mullins, 2006:199).

In contrast, Herzberg suggested, on the basis of multiple interviews with engineers and accountants during the 1950s, a two-factor theory: that job satisfaction and dissatisfaction had differing roots. He claimed that so-called hygiene factors such as conditions and pay were likely to cause negative attitudes if inadequate, while positive attitudes came from the nature of the job itself. In other words, workers were satisfied if they found their work intrinsically interesting, but would not be

---

motivated to work harder merely by good salaries or holiday allowances. Instead workers needed to be given more responsibility, more authority or more challenging tasks to perform (Vroom and Deci, 1992:252). Herzberg's work has probably been the most influential of all the theories in this field and is still widely used today, despite being the subject of some criticism, which will be considered later.

Process theories

Vroom's expectancy theory hypothesises a link between effort, performance and motivation. It is based on the idea that an employee believes that increased effort will result in improved performance. This requires a belief that the individual will be supported by the organisation in terms of training and resources (Mullins, 2006). In contrast, Locke emphasised the importance of setting clear targets to improve worker performance in his goal theory. Setting challenging but realistic goals is necessary for increasing employee motivation: 'goal specificity, goal difficulty and goal commitment each served to enhance task performance' (Steers *et al.*, 2004:382). This theory has implications for the design and conduct of staff appraisal systems and for management by objective methods focusing on the achievement of agreed performance targets.

Another approach was developed by Adams in his theory of equity, based on the concept that people value fairness. He argued that employees appreciate being treated in a transparently equitable manner in comparison with other workers doing similar functions and respond positively if this is made apparent (Mullins, 2006). This approach takes a wider view of the workplace situation than some other theories and stresses the balance each worker calculates between 'inputs' (i.e. the effort made) and 'outputs', which are the rewards obtained.

As many of these theorists did their research over 60 years ago, there has clearly been a huge change in the nature of employment since then. Therefore, it is worth asking whether they still have relevance to the situation of many workers in the modern, post-industrial economy, and this study attempts to answer that question.

a)   How many types of motivation theory are described?

b)   How many different theorists are mentioned?

c)   How many sources are cited?

d)   Why has the writer not referred to the work of the theorists directly but used secondary sources instead?

3 Book reviews

Writing a book review gives a student the opportunity to critically examine a topic in detail. Journals normally specify the length they require (often about 400 words). In general a review should contain two parts:

a) A description of the scope and organisation of the book. Who is the author and what has he/she written before? What kind of reader is the book aimed at? In the case of an edited volume, who are the editors and principal contributors?

b) The second part should evaluate how successful the book is in its aims. It is better to avoid excessive praise or criticism and to mention both positive and negative features. Is the book breaking new ground and adding significantly to current debates? It is also worth commenting on the author's style and how easy it is to read for specialist or non-specialist readers.

Writers are encouraged to first read a selection of reviews in their subject area before attempting their own reviews.

4 Model book review

■ **Study the following review and discuss with a partner whether there is anything else that you think the reviewer should have included.**

> *Atlantic Crossing: a comparison of European and American society*
> by Marcus Montero (ed.) York: York University Press, 2008. 378 pp., £35.00, ISBN 987 0 15 980456 3.
>
> ---
>
> This useful and important edited volume partly fills a gap in the comparative political science literature. The book compares the society and politics of the European Union (treated here as a single state) with the United States. The book examines 'convergences and divergences' between these two global powers, similar in size and economic weight 'but asymmetric in terms of political influence and military might' (p. 1).
>
> The book has eight chapters. The introductory and concluding chapters, which hold the volume together, are written by the editor. The first briefly outlines the adopted comparative approach and methodological challenges faced in producing this study. Montero then goes on to argue that the EU and the US offer two contrasting models of Western modernity. The final chapter argues that the process of constructing the EU has led to convergence, not divergence, between the EU and the

US. In between are six sectoral chapters; of particular interest is the third, by Kuhl, which argues that the *quality* of the democratic experience is in decline on both sides of the Atlantic.

This is a well-written work that breaks new ground in treating the EU as a single state. However, the book was published in 2008, a year after the EU had enlarged to 27 states. The authors fail to deal fully with this 'geographic boundary' problem. This neglect of the newest member states is repeated throughout the volume and brings into question the validity of the book's wider conclusions.

Writing Longer Papers

Long essays of 3,000–5,000 words may be required as part of a module assessment. These require more time, research and organisation than short essays, and this unit provides a guide to how such an assignment can be approached.

1 Planning your work

Longer assignments are normally set many weeks before their deadline, which means that students should have plenty of time to organise their writing. However, it is worth remembering that at the end of a semester you may have to submit several writing tasks, so it may be a good idea to finish one well before the deadline.

   You should also check the submission requirements of your department. These include style of referencing, method of submission (i.e. electronic, hard copy or both) and place and time of submission. Being clear about these will prevent last-minute panic.

a)   The first thing to do is to prepare a schedule for your work. An eight-week schedule might look like this:

Week	Stages of work	Relevant units in *Academic Writing*
1	Study title and make first outline. Look for and evaluate suitable sources.	1.2, 1.5
2	Reading and note-making. Keep record of all sources used.	1.2, 1.3, 1.6, 1.8
3	Reading, note-making, paraphrasing and summarising. Modify outline.	1.2, 1.3, 1.5, 1.7

4	Write draft of main body.	1.10
5	Write draft introduction and conclusion.	1.11
6	Rewrite introduction, main body and conclusion, checking for logical development of ideas and relevance to title.	1.12
7	Organise list of references, contents, list of figures and appendices if required. Check all in-text citations.	1.8
8	Proofread the whole essay before handing it in. Make sure that the overall presentation is clear and accurate (e.g. is page numbering correct?).	1.12

b) How you actually plan your schedule is up to you, but the important thing is to organise your time effectively. At some point you have to stop researching and start writing (Week 4 in the example above). Leaving the writing stage until the last minute will not lead to a good mark, however much research you have done. Although you may be tempted to postpone writing, the sooner you start, the sooner you will be able to begin refining your ideas. Remember that late submission of coursework is usually penalised.

c) Longer papers may include the following features, in this order:

Title page	Apart from the title, this usually shows the student's name and module title and number.
Contents page	This should show the reader the basic organisation of the essay, with page numbers.
List of tables or figures	If the essay includes visual features such as graphs, these need to be listed by title and page number.
Introduction	
Main body	If a numbering system is used, the chief sections of the main body are normally numbered 1, 2, 3 and then subdivided 1.1, 1.2 etc.
Conclusion	
Acknowledgements	A space to thank any teachers or others who have assisted the writer.
List of references	This is a complete list of all the sources cited in the text. Writers occasionally also include a bibliography, which is a list of sources read but not cited.
Appendices (Singular – appendix)	These sections are for data related to the topic which the reader may want to refer to. Each appendix should have a title and be mentioned in the main body.

2 Example essay

■ Read the following essay on the topic of nuclear energy. In pairs or groups, discuss the following points:

a) What is the writer's position on this issue?

b) How does the writer make his/her position clear?

c) What are the strengths and weaknesses of this work? How could it be improved?

EVALUATE THE RISKS OF USING NUCLEAR ENERGY AS AN ALTERNATIVE TO FOSSIL FUELS

Introduction

The search for sources of energy began when humans first started to burn wood or other forms of biomass to generate heat for cooking and smelting. This was followed by using hydropower from rivers and harnessing wind energy with windmills. Later the exploitation of chemical energy began with the burning of coal, oil and natural gas. Then, in the middle of the twentieth century, nuclear energy was harnessed for the first time with the hope that it would allow the efficient production of cheap, clean power (Bodansky, 2004).

Nuclear energy has, however, become the subject of considerable debate, with its proponents claiming that it is beneficial for the environment since its production does not create carbon dioxide (CO_2) which can lead to global warming. However, its opponents argue that it can damage the environment by creating radioactive waste. Radioactivity is also linked to diseases in humans, and there is the additional fear that it may be abused by terrorists in future. These critics further argue that other energy sources, such as solar power, could constitute safer alternatives to fossil fuels without posing an environmental threat.

This essay attempts to assess the risks of using nuclear power compared to other sources of energy. The main arguments for employing nuclear energy are first considered, followed by an examination of the safety issues around this source of power, including the safety and security concerns connected with nuclear waste.

1 Reasons for using nuclear energy

1.1 An alternative source of energy

The rationale behind using nuclear energy stems from the need to find alternative energy sources to fossil fuels (i.e. oil, gas and coal), which are finite. This is a growing concern, due to the increase in the global population, which is accompanied by an increase in energy demand. Mathew (2006) indicates that the annual energy consumption rate per capita in developed countries is between 4,000 and 9,000 kgs of oil, while the rate in less developed countries is around 500 kgs. As a result, the demand for total primary energy, which will accompany this population growth, is projected to increase from 12.1 Mtoe (million tons of oil equivalent) to 16.1 Mtoe in 2030. If this increase occurs, the total global stock of oil and gas would only be adequate for 250 years, thus requiring the urgent development of other energy sources which would not deplete the stock of natural resources available for future generations.

1.2 Limitations of other energy sources

Wind energy and solar power are frequently presented as alternative energy sources to fossil fuels. Both are freely available in many parts of the world, and their use involves no CO_2 emissions. Sterrett (1994) claims that sufficient wind energy exists to displace approximately eight billion barrels of oil. However, wind energy is unreliable, as wind turbines do not function if the wind speed is too high or too low. Similarly, solar power is only effective during the day and is uneconomic in cool and cloudy climates. Neither of these sources currently offers an efficient and reliable alternative to energy created from fossil fuels.

1.3 Reducing carbon dioxide emissions

An important reason for using nuclear energy is to reduce the emissions of CO_2, which are produced by burning fossil fuels. Bodansky (2004) points out that this type of fuel is the main source of the increase in atmospheric carbon dioxide. The amount of CO_2 produced by each source varies due to the differences in their hydrogen content. For example, natural gas contains one carbon atom and four hydrogen atoms which combine with oxygen to produce CO_2. The proportion of CO_2 is lower than with the other sources, because the emission depends on the mass of carbon inside the chemical compounds. Although natural gas is thus cleaner than the alternatives, burning all three fuels contributes to the greenhouse effect, which is causing the earth to heat up.

Nuclear energy, however, emits no carbon dioxide, sulphur dioxide (SO_2) or nitrous oxide (N_2O). It is estimated that in 2003, in the United States, nuclear energy prevented the release of 680 million tons of CO_2, 3.4 millions tons of SO_2 and 1.3 million tons of N_2O. If released from coal-burning plants, these gases would have caused the deaths of 40,000 people annually (Olah *et al.*, 2006:127). According to Richard

(2008:273), the use of nuclear energy in France between 1980 and 1987 reduced CO_2 emissions by 34%.

1.4 Cost efficiency

Nuclear energy could generate more electricity than other current sources. As Murray (2000:73) explains, a typical reactor, which consumes 4 kg/day of uranium U235, generates 3,000 MW of energy a day, while other sources such as natural gas, coal or oil require many times the equivalent of that amount of uranium to generate the same energy. Therefore, nuclear energy is relatively cost-efficient, as it uses a cheap raw material.

In recent years the price of oil and natural gas has risen sharply, and this trend seems likely to continue in future. Lillington (2004) suggests that the cost of purchasing fuel for nuclear energy is likely to remain low compared to other energy sources, so it seems likely that this cost advantage will become a significant factor in the comparison between nuclear and other energy sources.

2 Health and safety concerns

2.1 The impact of radiation on the human body

Especially since the Chernobyl accident in 1986, there has been persistent concern about the dangers to human health from nuclear power and nuclear waste. These were reinforced by the Fukushima disaster in Japan in 2011 (Hatamura, 2015). However, it must be understood that nuclear energy is not the only source of radiation, and that there are natural sources in the environment which may be more significant. According to Bodansky (2004:74), there is far more exposure to radiation from natural sources such as radon and cosmic rays than from all human sources, for example, X-rays and nuclear medicine.

Some researchers argue that radon is one of the main causes of cancer among uranium miners. However, radon may be found in all types of soil which contain uranium and radium. Bodansky (2004) points out that the concentration of radon in the soil depends on the type of soil. Hence people's exposure to radon depends on their surroundings, so that people living in houses made from limestone or wood are exposed to less radon than those living in houses built with granite. So it seems that it is not only uranium miners who are exposed to radiation but also people in certain geological districts.

According to US law, the maximum permissible exposure for those living close to nuclear plants is 1/200 rem (Roentgen equivalent man). However, according to

Hoyle (1979), this amount is just 1/20th of the radiation that can be experienced from natural background radiation. It has been estimated that nuclear energy is responsible for just 20 deaths per year worldwide, although these figures are disputed by anti-nuclear campaigners who claim that the true figure is as high as 600 deaths. Hoyle (*ibid*) claims that the average American's life-span is reduced by 1.2 hours as a result of nuclear accidents and contrasts that with the risk from smoking, which is a loss of eight years if one packet a day is smoked. Consequently, it can be seen that the risk to human health from the use of nuclear power is extremely low.

With regard to medical treatment, which is the next largest source of exposure to radiation, X-rays will expose a patient to radiation amounts from 0.4 to one rad (radiation absorbed dose). A broken wrist, for instance, is likely to require four X-rays with a total exposure of up to four rads. The unit of measurement for radiation exposure is the rem, and one rem is equal to the damage caused by one rad of X-rays; the maximum amount allowed for workers in nuclear plants is five rem per year: the same as the quantity received in the course of a routine medical check-up.

2.2 The impact of radioactive waste on the environment

Nuclear energy is not alone in producing dangerous waste. Lillington (2004) estimates that nuclear energy, in the course of producing 1000 megawatts (MWe) of electricity produces annually about 30 tons of highly radioactive waste and about 800 tons of intermediate and low-level waste. In contrast, a coal-burning plant producing the same quantity of electricity would generate about 320,000 tons of coal ash, of which nearly 400 tons would be hazardous waste such as mercury and vanadium, and at least 44,000 tons of sulphur dioxide. So it can be seen that nuclear energy only produces a fraction of the dangerous wastes emitted from coal-fired power stations and in addition does not produce greenhouse gases.

2.3 Risks of terrorism

There has been widespread concern that terrorists might steal plutonium to produce nuclear weapons. In general, nuclear facilities are tightly controlled, and in practice, it would be very difficult for terrorists to use such stolen material effectively. There are alternative materials such as toxic gas which could produce equally lethal terrorist weapons. However, these concerns could be solved by keeping U233 mixed with U238, which would prevent terrorist groups extracting the plutonium and fabricating a bomb.

Conclusion

The risks of nuclear energy in terms of both human health and the environment have been the subject of widespread debate and controversy. This essay has attempted to examine these risks both in terms of human health and environmental damage. It appears that many of these concerns are exaggerated and that nuclear energy can be seen as a safe, reliable and cost-effective alternative to using fossil fuels.

While all energy sources have drawbacks, nuclear should be viewed as a useful and relatively safe component in a mix of sources which can include renewables such as hydro and wind energy and non-renewables such as natural gas. The steady depletion of reserves of oil and the subsequent rise in prices is liable to emphasise this position. Clearly more could be done to make nuclear plants safer and more efficient in the future, but until their value is recognised and more work is done on their design and construction, their full potential is unlikely to be realised.

REFERENCES

Bodansky, D. (2004) *Nuclear Energy: Principles, Practices and Prospects*. New York: Springer.

Hatamura, Y. *et al* (2015) *The 2011 Fukushima Nuclear Power Plant Accident*. Cambridge: Woodhead.

Hoyle, F. (1979) *Energy or Extinction?* London: Heinemann.

Lillington, J. N. (2004) *The Future of Nuclear Power*. Oxford: Elsevier.

Mathew, S. (2006) *Wind Energy: Fundamentals, Resource Analysis and Economics*. Berlin: Springer.

Murray, L. R. (2009) *Nuclear Energy. An Introduction to the Concepts, System and Application of the Nuclear Process*. Oxford: Butterworth.

Olah, A.G., Goeppert, A. and Parakash, S. (2006) *Beyond Oil and Gas: The Methanol Economy*. Wienheim: Wiley.

Sterrett, T. (1994) *The Energy Dilemma*. London: Multivox.

3 Revision

■ **Look back at the text and find examples of the following features:**

a)   Background information

b)   A purpose statement

c)   An outline

d)   A definition

e)   A generalisation

f)   The use of brackets to give extra detail

g)   A passive structure

h)   A phrase showing cause and effect

i)   A synonym for 'energy'

j)   An example of tentative or cautious language

k)   An example to support the writer's argument

l)   A counter-argument

m)   A citation

n)   A synopsis

NB: Formatting of written assignments

Some departments may expect essays to be written in the style illustrated above, with numbered sections and headings, while other may require essays to be written without these. It is important to check with your teachers what the preferred style is.

UNIT 5.4   Reports

Although essays are the most common assignments in many academic disciplines, students of subjects such as the sciences or business may often have to write reports. Reports and essays are similar in many ways, but this unit explains and illustrates the differences.

1 Writing reports

While essays are often concerned with abstract or theoretical subjects, a report is a description of a situation or something that has happened. In academic terms it might describe:

a)   an experiment you have conducted

b)   a survey you have carried out

c)   a comparison of alternative proposals to deal with a situation

Clearly there is a big difference between describing a scientific laboratory experiment and reporting on students' political opinions. In some areas (e.g. laboratory work), your teachers will make it clear what format you should follow. However, most reports should include the following features:

Introduction
–   background to the subject
–   reasons for carrying out the work
–   review of other research in the area

Methods
–   how you did your research
–   description of the tools/materials/equipment used

Results
- – what you discovered
- – comments on likely accuracy of results

Discussion
- – of your main findings
- – comments on the effectiveness of your research

Conclusion
- – summary of your work
- – suggestions for further research

2 Essays and reports

In comparison with essays, reports are likely to:

a) be based on primary as well as secondary research

b) use numbering (1.1, 1.2) and sub-headings for different sections

c) be more specific and detailed

In most other respects reports are similar to essays since both:

a) have a clear and logical format

b) use objective and accurate academic style

c) include citations and references

d) make use of visual information in the form of graphs, diagrams and tables

e) include appendices where necessary

■ **Decide whether the following titles are more likely to be written as reports or essays.**

Topic	Report	Essay
1 The development of trade unions in South Africa (1900–2015)		
2 Two alternative plans for improving the sports centre		
3 A study you conducted to compare male and female attitudes to writing essays		
4 An overview of recent research on the human genome		
5 The arguments for and against capital punishment		

3 Practice

The following plans illustrate two proposals for redeveloping a site on a university campus.

■ Study the plans and then read the five sentences (a-e), which are the introduction to a report on the redevelopment. The order of the sentences has been mixed up. Put them in the correct order. Then write the rest of the report in about 250 words, under these three headings: Proposals, Discussion, Recommendations.

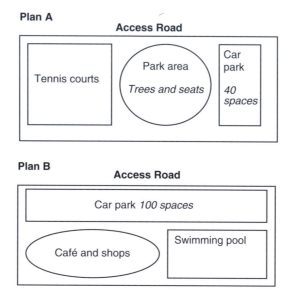

a) The report takes into account a consultation exercise with staff and students carried out last autumn.

b) Two alternatives schemes for redevelopment have been put forward, as can be seen in Plans A and B above.

c) This report attempts to compare the two schemes and to establish which is the more suitable.

d) The aim of the redevelopment is to improve facilities for both staff and students and at the same time enhance the appearance of this part of the campus.

e) Due to the recent closure of the maintenance depot, a site approximately 250 metres long and 100 metres wide has recently become vacant on the west side of the university campus and is ready for redevelopment.

4 Scientific reports

Scientific research is usually conducted in order to support a hypothesis or to validate the work of others. An accurate written record of the experiment is important because it allows other researchers to share your work. At graduate level or above, your research is adding to an international body of data on your particular area of study.

In general, scientific reports follow the same guidelines as other academic writing in terms of style and vocabulary. However, your department may well have its own requirements for the organisation of a report, so it is advisable to ask if these exist.

Format

Reports of laboratory experiments in disciplines such as biology, chemistry and physics generally include the following sections:

a) **Title**

This should contain the essential elements of the report in (ideally) no more than 12 words:

The effect of temperature changes on the germination of wheat (Triticum aestivum)

b) **Abstract**

The function of an abstract is to help potential readers identify whether your report is relevant to their research interests. It is essentially a summary in about 200 words of each part of the report, and so it is commonly written after the last draft is finalised. It should include the principal conclusions and be written in the same tenses as the main report.

c) **Introduction**

The introduction should contextualise your work with reference to other similar research. It should cite previous research papers which you have studied, in order to explain the purpose of your work (e.g. to confirm or extend their findings). It must contain a purpose statement (why you did this experiment) or a hypothesis you wished to evaluate, or both.

d) **Method**

This section explains how you did the research. It should allow another researcher to repeat your work, so it needs to include a description of equipment and materials used, as well as the process you followed. You may wish to include diagrams or photographs to illustrate the set-up in the laboratory. The passive is normally used ('three samples were prepared') rather than the active ('we prepared'). As the research is concluded, the past tense should be used throughout.

e) **Results**

Again using the past tense, here you summarise all the results obtained. Detailed data may be presented in tables and graphs, with only the most important features highlighted in the text. You must include all results, including unexpected ones which do not conform to your hypothesis.

f) Discussion

This section links back to the introduction by comparing your results with the original purpose or hypothesis. It aims to evaluate the experiment in terms of your findings and compare them to your expectations. It may be necessary to refer to the relevant literature. The conclusion should make it clear whether you feel that your hypothesis has been supported and whether there are changes that you would make to the design of the experiment if you were to repeat it.

g) References

As in all academic writing, this is a list of all the sources you have specifically mentioned in your report.

▶ **See Unit 1.8 References and Quotations**

5 Example report: Student experience of part-time work

■ Study the report of a survey carried out on a university campus. Complete the report by inserting suitable words from the following box into the gaps (more words than gaps).

> sample   conducted   method   respondents   random   questions
>
> majority   questioned   mentioned   interviewees   common
>
> questionnaire   unusual   generally   minority   slightly

A Introduction

With the introduction of course fees and the related increase in student debt, more students are finding it necessary to work part-time. This has led to concern that this work may have a detrimental effect on students' academic performance. Consequently, the survey was a) _____ to find out exactly how this work affects student life and study.

B Method

The research was done by asking students selected at b) _____ on the campus to complete a c) _____ (see Appendix A). 50 students were d) _____ on Saturday April 23rd, with approximately equal numbers of male and female students.

Table 1 Have you had a part-time job while studying?

	Men	Women	Total	%
Have job now	8	7	15	30
Had job before	4	6	10	20
Never had job	14	11	25	50

C Results

Of the e) _____, 30% currently had part-time jobs, 20% had had part-time jobs, but half had never done any work during university semesters (see Table 1). f) _____ who were working or who had worked were next asked about their reasons for taking the jobs. The most common reason was lack of money (56%), but many students said that they found the work useful experience (32%) and others g) _____ social benefits (12%).

The 25 students with work experience were next asked about the effects of the work on their studies. A significant h) _____ (64%) claimed that there were no negative effects at all. However, 24% said that their academic work suffered i) _____, while a small j) _____ (12%) reported serious adverse results, such as tiredness in lectures and falling marks.

Further k) _____ examined the nature of the work that the students did. The variety of jobs was surprising, from van driver to busker, but the most l) _____ areas were catering and bar work (44%) and secretarial work (32%). Most students worked between 10 and 15 hours per week, though two (8%) worked over 25 hours. Rates of pay were m) _____ near the national minimum wage and averaged £6.20 per hour.

The final question invited students to comment on their experience of part-time work. Many (44%) made the point that students should be given grants so that they could concentrate on their studies full-time, but others felt that they gained something from the experience, such as meeting new people and getting insights into various work environments. One student said that she had met her current boyfriend while working in a city centre restaurant.

D Discussion

It is clear that part-time work is now a common aspect of student life. Many students find jobs at some point in their studies, but an overwhelming majority (88%)

of those deny that it has a damaging effect on their studies. Most students work for only 2–3 hours per day on average, and a significant number claim some positive results from their employment. Obviously, our survey was limited to a relatively small n) _____ due to time constraints, and a fuller study might modify our findings in various ways.

Writing Letters and Emails

Letters are still used for formal matters, or when an email address is unknown, and are considered to be more reliable than emails. However, due to its convenience, email is increasingly used for semi-formal as well as informal communication. It is widely seen as a way of having a permanent record of an arrangement or discussion.

1 Letters

You have applied for a place on an MSc course at a British university. This is the letter you have received in reply.

a)

Central Admissions Office
Wye House
Park Campus
University of Mercia
Borchester BR3 5HT
United Kingdom

b) Ms P Tan
   54 Sydney Road
   Rowborough RB1 6FD

c) Ref: MB/373

d) 3rd May 2017

e) Dear Ms Tan,

f) Application for MSc Sustainable Building Technology

g) Further to your recent application, I would like to invite you to the university for an informal interview on Tuesday 21st May at 11 am. You will be able to meet the course supervisor, Dr Schmidt, and look round the School of the Built Environment.

h) A map of the campus and instructions for finding the university are enclosed.

i) Please let me know if you will be able to attend on the date given.

j) Yours sincerely,

k) *M. Bramble*

l) Mick Bramble
Administrative Assistant
Central Admissions Office

Enc.

■ **Label the following features of formal letters with the letters (a-l) from the left margin.**

(*d*) Date   ( ) Ending   ( ) Request for response

( ) Greeting   ( ) Address of recipient   ( ) Address of sender

( ) Further details   ( ) Reason for writing   ( ) Sender's reference

( ) Subject headline   ( ) Signature   ( ) Writer's name and job title

Note the following points:

a)   The example above is addressed to a known person and the ending is 'Yours sincerely'. However, when writing to somebody whose name you do not know (e.g. The Manager), use *Dear Sir* and *Yours faithfully*.

b)   A formal letter generally uses the family name in the greeting (*Dear Ms Tan*). Certain organisations may, however, use a first name with a family name or even a first name alone (*Dear Polly Tan, Dear Polly*).

c)   If the sender includes a reference it is helpful to quote it in your reply.

2 Practice A

■ **You are Ms Tan. Write a letter in reply to Mr Bramble that makes the following points:**

a) You will attend the interview on the date given.

b) You would like to have the interview one hour later, due to train times.

3 Emails

Starting and finishing

The following forms are acceptable ways to begin an email if you know the recipient:

Hi Sophie, Dear Sophie, Hello Sophie

If you have not met the recipient it may be safer to use:

Dear Sophie Gratton, Dear Ms Gratton, Dear Dr Gratton

If you need to send an email to a large group (e.g. colleagues) you may use:

Hi everyone, Hello all

In all cases to close the message you can use:

Regards, Best wishes, Best regards

You may also add a standard formula before this:

Look forward to meeting next week/Let me know if you need further information

The main text

Here you can use common contractions (I've, don't) and idiomatic language, but the normal rules for punctuation should be followed to avoid confusion. Spelling mistakes are just as likely to cause misunderstanding in emails as elsewhere. Always check for spelling and grammar problems before clicking 'Send'. Note that emails tend to be short, although longer documents may be added as attachments.

Replying to emails

If you receive an email telling you about an arrangement such as a meeting or lecture that you expect to attend, or giving you some information relevant to your studies, it is good practice to acknowledge receipt of the email. It only takes a minute to reply:

Thanks for letting me know.

That's interesting, but I'm busy that morning.

Your response will tell the sender that you have read and understood their message.

4 Practice B

■ Read the following and decide who the sender and recipient might be. Would Rachel expect a reply?

Hello Dr Hoffman,

I'm afraid I can't attend your Accounting Methods class this week, as I have to go for a job interview then. However, I will be there next Tuesday, when I am giving my paper (attached, as requested).

See you then,
Rachel

---

5 Practice C

■ Write suitable emails for the following situations:

a) You are writing to Mark, a colleague at work, to ask him to suggest a time to meet you tomorrow.

b) Write to your teacher, Tricia James, to ask her to recommend another book for your current essay.

c) Write to a group of classmates asking them how they want to celebrate the end of the course.

d) Write an email in response to the following message. You have never had this book.

According to our records, the copy of *Special Needs in Education* you borrowed from the library on October 12th is now overdue. Your fine is currently £2.15. Please arrange to return this book as soon as possible.

Best wishes,

Tim Carey

Library services

Writing in Groups

Courses in business and other subjects may expect students to complete written tasks as part of a group of four to eight students. This unit explains the reasons for this and suggests the best way to approach group work in order to achieve the maximum benefit from the process.

1 Why write in groups?

■ Read the text and complete the following exercise.

THE IMPORTANCE OF GROUP WORK

Some students, especially those from other academic cultures, may be surprised to find they are expected to work in groups to complete some academic assignments. For those who have always worked on their own, this may cause a kind of culture shock, especially as all the students in the group will normally be given the same mark for the group's work. In addition, students are normally told with whom they will have to work and the topic they must write about, although with some kinds of projects, groups may be able to choose their own topics. There are several good reasons for this emphasis on group work in many English-speaking institutions.

First of all, employers are generally looking for people who can work in a team. Most managers are not looking for brilliant individuals; instead they want employees who are comfortable working with a mixed group having different skills and backgrounds. So familiarity with teamwork has become an essential qualification for many jobs, and this group writing task provides students with an opportunity to strengthen their experience of working in this way.

Furthermore, working in groups allows individuals to achieve more than they could by working on their own. A team can tackle much larger projects than individual students can, and this applies to most research projects at university as well as business development in companies. Therefore, by taking part in these activities students are able to provide evidence in their portfolio and CV that they have succeeded in this critical area.

Finally, in the academic world, many journal articles and other publications are the product of a group of researchers. By collaborating, academics are able to pool their knowledge and bring their varied expertise and backgrounds to focus on an issue, thereby often achieving more credibility than they could when working alone.

■ Working in pairs, decide if the following statements are true or false.

a) Most students react positively to the idea of group work.

b) All the group members receive the same mark.

c) Students in groups can normally choose who they work with.

d) There are two main reasons for setting group work.

e) Most employers look for successful team members.

f) Group work on university courses has no connection to teamwork in companies.

2 Making group work successful

■ The following is a list of suggestions for organising the process of completing group work successfully. The correct order (1–7) has been mixed up. Working with a partner, put the list into the most logical sequence, using the table on page 255.

A Analyse the task
Get everyone to discuss the assignment and agree on the best methods to complete it. At this stage it is important to have complete agreement on the objectives.

B Divide up the work fairly, according to the abilities of the members
Your group may include a computer expert or a design genius, so make sure that their talents are used appropriately. It is most important to make sure that everyone feels they have been given a fair share of the work.

C Make everyone feel included
Nobody should feel like an outsider, so make special efforts if there is only one male student, or one non-native speaker, for instance. Make a list of all members' phone numbers and email addresses and give everyone a copy.

D Finish the assignment on time
This is the most important test of your group's performance. When you have finished and handed in your work, it may be helpful to have a final meeting to discuss what you have all learned from the task.

E Get to know the other members
Normally you cannot choose with whom you work, so it is crucial to introduce yourselves before starting work. Meet informally in a café or somewhere similar (but be careful not to choose a meeting place which may make some members uncomfortable, such as a bar).

F Select a co-ordinator/editor
Someone needs to take notes about what was agreed at meetings and send these to all members as a reminder. The same person could also act as editor, to make sure that all the individual sections conform to the same layout and format. However, you should all be responsible for proofreading your own work.

G Plan the job and the responsibilities
Break down the task week by week and allocate specific roles to each member. Agree on times for regular meetings – although you may be able to avoid some meetings by using group emails. You may want to book a suitable room, for example in the library, to hold your meetings.

	Schedule for successful group work
1	*E. Get to know the other members*
2	
3	
4	
5	
6	
7	

3 Dealing with problems

■ **Working in groups of three, discuss the best response to the following situations. You may choose an alternative strategy to the ones provided.**

a) In a group of six, you find that two students are not doing any work. They not only do not come to meetings but have also not done the tasks they were given at the beginning. Should you. . .

   i) decide that it's simplest to do the work of the missing students yourself?

   ii) find the students and explain that their behaviour is going to damage the chances of all six members?

   iii) tell your lecturer about the problem?

b) You are the only non-native speaker in the group. Although you can understand normal speech, the other students speak so fast and idiomatically that you have difficulty taking part in the discussions. Should you. . .

   i) tell your lecturer about the problem?

   ii) keep quiet and ask another student in the group to explain decisions later?

   iii) explain your problem to the group and ask them to speak more slowly?

c) One member of the group is very dominant. He/she attempts to control the group and is intolerant of the opinions of others. Should you. . .

   i) explain to them, in a group meeting, that their behaviour is having a negative effect on the group's task?

   ii) tell your lecturer about the problem?

   iii) let them do all the work, because that's what they seem to want?

4 Points to remember

Remember that:

- Working in groups is an ideal opportunity to make new friends – make the most of it.
- You may learn a lot by listening to other people's ideas.
- Negotiation is important in a group – nobody is right all the time.
- Respect the values and attitudes of others, especially people from different cultures – you may be surprised what you learn.

Glossary

Abbreviation
The short form of a word or phrase (see 4.2)

Abstract
A short summary of the aims and scope of a journal article (see 1.3)

Acknowledgements
A list of people the author wishes to thank for their assistance, found in books and articles

Appendix (plural – appendices)
A section at the end of a book or article containing supplementary information

Assignment
A task given to students, normally for assessment

Authority
A well-known expert or reference work on a subject

Back issue
A previous issue of a journal or magazine

Bias
A subjective preference for one point of view

Bibliography
A list of sources an author has read but not specifically cited

Brainstorm
A process of collecting ideas on a topic at random (see 1.5)

Case study
A section of an essay which examines one example in detail (see 5.1)

Citation
An in-text reference providing the name of the source (see 1.4 and 1.8)

Cohesion
Linking ideas in a text together by use of reference words (see 3.1)

Conclusion
The final section of an essay or report (see 1.11)

Contraction
A shortened form of pronoun and verb (e.g. she's, I'd [see 3.5])

Coursework
Assessed assignments given to students to complete during a course

Criteria (singular – criterion)
The principles on which something is judged or based

Deadline
The final date for completing a piece of work

Draft
An unfinished version of a piece of writing

Edited book
A book with contributions from a number of writers, controlled by an editor

Extract
A piece of text taken from a longer work

Flowchart
A diagram that illustrates the stages of a process

Formality
In written work, the use of a non-idiomatic style and vocabulary

Format
The standard organisation of a text

Heading
The title of a section of text

Higher degree
A Master's degree or Doctorate

Hypothesis
A theory which a researcher is attempting to explore or test

Introduction
The first part of an essay or article (see 1.11)

Journal
   An academic publication in a specialised area, usually published quarterly (see 1.2)

Literature review
   A section of an article describing other research on the topic in question (see 5.2)

Main body
   The principal part of an essay after the introduction and before the conclusion

Margin
   The strip of white space on a page around the text

Module
   Most academic courses are divided into modules, each of which focuses on a specified topic

Outline
   A preparatory plan for a piece of writing (see 1.5)

Paraphrase
   A rewriting of a text with substantially different wording and organisation but similar ideas

Peer review
   The process of collecting comment from academic authorities on an article before publication in a journal. This system gives increased validity to the publication.

Phrase
   A few words which are commonly combined (see 1.1)

Plagiarism
   Using another writer's work without acknowledgement in an acceptable manner (see 1.4)

Primary research
   Original research (e.g. a laboratory experiment or a sociological enquiry)

Quotation
   Use of the exact words of another writer to illustrate an argument or idea (see 1.8)

Redundancy
   The unnecessary repetition of ideas or information (see 3.7)

References
   A list of all the sources cited in a paper (see 1.8)

Register
   The level of formality in language

Restatement
   Repeating a point in order to explain it more clearly

Scan
A method of reading in which the eyes move quickly over the page to find a specific item

Skim
A reading technique to quickly find out the main ideas of a text

Source
The original text used to obtain an idea or piece of information

Summary
A shorter version of something (see 1.7)

Synonym
A word with a similar meaning to another word (see 4.8)

Synopsis
A summary of an article or book

Term
A word or phrase used to express a special concept

Word class
A grammatical category (e.g. noun, adjective)

Answers

Providing answers for a writing course is less clear-cut than for other language areas. In some exercises there is only one possible answer, but in other cases several possibilities exist. Teachers need to use common sense and accept any reasonable answer. In the case of exercises where students can choose their own topic and it is therefore impossible to provide a definite answer, students may still appreciate having a model answer, and so some have been given.

Academic writing quiz

1	b (see Unit 1.1)	2	c (see Unit 1.1)	3	a (see Unit 1.5)	4	c (see Unit 1.11)
5	a (see Unit 1.11)	6	c (see Unit 1.6)	7	a (see Unit 1.8)	8	b (see Unit 1.7)
9	c (see Unit 1.10)	10	b (see Unit 1.12)	11	c (see Unit 1.3)	12	c (see Unit 3.5)
13	a (see Unit 4.8)	14	b (see Unit 4.4)	15	b (see Unit 1.3)	16	c (see Unit 4.6)
17	b (see Unit 1.6)	18	b (see Unit 2.8)	19	c (see Unit 1.1)	20	a (see Unit 1.11)

PART 1 THE WRITING PROCESS

1.1 Basics of Writing

1   The purpose of academic writing

Other reasons might include:
- To present a hypothesis for consideration by others
- To make notes on something read or heard or seen

2   Features of academic writing

Possibilities include:
- Semi-formal vocabulary, lack of idioms
- Use of citation/references
- Use of both passive and active voices
- Precision
- Caution

3   Common types of academic writing

Notes – A written record of the main points of a text or lecture for a student's personal use
Report – A description of something a student has done (e.g. conducting a survey or experiment)
Project – A piece of research, either individual or group work, with the topic chosen by the student(s)
Essay – The most common type of written work, with the title given by the teacher, normally 1,000–5,000 words
Dissertation/Thesis – The longest piece of writing normally done by a student (20,000+ words) often for a higher degree on a topic chosen by the student
Paper – A general term for any academic essay, report, presentation or article

4   The format of short and long writing tasks

a) abstract
b) references
c) appendix
d) acknowledgements

e) literature review
f) case study
g) foreword

5 **The components of academic writing**
a) title
b) subtitle
c) heading
d) sentence
e) phrase
f) paragraph

7 **Simple and longer sentences**
(*Example sentences*)
a) In 2016 the Education Faculty had predominantly female students.
b) There was a small majority of female students in the Law Faculty.
c) The Engineering Faculty had the greatest imbalance: over 80% of the students were male.
d) There was a significant majority of female students studying Business, but the situation in Computer Sciences was the opposite, with a substantial majority of males.

8 **Writing in paragraphs**
See Unit 1.10.1 Organising Paragraphs for initial questions

para 2 begins: But a new use for charcoal. . .
para 3 begins: The other benefit of biochar. . .
para 4 begins: But other agricultural. . .

9 **Practice**
(*Example sentences*)
a) Biochar is the new name for charcoal.
b) Recent research shows that making biochar may benefit agriculture.
c) Mixing burnt plants into the soil improves fertility and also slows the release of carbon dioxide.
d) The process has been criticised by scientists, since it may reduce the quantity of food being grown.

1.2 Reading: Finding Suitable Sources

1 **Academic texts**

1 Worldwide pressures – Possibly – it mentions two sources and contains a lot of information, but some of the language is subjective (e.g. 'reckless lack of control', 'shrinking alarmingly').
2 A drying world? – No – no sources are mentioned and the style is very informal (e.g. 'the stuff we drink').
3 Measuring scarcity – Yes – a more critical, formal and objective style and a citation provided.
(*Possible answers*)

Feature	Examples
1 Formal or semi-formal vocabulary	The more complex indicators are not widely applied because data are lacking to apply them and the definitions are not intuitive.
2 Sources are given	Rijsberman (2006)

3 Objective, impersonal style It is surprisingly difficult to determine whether water is truly scarce in the physical sense at a global scale (a supply problem) or whether it is available but should be used better (a demand problem).

2   Types of text

(*Possible answers*)

Text type	Advantages	Disadvantages
Website	Easily accessed, probably up to date	Possibly unreliable and/or unedited
Journal article	Often focuses on a specialist area	May be too specialised or complex
Official report (e.g. from government)	Contains a lot of detail	May have a narrow focus
Newspaper or magazine article	Easy to read and up to date	May not be objective and not give sources
E-book	Easily accessible	Must be read on screen
Edited book	A variety of contributors provide a range of views	May lack focus

4   Using library catalogues

Titles 1 and 2 are up to date and appear to be relevant to construction issues. The other titles are more general, but title 4 is also recent and might contain some relevant sections. The others seem more focused on the appearance of the buildings.

1.3 Reading: Developing Critical Approaches

1   Reading methods

Choosing suitable texts

Read title and sub-title carefully

Survey text features (e.g. abstract, contents, index)

Skim text for gist – is it relevant?

Scan text for information you need (e.g. names)

Read extensively when useful sections are found

Read intensively to make notes on key points

Other reading skills – possible answers:
*   Text genre recognition
*   Dealing with new vocabulary

3 **Reading abstracts**
   a) Background position – A growing chorus of scholars . . . American democracy.
   b) Aim and thesis of paper – This article questions . . . engaged citizenship.
   c) Method of research – Using data from . . . political participation.
   d) Results of research – Rather than the erosion . . . in America.

4 **Fact and opinion**
   a) fact (not true)
   b) opinion
   c) fact (not true)
   d) opinion
   e) fact (true) + fact (true)
   f) fact (true) + opinion

(Objective version with facts corrected)

New Zealand is an island nation in the southern Pacific Ocean, consisting of two main islands. Nearly 1,000 miles east of Australia, it was one of the last places on Earth to be settled by man: Polynesians who arrived in about 1250 CE and who developed the Maori culture. In the eighteenth century European settlers started to land, and in 1841 New Zealand became part of the British Empire. Due to its long period of isolation, many distinctive plants and animals evolved, such as the kiwi, now the nation's symbol. The country suffers from frequent earthquakes, such as the one that hit Christchurch in 2011, causing serious damage and loss of life.

6 **Practice**

Educating the poorest

Positive aspects: Contains some relevant ideas. The studies mentioned could be followed up using a search engine.
Negative aspects: Rather superficial and informal in style (e.g. use of question form in first sentence). Some points not relevant to sub-Saharan Africa. No citations.

7 **Critical thinking**

The responses to these questions will vary from student to student, which is the nature of the critical approach.

(*Model Answer*)

Statements	Comments
A	
It is claimed that in one year nearly half of Harvard's history professors were on sabbatical leave. As a consequence, students work less. . .	The link between these two situations is not made clear.
B	
. . . it has been calculated that the average UK university graduate will earn £400,000 ($520,000) more over his or her lifetime compared to a non-graduate.	Who has made this calculation? What basis is there for this claim?

1.4 Avoiding Plagiarism

3 Degrees of plagiarism

1	Y	6	N
2	Y	7	Y
3	Y	8	N
4	N	9	Y/N
5	Y	10	Y

4 Avoiding plagiarism by summarising and paraphrasing

a) Acceptable – a correctly referenced summary
b) Plagiarised – original wording with minor changes to word order
c) Acceptable – a correctly referenced quotation
d) Technically plagiarism – mistake in date means the citation is incorrect
e) Plagiarised – some original wording and no citation

5 Avoiding plagiarism by developing good study habits

(*Possible further suggestions*)

- Check that your quotations are exactly the same wording as the original.
- When paraphrasing, alter the structure as well as the vocabulary.
- Make sure your in-text citations are all included in the list of references.

6 Practice

Kaufman (2017) argues that wealth (expressed as GDP per head) rather than size of population is the key to national success in the Olympics.

Large populations alone do not guarantee good national results at the Olympics. Countries must also be wealthy enough to have healthy citizens and be able to provide resources for training. As Kaufman points out: 'When many people are affected by poverty and illness it is not easy to be ordinarily healthy, let alone be an Olympic athlete' (Kaufman, 2017:3).

7 Further practice

Source – The origin of ideas and information
Citation – Short in-text note giving the author's name and publication date
To summarise – To reduce the length of a text while keeping the main points
Quotation – Using the exact words of the original text in your work
Reference – Full publication details of a text or other source
To cheat – To gain advantage dishonestly
Paraphrase – Using different words or word order to restate a text

1.5 From Understanding Essay Titles to Planning

2 Analysing essay titles

Analyse – Break down into the various parts and their relationships
Assess/Evaluate – Decide the value or worth of a subject

Describe – Give a detailed account of something
Discuss – Look at various aspects of a topic and compare benefits and drawbacks
Examine/Explore – Divide into sections and discuss each critically
Illustrate – Give examples
Outline/Trace – Explain a topic briefly and clearly
Suggest/Indicate – Make a proposal and support it
Summarise – Deal with a complex subject by reducing it to the main elements
(NB: 'summarise' and 'outline' are very similar)

3   Practice

a)   Summarise/discuss
Give the factors behind the development and explore the possible consequences.
Context: since 2010

b)   Describe
List the most likely causes of this situation.

c)   What/Are there
Give the advantages and disadvantages.
Context: at primary school (age 6–10)

d)   What/Evaluate
List the most important sources and say how useful they are in reducing CO_2 emissions.
Context: in the last fifteen years

e)   Discuss/indicating
Describe how earthquakes affect different types of structures with reference to the soil characteristics and explain how the structures can be made more resilient.

4   Brainstorming

(*Model answers*)
Possible benefits
Young children more open, less inhibited
They appear to have better memories
May improve understanding of their own language

Possible drawbacks
Young children may not understand the necessary grammar
They may not grasp the cultural context of a second language

5   Essay length

(NB: These figures are only a guide and individual students may have a different approach.)
a)   Describe/How
Context: in developing countries
Approximately 50:50

b)   How/Illustrate
Context: in one country
Approximately 40:60

c)   Outline/Suggest
Context: in South East Asia
Approximately 50:50

d) What/How
Context: in international aid
Approximately 30:70

6 Writing outlines

c) Lists can help develop a logical structure and make it easier to allocate space but are rather inflexible.
Mind maps are more flexible, as extra items can be added easily.

7 Practice

(*Model outline – list*)

The main reasons

- In UK most homes accessible from central warehouses
- Smartphones common, make shopping simple
- E-commerce saves time and is often cheaper

The likely results

- Retailers must compete on logistics (delivery times)
- Increased demand for warehouse space esp. near big cities
- New businesses created (e.g. returns)
- More delivery traffic > demand for drivers
- Many stores will close
- Character of shopping streets will change > more cafés and entertainment

1.6 Finding Key Points and Note-making

1 Finding key points

(*Example titles*)

Treasure hunters
Buried wealth
Key points:

1   . . . in Britain thousands of people are doing that every year. Treasure hunting has become a popular hobby. . .
2   In 1996 the law on finding treasure was clarified by the Treasure Act, which imposed severe penalties for not reporting new finds. . .

2 Finding relevant points

Key points:

2   . . . since the start of the twenty-first century this level has hardly changed, making scientists believe that some process is extracting the extra CO_2 from the air.
3   This appears to be a likely reason for the CO_2 concentration levelling off and might be seen as a check on global warming. . .
4   . . . the effects are likely to be temporary, since plant growth is also dependent on water, and as rainfall patterns change droughts and floods are likely to become more severe.
5   Other researchers claim that other consequences of human activity, such as the loss of tropical forests, will counter the beneficial effects of extra plant growth in polar areas by releasing the CO_2 stored in the rainforests.

3   **Practice A**

(*Model notes*)

Can plants limit global warming?

1)   New research: extra plant growth > slowing global warming
2)   Amount CO_2 in air stabilised at start 21C.
3)   Photosynthesis speeded up by higher CO_2 levels > more plant growth
4)   But other factors e.g. lack of water may have opposite effect
5)   Human activity e.g. cutting rainforest also releases CO_2

(Source: Suarez, M. (2016) *Earth Matters* 3:176)

4   **Why make notes?**

b)   To avoid plagiarism
c)   To keep a record of reading/lectures
d)   To revise for exams
e)   To help remember main points

5   **Note-making methods**

(*Other answers possible*)

The notes are paraphrased, not copied from the text
The source is included
Symbols are used (>)
Abbreviations (esp.) to save space
Notes are organised in lists

7   **Practice B**

(*Example notes*)

Sleep and the memory process

1)   Siesta can help improve memory > learning
2)   New memories > hippocampus (short term) > Pre-frontal cortex (long-term)
3)   Process happens during Stage 2 non-REM sleep
4)   Univ. Calif. team researched process:
      •   2 groups: a) stayed awake b) had siesta
      •   group b) performed better at memory tasks in evening

(Source: Kitschelt, P. (2006) *How the Brain Works*, p. 73)

1.7 Summarising and Paraphrasing

1   **What makes a good summary?**

A good summary requires:
•   selection of most important aspects
•   clear organisation
•   accuracy

2   Stages of summarising

1   c)
2   d)
3   b)
4   a)
5   e)

3   Practice A – Mechanical pickers

1 = a (contains all key points)
2 = c (includes unnecessary examples)
3 = b (includes information not in original [e.g. increase in profits] and fails to describe the machines)

4   Practice B

(*Model answers*)

b)
    i)   Mobile phones have helped to establish new businesses in Africa.
    ii)   There is a link between higher phone ownership and increase in GDP.
    iii)   Only half of Africans (wealthier and urban) have a mobile phone.
    iv)   New developments should reduce costs and increase availability of telecom services.
    v)   But growth is still held back by high levels of taxation on telecom companies.

c)   (*Model summary*)

The impact of mobile phones in Africa

Recently, mobile phones have helped to establish new businesses in Africa, and there is a link between higher phone ownership and an increase in GDP. However, only half of Africans (mainly the wealthier and urban ones) currently have a mobile phone. New technical developments should reduce costs and increase the availability of telecom services, but growth is still held back by high levels of taxation on telecom companies.

d)   (*Example summary*)

Although mobiles help create new African businesses, their use is limited to richer people. Advanced technology may make them more accessible, but high taxes threaten the providers.

5   Practice C – The last word in lavatories?

(*Example summary*)

The Washlet is an expensive lavatory with a range of special features which is popular in Japan, where homes are crowded. Its maker, the Toto company, is hoping to expand sales in the West, but European regulations about toilet design and electrical fittings make this a challenging goal.

7   Practice D – The causes of the Industrial Revolution

1)   b. The best paraphrase, with all main points included and a significantly different structure.
2)   a. Quite good, but lack of precision (at that time) and unsuitable register (bosses).
3)   c. A poor paraphrase, with only a few words changed and extra and inaccurate information added (Britain was the only country. . .).

9   Practice E – Brains and sex

(*A number of possibilities are acceptable here. These are suggestions*)

a) It is **generally considered** that **males and females** think and **behave** in different ways. Women **seem** to have **superior** memories, better social **abilities** and are more **successful** at multitasking. Men, **by comparison**, seem to focus better on single **subjects** and have superior motor and spatial **abilities**, although **obviously** many people **do not follow** these patterns.

b) **The explanation** for these differences may be the way people **behaved** thousands of years ago, when men were **hunters** while women stayed at home as **carers** for their children. But another approach is to see the behaviour **as resulting from** the way our brains function.

c) The brain functioning of 428 men and 521 women has been compared using brain scans in recent research by Ragini Verma's team at Pennsylvania University. Fascinating differences were found by tracking the pathways of water molecules around the brain area.

d) The cerebrum is the name for the upper part of the brain, and this consists of left and right halves. It is believed that logic is controlled from the left half, while the right side deals with intuition. Dr Verma's research discovered that the female molecule pathways were mainly between the two parts, but the male pathways were generally within the halves. Her conclusion is that these findings are an explanation for differences in skills between the sexes, for example, greater social ability in women in contrast to stronger male focus on limited areas.

10 Practice F – The past below the waves

(*Example answers*)

a) Archaeologists can learn about multiple aspects of historic societies by studying shipwrecks, but most of the millions lying on the ocean floor are too deep for divers to examine. They can only work above 50 metres, restricting them to coastal wrecks which are more likely to have been disturbed. Research in mid-ocean has required expensive submarines with their support vessels, limiting the number of wrecks that can be explored. But this may change due to the latest craft, called an automatic underwater vehicle or AUV. Not requiring a support ship and operating independently, this will be used by an American team to examine part of the sea bed off the northern Egyptian coast close to the site of a harbour used around 2000 BCE.

b) There are millions of shipwrecks on the sea floor, providing historians with a vital insight into past trade and technology. Previously, most wrecks were too deep to explore economically, but a new small automatic submarine (called an AUV) has been developed which should allow these deeper sites to be investigated.

1.8 References and Quotations

1   Why use references?

a) N
b) Y
c) Y
d) N
e) Y
f) N
g) Y

2   Citations and references

Smith (2009) argues that the popularity of the Sports Utility Vehicle (SUV) is irrational, as despite their high cost most are never driven off-road. In his view 'they are bad for road safety, the environment and road congestion' (Smith, 2009:37).

The first is a summary, the second a quotation.

A summary allows the writer to condense ideas, while a quotation uses the words of the original author, which have authenticity and may be difficult to improve.

6   **Practice**

(*Example answers*)

a)   According to Kelman (2016), McEwan (2015) points out that with an increasingly diverse body of both students and teaching staff, the need to reduce the gap in their distinct expectations is vital.

b)   McEwan maintains that 'student success at university level is partly dependent on narrowing the difference between student and staff expectations' (Kelman, 2016:45).

c)   According to Kelman, McEwan (2015) points out that with an increasingly diverse body of both students and teaching staff, the need to reduce the gap in their distinct expectations is vital: 'the student body includes an increasing proportion of international students, who may take longer to adapt to the university culture' (Kelman, 2016:45).

9   **Organising the list of references**

a)

i)   Bryman, A. (2004). *Social Research Methods*
Carroll, J. (2007). *A Handbook for Deterring Plagiarism in Higher Education*
Tinto, V. (1987). *Leaving College: Rethinking the Causes and Cures of Student Attrition*

ii)   Crisp, G., Palmer, E., Turnbull, D., Nettelbeck, T., Ward, L., LeCouteur, A., Sarris, A., Strelan, P. and Schneider, L. (2009). 'First year student expectations: results from a university-wide student survey.'

iii)   Ryan, J. and Carroll, J. (2005). 'Canaries in the coalmine: international students in Western universities.' In J. Carroll & J. Ryan (Eds). *Teaching International Students – Improving Learning for All*

iv)   White, P. (2013). Embracing Diversity. 7th Annual Learning and Teaching Conference, 9th January 2013, [online]

v)   Killen, R. (1994). 'Differences between students' and lecturers' perceptions of factors influencing students' academic success at university.' *Higher Education Research and Development*
Leese, M. (2010). 'Bridging the gap: supporting student transitions into higher education.' *Journal of Further and Higher Education*

vi)   Moore, D. and McCabe, G. (2006). *Introduction to the Practice of Statistics*

b)

Books: Author/Date/Title/Edition/Place of publication/Publisher
Journal articles: Author/Date/Article title/Journal title/Issue/Page numbers

c)   Book and journal titles

d)   Book and journal titles are capitalised, journal article titles are not

e)   Name of publication (e.g. *The Times*)

f)

i)   Bryman (2004)

ii)   Carroll (2007)

iii)   Cook and Leckey (1999)

iv)   Crisp *et al.* (2009)

v)   Killen (1994)

1.9 Combining Sources

1   **Referring to sources**

a)   6

b)   Dalglish and Chan

c)   Academic support

d)   Ramsden

e) His work is referred to twice for different topics
f) Difficulties faced by international students
g)
    ii) Period of adjustment to new academic environment needed by international students
    iii) Cultural adjustments international students must make
    iv) Linguistic adjustments
    v) Length of time these adjustments require

2 Taking a critical approach

a) (*Example answers*)

Summary	Original
. . . steps should be taken . . . such as carbon dioxide.	. . . it can be expected that . . . burning of fossil fuels. (2.1)
she mentions evidence of . . . levels of CO_2	Some critics claim . . . unrelated to CO_2 levels. (2.2)

b) puts forward/maintains/presents/mentions/discusses/considers
c) However
d) But/on the other hand

3 Combining three sources

(*Example answer*)

Additionally, Lahav (2010) raises the issue of the computer models which are used to predict future climate and argues that these may be unreliable instruments for making critical decisions. He points out that climate-change critics suggest that, given the uncertainty involved, it might be better to allocate resources to social improvements rather than green technology.

4 Practice

(*Example answer*)

There is good evidence that globalisation has resulted in a considerable increase in world trade over the past 20–30 years (Costa, 2008). However, it has been pointed out (Lin, 2012) that the benefits of this are not evenly shared. While multinationals are able to use the cheapest labour for manufacturing, people in the poorest countries are no better off than they were 40 years ago. In addition, Brokaw (2014) maintains that these large companies benefit from reduced import duties and so can compete more successfully with local businesses, further strengthening their market dominance. Moreover, they are often able to cut their tax payments by basing themselves where taxes are lowest.

1.10 Organising Paragraphs

1 Paragraph structure

a) The topic is Spanish as a world language.
   See iv).

2 Practice A

a)

Topic sentence   iv

Example 1   v

Example 2   iii
Reason   i
Summary   ii

3   Practice B

a)

Topic sentence	Despite this, many countries encourage the growth of home ownership.
Example	Ireland and Spain, for instance, allow mortgage payers to offset payments against income tax.
Reason	It is widely believed that owning your own home has social as well as economic benefits.
Supporting point 1	Compared to renters, homeowners are thought to be more stable members of the community who contribute more to local affairs.
Supporting point 2	In addition, neighbourhoods of owner-occupiers are considered to have less crime and better schools.
Supporting point 3	But above all, home ownership encourages saving and allows families to build wealth.

b)   for instance/It is widely believed/In addition/But above all
c)   Despite this

5   Practice C

(*Example answer*)

Trams

Trams were first introduced in the late nineteenth century, when they provided cheap and convenient mass transport in many cities in America and Europe. But their drawbacks were that the rail-based systems were expensive to maintain, and the fixed tracks made them inflexible as cities developed. Consequently, by the 1950s many European and Asian cities had closed their tramway systems.

Today, however, trams are regaining their popularity. They are seen as less polluting than cars and relatively cheap to operate. As a result, cities such as Paris and Manchester have built new systems. Despite this, the high cost of constructing tramways and difficulties with traffic congestion blocking the tracks mean that trams remain a controversial transport option.

6   Practice D

(*Example answer*)

Rainfall in the UK in 2016 was slightly above average, with 105% of the long-term average. However, the first half of the year, January to June, was significantly wetter than the second part, July to December. October was the driest month, with only 44% of average rainfall, while January was the wettest, with nearly 160%.

1.11 Introductions and Conclusions

1   Introduction components

a)

	Y/N
i) A definition of any unfamiliar terms in the title	Y
ii) Your personal opinion on the subject of the essay	N
iii) Mention of some sources you have read on the topic	Y
iv) A provocative idea or question to interest the reader	N
v) A suitable quotation from a famous authority	N
vi) Your aim or purpose in writing	Y
vii) The method you adopt to answer the question	Y
viii) Some background or context of the topic	Y
ix) Any limitations you set yourself	Y
x) An outline of the main body	Y

b)
  A) Background (viii)
  B) Outline (x)
  C) Method (vii)
  D) Mention of sources (iii)
  E) Definition (i)
  F) Limitation (ix)
  G) Purpose (vi)

2 Introduction structure

a) Definition: . . . *in this paper 'e-learning' refers to any type of learning situation where content is delivered via the internet.*

b) Context: *Learning is one of the most vital components of the contemporary knowledge-based economy. With the development of computing power and technology, the internet has become an essential medium for knowledge transfer.*

c) Reference to other researchers: *Various researchers (Webb and Kirstin, 2003; Honig et al., 2006) have evaluated e-learning in a healthcare and business context . . .*

d) Aim: *The purpose of this study was to examine students' experience of e-learning in an HE context.*

e) Method: *A range of studies was first reviewed, and then a survey of 200 students was conducted to assess their experience of e-learning.*

f) Limitations: *Clearly a study of this type is inevitably restricted by various constraints, notably the size of the student sample . . . students of Pharmacy and Agriculture.*

g) Outline: *The paper is structured as follows . . .. the delivery of e-learning programmes.*

3 Opening sentences

(*Example answers*)

a) In recent years, there has been steady criticism of the lack of women in senior management positions.

b) In the past decade, global warming or climate change has become one of the most pressing issues on the international agenda.

c) In the developing world, there has been some decline in rates of infant mortality over the last twenty years, but in many countries progress has been slow.

d) Steady internal migration from the countryside to the cities is a feature of many developing societies.

4 **Conclusions**
   a) Yes
   b) Yes
   c) No
   d) Yes
   e) Yes
   f) Yes
   g) Yes
   h) No
   i) f
   ii) b
   iii) e
   iv) d
   v) g

6 **Practice A**
   1 e
   2 c
   3 a
   4 b
   5 d

1.12 Rewriting and Proofreading

2 **Practice A**

Comments on the first draft might include some of the following:

   a) Too much space given to basic points
   b) No references are given
   c) Sentences are too short
   d) Style (e.g. *I personally think* not suitable)
   e) Question in title not properly addressed

3 **Practice B**

(*Example rewrite*)

Organisations inevitably face risks by permitting researchers to interview employees, so these must be understood and minimised by the design of the research project. If employees criticise other workers in the organisation, they may be punished, or alternatively, they may feel unable to express their true feelings and so invalidate the interviews. Consequently, researchers must protect the reputation of the organisation and the value of their own work by carefully explaining the purpose of the study and insisting on strict anonymity through the use of false names. By doing this, both parties should benefit from the research.

5 **Practice C**

   i) Africa is not a country: *such as Nigeria*
   ii) Innocence is a noun: *Young and innocent*
   iii) Question mark needed
   iv) Present perfect needed with 'since': *Since 2005 there have been . . .*

v)   'Successfulness' is not a word: *success*
vi) 'pervious' is incorrect: *previous*
vii) 'one of the. . .' needs plural noun: *one of the largest companies . . .*
viii) Repetition: *the essay will conclude with an analysis of . . .*
ix) Time periods need definite article: *the nineteenth century*
x)   *Three skills are needed for success . . .*

6   Practice D

a)   Style – use 'children'
b)   Singular/plural – their lines
c)   Vocabulary – torment is too strong, use inconvenience
d)   Word ending – different effects
e)   Factual – 1973
f)   Word order – overcome
g)   Punctuation – its
h)   Spelling – Hungary
i)   Missing word – the world
j)   Tense – were

7   Practice E – Bicycles

(*Corrected version*)

The bicycle is one of <u>the</u> most efficient <u>machines</u> ever designed. Cyclists can travel <u>four</u> times faster than walkers <u>while</u> using less <u>energy</u> to do so. Various people invented early versions of the bicycle, but the first <u>model</u> with pedals which was <u>successfully</u> mass-produced was made by a <u>Frenchman</u>, Ernest Michaux, <u>in</u> 1861. Later <u>additions</u> included pneumatic tyres and gears. Today hundreds of <u>millions</u> of bicycles are in use all over <u>the</u> world.

PROGRESS CHECK 1

1   (*Other answers may be possible*)
a)   title
b)   schedule, timetable
c)   outline, plan
d)   sources
e)   making, taking
f)   techniques, skills
g)   draft
h)   plagiarism
i)   conclusion
j)   carefully/thoroughly
k)   references
l)   proofread

2

a)	T see p. 4	f)	T see p. 19	k)	T see p. 51	p)	T see p. 82
b)	F see p. 5	g)	T see p. 26	l)	F see p. 56	q)	F see p. 84
c)	T see p. 6	h)	T see p. 76	m)	F see p. 72	r)	T see p. 80
d)	F see p. 17	i)	F see p. 36	n)	F see p. 46	s)	T see p. 13
e)	F see p. 14	j)	T see p. 44	o)	T see p. 80	t)	F see p. 37

3
(*Model summary*)
Although tool-making ability had been thought unique to primates, recent research by an Oxford University team has demonstrated that crows can also develop tools (Grummitt, 2010). The birds had previously been observed in the wild using sticks to reach food, but the Oxford team gave crows lengths of wire which the birds bent to extract chunks of meat from inside a glass tube. As Grummitt explains: 'The Oxford experiment was designed to see if the same kind of bird could modify this ability to make a tool out of a material not found in their native forests (i.e. wire)' (Grummitt 2010:15).

Reference

Grummitt, F. (2010) *What Makes Us Human?* Dublin: Roseberry Press.

PART 2 ELEMENTS OF WRITING

2.1 Argument and Discussion

1   Discussion vocabulary
(*Model paragraph*)
Every year millions of students choose to study in a foreign country. This can have considerable benefits, such as the chance to experience another culture and the opportunity to improve language fluency. But it also involves certain disadvantages, which may include feelings of isolation or homesickness. Another negative aspect may be the high cost, involving both fees and living expenses. However, most students appear to find that the benefits outweigh the negatives and that the chance to join an international group of students is a major advantage in developing a career.

2   Organisation
Vertical: a simpler pattern suitable for short essays
Horizontal: this allows a more complex approach in longer essays

3   Practice A
Possible ideas include:

+	–
No time wasted commuting to work	Employees may feel isolated
Gives employees more flexibility	May not suit all employees
Saves expensive office space	Home may contain distractions
	Requires different management style

Example outline with vertical structure:
a)   Introduction: Reasons for growth of home-working: development in communication technology, demand for more flexible work patterns.
b)   Drawbacks: Employees may feel isolated and be distracted by activities at home. May not suit all employees, some prefer more direct management.

c) Benefits: Companies need to provide less office space, less time spent on commuting = more work time, employees have more flexibility.

d) Discussion: Of benefit to certain employees in some roles, but necessary to have regular contact with colleagues and managers.

5   Counter-arguments

The writer's position is essentially critical of the way prisons currently work.
(*Example answers*)

Counter-argument	Your position
It has been claimed that employees may waste time at home,	but in practice there seems little evidence for this.
Although home-working may save companies money by reducing the need for expensive office space,	employees need to have a well-equipped workspace in their home.

6   Providing evidence

a) 2
b) Education system
c) Many young people do not use 'digital tools'
d) Sceptical of the 'digital native' theory

7   Practice B

(*Example answer*)

As social media such as Facebook and Snapchat have become more important, and also more available through widespread ownership of 4G mobile phones and other devices, the age at which children start using these media has tended to become lower. But various critics have warned of the negative consequences of allowing young children, at primary school age or less, to access these websites.

Yet it is argued (Dobrowsky, 2012) that in fact using these media has many benefits. Dobrowsky claims that it is a harmless and enjoyable way of keeping in touch with friends and family, and moreover it is safer for children to be indoors using their mobile phones than being out on the streets. A further claim is that using social media sites allows children to develop computer skills that will benefit them in later life.

However, others such as Campbell and Childs (2014) strongly disagree, pointing out that young children have no understanding of the potential dangers of the virtual world. They also warn that too much time looking at a screen would reduce a child's chance of gaining real-life experience, and that such passive activity is unhealthy at an age when children need to be physically active. In addition, they say that such behaviour may become addictive and lead to poor sleep patterns. Overall, these arguments are convincing and suggest that parents should be cautious of these media.

2.2 Cause and Effect

2   Practice A

(*Example answers*)

a) Higher rates of literacy often lead to greater demand for secondary education.
    Greater demand for secondary education may result from higher literacy rates.

b)   As a result of the airport construction, more tourists arrived.
     More tourist arrivals were due to the construction of a new airport.
c)   Due to last year's national election, a new government was formed.
     A new government was formed because of the national election last year.
d)   Installing speed cameras on main roads leads to a fall in the number of fatal accidents.
     A fall in the number of fatal accidents results from installing speed cameras on main roads.
e)   Opening a new hospital in 2012 reduced infant mortality.
     The reduction in infant mortality was due to the opening of a new hospital in 2012.
f)   More people shopping on the internet results in stores closing on the high street.
     Stores are closing on the high street owing to more people shopping on the internet.

3   **Practice B**
    (*Example answers*)
    a)   Increasing use of email for messages has caused a decline in letter writing.
    b)   The violent storms last week damaged power lines in the region.
    c)   The new vaccine for tuberculosis (TB) will result in lower child mortality.
    d)   Building a high-speed railway line caused journey times to fall by 25%.
    e)   The invention of the jet engine made cheap mass travel possible.
    f)   The serious motorway accident was due to thick fog.
    g)   The high price of bread is owing to the poor harvest last summer.
    h)   The increase in obesity is a result of a more sedentary lifestyle.
    i)   Earthquakes are often caused by movements in tectonic plates.
    j)   The rising prison population was due to a harsher sentencing policy.

4   **Practice C – Why do women live longer?**
    (*Other answers possible*)
    a)   because
    b)   consequently/therefore/which is why/
         hence/so
    c)   because
    d)   because of/due to/owing to
    e)   due to/owing to/because of
    f)   as a result of/because of/due to
    g)   owing to/because of/due to

5   **Practice D**
    a)   (*Example paragraph*)
    An increase of 25% in the price of oil would have numerous results. First, it would lead to sharp rises in the cost of transport and freight, thus affecting the price of most goods. Clearly, businesses for which fuel was a significant proportion of their costs, such as airlines, would find it difficult to maintain profitability. Another consequence would be a reduction in oil consumption as marginal users switched to alternative fuels, such as gas, or made economies. There would also be increased investment in exploration for oil, as the oil companies attempted to increase supply, and this in turn would stimulate demand for equipment such as oil rigs. Finally, there would be a number of more localised effects, for instance, a change in demand from larger to smaller and more economical vehicles.

2.3 Comparisons

2   **Practice A**
    a)   Residential property in London is twice as expensive as in Rome.
    b)   Property in Moscow is slightly cheaper than in New York.
    c)   Tokyo property is nearly as expensive as property in Paris.

d) Singapore has significantly cheaper property than New York.
e) London is the most expensive of the eight cities, while Sydney is the cheapest.

(*Possible answers*)

f) Property in Paris is slightly cheaper than Moscow property.
g) Property in Sydney is 50% cheaper than in New York.

5 Practice B

a) Manchester United had the highest income **in European football.**
b) Bayern Munich's income was almost twice **as** much as Tottenham's.
c) FC Barcelona earned **considerably** more than Juventus.
d) Juventus had less revenue **than** Liverpool.
e) Arsenal's income was **slightly** less than Manchester City's.
f) Arsenal earned approximately **the** same as Chelsea.

6 Practice C

a) rate
b) varies/fluctuates
c) same
d) substantially/significantly
e) than
f) over/approximately
g) high

2.4 Definitions

2 Category words

(*Model examples*)

A lizard is a four-legged reptile with a long tail.
A chain saw is a power tool used for felling trees.
Malaria is a disease transmitted by mosquito bite.
Autocracy is a political system in which the ruler has total power.
Weaving is the process of making cloth from threads.
Oats is a cereal crop that grows in cool damp climates.
A limited company is a type of business organisation with limited liability.
A parking fine is a penalty imposed for breaking parking rules.
Sculpture is a branch of the visual arts that employs metal, wood or stone.

a) instrument
b) organs
c) organisation
d) fabric
e) behaviour
f) process
g) period
h) root vegetables

(*Example answers*)

i) A lecture is an academic talk used for teaching purposes.
j) Tuberculosis (TB) is a disease mainly affecting the lungs.

k)   The Red Cross is a humanitarian organisation which helps people affected by disasters.
l)   An idiom is a colloquial phrase.

3   Complex definitions

a)   a failed project
b)   development
c)   attachment
d)   self-brightening
e)   globalisation
i)   c
ii)   a, e
iii)   b, d
iv)   b (process), c (system), d (effect)

4   Practice

(*Example definitions*)

a)   **Capital punishment** means the execution by the state of convicted criminals.
b)   An **entrepreneurial business** is set up by somebody who demonstrates the effective application of a number of enterprising attributes, such as creativity, initiative, risk taking, problem solving ability and autonomy, and who will often risk his or her own capital.
c)   **E-books** are books in digital form which can be read on electronic devices.
d)   **Urban areas** are predominantly built-up areas in which roads, housing or commercial buildings are found.
e)   **Obesity** is a medical term meaning unhealthily overweight.

2.5 Examples

2   Phrases to introduce examples

(*Example answers*)

a)   Some twentieth-century inventions, such as TV and the internet, affected the lives of most people.
b)   Lately many countries, for instance China, have introduced fees for university courses.
c)   Various companies have built their reputation on the strength of one product; a case in point is Microsoft Windows.
d)   In recent years more women (e.g. Angela Merkel) have become political leaders.
e)   Certain countries such as Japan are frequently affected by earthquakes.
f)   Many musical instruments, for example guitars, use strings to make music.
g)   Ship canals, for instance the Panama Canal, facilitate world trade.
h)   Politicians have discussed a range of possible alternative punishments to prison, for instance community work.

3   Practice A – Eating for health

(*Model answer*)

A hundred years ago most people's diets consisted of a few staple items that were cheap and also filling, for example, bread or rice. Today many people are able to afford more variety, and regularly eat more expensive foods, such as fruit and meat. But along with the wider choice has come anxiety about the possible threats to health contained in certain foods. In recent years a broad range of products, including eggs, butter, salt, sugar, fats and smoked meat have been considered a risk to health. This has left many people confused, as much of the 'research' behind these claims is contradictory; in other words, a food may be condemned by one scientist but approved by another. One beneficiary of this process is the health food industry, a booming sector which promotes food and drink products to health-conscious young people. However, many doctors argue that instead of focusing exclusively on what they eat or drink, people's health would be improved by doing more exercise (e.g. swimming, running or cycling).

4   **Practice B**

(*Model paragraph*)

A new perspective

Students who go to study abroad often experience a type of culture shock when they arrive in the new country. Of course, there are always different things (e.g. public transport systems) to learn about in a new town or city. But in addition, customs which they took for granted in their own society, such as holidays and festivals or ways of greeting people, may not be followed in the host country. Even everyday patterns of life, for instance types of shops and shop opening times, may be different. When these are added to the inevitable differences which occur between every country, such as language and currency, students may at first feel confused. They can experience rapid changes of mood, for example depression or elation, or even want to return home. However, most soon make new friends and, in a relatively short period of two or three months, are able to adjust to their new environment. They may even find that they prefer some aspects of their new surroundings, such as freedom and independence, and forget that they are not at home for a while!

5   **Restatement**
   a)   The company's overhead, in other words the fixed costs, doubled last year.
   b)   The Roman Empire (27 BCE – 476 CE) was an empire in which there was autocratic rule.
   c)   The Indian capital, namely, New Delhi, has a thriving commercial centre.
   d)   Survival rates for the most common type of cancer (i.e. breast cancer) are improving.
   e)   Voting rates in most democracies are in decline, that is to say, fewer people are voting.

2.6 Generalisations

1   **Using generalisations**
   a)   Invalid: England is not a particularly wet country.
   b)   A widely accepted fact, supported by evidence.
   c)   Similar to b), this is a well-researched link.
   d)   This may be true in some cases but is a very sweeping generalisation.
   e)   Clearly true in many cases but not valid for every situation (e.g. short journeys).

3   **Practice A**

(*Example answers*)
   a)   Regular rainfall is necessary for good crop yields.
   b)   Honest judges are needed to ensure respect for the law.
   c)   Adequate sleep is vital for academic success.
   d)   Industrial growth tends to cause pollution.
   e)   Cold weather is likely to increase demand for gas.
   f)   Job satisfaction depends on having interesting work.

g)   Regular training is essential for sporting success.
h)   Creativity and skill are both needed to produce great art.

4   Practice B

(*Example generalisations*)

a)   Graduates are more likely than undergraduates to study in the library.
b)   Female undergraduates generally prefer to work in silence.
c)   Few students choose to study outdoors.
d)   Male graduates prefer to study in the library, while females prefer their own room.
e)   More undergraduates than graduates work in bed.

5   Building on generalisations

a)   To introduce the topic
b)   The study which compared the preferences of women in a range of countries
c)   To summarise the findings of the research

6   Practice C

(*Example*)

a)   The growth of tourism is often seen as being detrimental to the host society. It is claimed that growth in visitor numbers causes pollution, overcrowding and even leads to crime. But the weakness of this argument can be shown by comparing several countries which have experienced rapid growth in tourist numbers, with very different results, both positive and negative.

2.7 Problems and Solutions

4   Practice A – The housing dilemma

(*Example answer*)

In many expanding urban areas, there is a serious housing shortage, caused by people moving from the country to seek urban opportunities. There are various possible answers to this problem, but each has its drawbacks. The traditional response is to build family houses with gardens, which offer privacy and space but require a lot of land. Building these is slow and the growth of suburbs creates longer journeys to work.

A second option is to build prefabricated three-storey houses, which can be erected more quickly and cheaply than traditional houses and can be designed to achieve a higher density of population. In some places these may be the best solution, but they also require a lot of space and are too expensive for the average citizen.

A better solution is to construct tall blocks of flats, which will accommodate more people at high density quite cheaply while preventing cities from sprawling too widely. Although some families may find them cramped, for the majority they are a convenient and affordable answer to the housing problem.

5   Practice B – University expansion

(*Example argument*)

Currently there is increasing demand for university places, which frequently leads to overcrowding of student facilities, such as lectures. It has been argued that fees should be increased to reduce demand for places, but this would discriminate against students from poorer families. Another proposal is for the government to pay for the expansion of universities, but against this is the view that this would unfairly benefit the minority who attend university, who in any case go on to earn higher salaries. A fairer solution might be for the government to subsidise the fees of the poorest students.

2.8 Visual Information

1 Types of visuals

TYPES	USES	EXAMPLE
1 Diagram	g	F
2 Table	h	B
3 Map	a	H
4 Pie chart	f	D
5 Flow chart	d	E
6 Line graph	c	A
7 Bar chart	e	C
8 Plan	b	G
9 Scatter graph/plot	i	I

3 Describing visuals

a)

i) is better. It comments on the main features of the chart but does not repeat the statistics.

b)

a) density
b) demonstrates/illustrates/shows
c) between
d) less crowded/less densely populated
e) role/part
f) since/as/because
g) tend

5 Practice A

a) shows/illustrates
b) between
c) majority
d) substantially/significantly
e) Spain
f) rise/increase
g) than

6 Practice B

(*Example paragraph*)

The bar chart compares the maximum speeds attained by some of the fastest mammals on earth. Humans are only capable of running at about 28 mph, while the fastest creature, the cheetah, can reach 70 mph. This speed is much greater than lions or hares can reach (50 mph), while animals such as greyhounds, horses and tigers are only capable of speeds in the 40–45 mph range.

PROGRESS CHECK 2

1 advantage/positive aspect
2 horizontal – more suitable for short essays
   vertical – allows consideration of multiple perspectives, better for longer papers
3 a position in opposition to the writer's views
4 (*Model examples*)
   a) Unemployment rose due to the economic recession.
   b) The railway accident was caused by a faulty signal.
   c) The power cut was due to the hurricane.

5

(*Model examples*)

Australia is approximately thirty times larger than New Zealand.
The population density of New Zealand is substantially higher than Australia's.
Australians are significantly wealthier than New Zealanders.

6

(*Model examples*)

a) A semester is one of the two divisions of the academic year.
b) A hammer is a tool with a metal head used for driving in nails.
c) A midwife is a medical professional specialising in delivering babies.

7

(*Model examples*)

a) Certain capital cities (e.g. Canberra) are smaller than the commercial centres of their country.
b) Many varieties of fruit, such as oranges, contain vital vitamins.
c) A few kinds of mammals (e.g. whales and seals) live in the sea.
d) Most planets in our solar system, for example Jupiter, have moons.

8

In the past century, photography has gone from being an exclusive hobby to something accessible to everyone. This is largely due to the invention of the digital camera. In the last twenty years this has made it simple to take colour photographs cheaply and to modify pictures easily by using editing programmes. So <u>now that everyone has a smartphone</u>, with its built-in camera, photography has become democratic and <u>high-quality photographs can be produced by anybody</u>.

9

(*Other synonyms may be possible*)

a) The main challenge/difficulty/issue facing the engineers was the extreme cold.
b) The only answer/remedy/option was to repeat the experiment.
c) Sherlock Holmes found an unusual answer/solution to the mystery of the Missing Mask.
d) The safe disposal of nuclear waste is a(n) issue/concern without an easy answer.

10

(*Model example*)

The table illustrates the results of a survey of student evaluation of library facilities, contrasting undergraduate with graduate opinion. Most facilities are rated highly by both groups, especially the café and staff helpfulness. Both student groups are least satisfied with the availability of short-loan stock. In most areas, graduates seem slightly more critical of facilities than undergraduates.

PART 3 LANGUAGE ISSUES

3.1 Cohesion

2 Practice A

Reference	Reference word/phrase
La Ferrera	She
new business start-ups	they
average life of only 3.4 years	this
one economic	the former
the other social	the latter
the former. . . ., the latter. . .	these
. . . sufficient market research	
The failure to do market research	this

4 Practice B – Famous for?

a) he
b) his
c) his
d) it/this
e) his

f) he
g) they/he
h) This
i) He
j) his

6 Practice C – Velcro

Velcro is a fabric fastener used with clothes and shoes. **It** was invented by a Swiss engineer called George de Mestral. **His** idea was derived from studying the tiny hooks found on some plant seeds. **They** cling to animals and help disperse the seeds. Velcro has two sides, one of which is covered in small hooks and the other in loops. When **they** are pressed together they form a strong bond.

Mestral spent eight years perfecting **his** invention, which **he** called 'Velcro' from the French words 'velour' and 'crochet'. **It** was patented in 1955, and today over 60 million metres of Velcro are sold annually.

7 Practice D – Nylon

(Example answer)

Wallace Carothers, the director of research at the American DuPont Corporation, patented nylon in 1935. He had previously studied chemistry and specialised in polymers, which are molecules composed of long chains of atoms. Nylon was a strong but fine synthetic fibre which was first mass produced in 1939. It is used to make a wide range of products which include stockings, toothbrushes, parachutes, fishing lines and surgical thread.

3.2 Definite Articles

3 Practice A

a) Engineering is the main industry in **the** northern region.
b) Insurance firms have made record profits in **the** last decade.
c) Global warming is partly caused by fossil fuels.

d) **The** mayor has been arrested on suspicion of corruption.
e) **The** moons of Jupiter were discovered in **the** eighteenth century.
f) Tourism is **the** world's biggest industry.
g) **The** forests of Scandinavia produce most of Britain's paper.
h) **The** Thai currency is **the** baht.
i) Computer crime has grown by 200% in **the** last five years.
j) **The** main causes of **the** Industrial Revolution are still debated.
k) Three percent of **the** working population are employed in call centres.
l) **The** latest forecast predicts warmer winters in the next decade.
m) Research on energy saving is being conducted in **the** Physics Faculty.
n) **The** best definition is often **the** simplest.
o) During **the** last recession there was a sharp increase in child poverty.

4   Practice B

A Northern model?

Norway is **a/the** global leader in **the** use of electric cars: in 2016 nearly 30% of vehicle sales were battery-powered or hybrid models. In **the** past five years, sales have increased sharply due to **the** development of better batteries, so now **the** country's five million people are **the** world's largest electric car market. **The** Transport Minister talks of ending sales of cars powered by fossil fuels by 2025. **The** government is subsidising **the** installation of charging points on main roads and shopping centres. In addition, drivers of zero-emission vehicles pay no sales tax or parking fees, and may use bus lanes in cities. But this pattern may not be **a/the** model for other countries: Norway has **a** surplus of cheap electricity thanks to hydropower, and it taxes petrol and diesel fuel heavily.

3.3 Numbers

2   Percentages
a)   50%
b)   100%
c)   400%

3   Simplification
a)   Scores of students applied for the scholarship.
b)   Since 1975 dozens of primary schools have been rebuilt.
c)   The students thought of a few/several good topics for their project.
d)   Various names were suggested but rejected for the new chocolate bar.
e)   Last year dozens of books were published on biogenetics.

4   Further numerical phrases
(Example answers)
a)   The price of petrol has increased tenfold since 1975.
b)   Two-thirds of the students in the group were women.
c)   The new high-speed train halved the journey time to Madrid.
d)   The number of students applying for the Psychology course has risen by 50% since last year.
e)   More than twice as many British students as Italian students complete their first degree course.
f)   Tap water is 700 times cheaper than bottled water.

g) The highest rate of unemployment in Europe is in Greece and the lowest in Norway.
h) A majority of members supported the suggestion, but a large proportion of these expressed some doubts.

5 Practice

(*Example answers*)

b) There were twice as many sports at the Paris Olympics compared to the Athens games.
c) The number of athletes competing doubled between the Tokyo and Beijing Olympics.
d) In the Barcelona Olympics nearly a third of the athletes were women.
e) The number of Olympic sports rose threefold between 1896 and 2008.
f) A substantial minority of athletes at the London Olympics were women.

3.4 Passives

2 Structure

a) The data was collected and the two groups (were) compared.
b) 120 people in three social classes were interviewed.
c) The results were checked and several errors (were) found.
d) An analysis of the findings will be made.
e) Four doctors were asked to give their opinions.
f) The report was written and ten copies (were) distributed.

3 Use of the passive

a) The vaccines were exposed to temperatures below the limit.
b) It is believed that the Atacama desert was too dry for animal life.
c) It is suggested that they can be damaged by foreign competition.
d) The life cycles of three main bee species were researched.
e) It was argued that prisons had a negative effect on the inmates.

4 Adverbs with passives

Mars mania

In the past it was commonly believed that creatures lived on Mars. Due to the similarity of size with Earth, the planet was generally thought to have a climate that would permit life. It was additionally discovered that Mars had four seasons, although they were longer than their equivalents on Earth. Straight lines seen on the surface of Mars were ridiculously considered to be canals built by Martians. An invasion of Earth by superior beings from Mars was graphically described by H.G. Wells in his novel *War of the Worlds*. Even today it is occasionally claimed that primitive life exists on the planet.

5 Practice

(*Model answer*)

Making bread

Bread is traditionally made from wheat flour, salt, water and yeast. You mix the wholemeal or white flour with a little salt and yeast, and then gradually add lukewarm water. Other ingredients such as chopped nuts or seeds may be included. Then mix the dough until a soft ball is formed, which you can knead by hand. In the kneading process the dough is vigorously pounded and reshaped so that all the ingredients are fully combined. After thoroughly kneading the dough, leave it for a few hours to rise. When this is finished work the dough by hand to shape it into loaves or rolls. After two more hours the loaves will have risen again, due to the action of the yeast. Bake them in a hot oven for about half an hour and then allow them to cool.

3.5 Punctuation

9 **Practice A**
   a) The study was carried out by Christine Zhen-Wei Qiang of the National University of Singapore.
   b) Professor Rowan's new book 'The End of Privacy' (2017) is published in New York.
      or
      Professor Rowan's new book *The End of Privacy* (2017) is published in New York.
   c) As Keynes said: 'It's better to be roughly right than precisely wrong'.
   d) Banks such as HSBC and Barclays were in penny-pinching mode in the 1990s.
   e) As Matheson (1954) wrote: 'It was the germ that was the villain'.
   f) Thousands of new words such as 'app' enter the English language each year.
   g) The BBC's World Service is broadcast in 33 languages, including Somali and Vietnamese.
   h) She scored 56% on the main course; the previous semester she had achieved 67%.

10 **Practice B**
   Studying will play a vital part in your life as an Oxford student, but you will also find an enormous amount to do in Oxford in your spare time. Oxford is the youngest city in England and Wales and has two universities: Oxford University and Oxford Brookes. Thirty-five percent of people who live here are aged 15–29, and 27% (40,000 of a total population of 150,000) are university students. If you ever feel like a change of scene, the bus to London takes around 90 minutes and runs 24 hours a day. There are now two railway stations: the central Oxford station and the recently opened Oxford Parkway. Oxford is a youthful and cosmopolitan city with plenty to see and do. There are dozens of historic and iconic buildings, including the Bodleian Libraries, Ashmolean Museum, Sheldonian Theatre, the cathedral and the colleges. In the city centre you will find lots of shops, cafés, restaurants, theatres, cinemas, pubs and clubs. There are plenty of green spaces too: riverside walks, England's oldest botanic garden, the University Parks and college gardens.

3.6 Singular or Plural?

1 **Five difficult areas**
   i)   . . . and disadvantages   (e)
   ii) are vaccinated   (a)
   iii) rural areas   (c)
   iv) . . . in crime   (b)
   v)   Each company has its own policy (d)

4 **Practice A**
   a) Little   f) much advice
   b) businesses   g) few interests
   c) experience/is   h) civil war
   d) travel broadens   i) Irons were
   e) stone   j) work

5   **Practice B**

traffic	Research	lives	stress
travel	capitals	petrol	advice
work	vehicles	jams	is
staff	day	factor	music

3.7 Style

3   **Practice A**

(Example sentences)

a)   Another factor to consider is the possibility of crime increasing.
b)   Currently the rate of unemployment is high.
c)   In the near future a vaccine for malaria may be discovered.
d)   The firefighters were quickly able to control the fire.
e)   The numbers in that report are unreliable.
f)   The severe inflation led to poverty and social unrest.
g)   He was delighted to win the prize.
h)   Students should be paid to study.
i)   Women were enfranchised in 1987.
j)   The main causes of the Russian Revolution were war and misgovernment.

4   **Avoiding repetition and redundancy – Fast food**

(Example answer)

Currently, fast food is growing in popularity. This is food that people can buy ready to eat or cook quickly. This essay examines its advantages and drawbacks. First, it is very convenient; most people who work in offices are very busy, so they do not have time to go home for lunch, but can eat in restaurants such as McDonald's. The second benefit is cheapness. As it is produced in large quantities, the companies can keep costs down. As a result, it is usually less expensive than a meal in a conventional restaurant.

5   **Varying sentence length**

(Example answers)

Worldwide, enrolments in higher education are increasing. In developed countries over half of all young people enter college, while similar trends are seen in China and South America. This growth has put financial strain on state university systems, so that many countries are requiring students and parents to contribute to the cost. This leads to a debate about whether students or society benefit from tertiary education. China is one developing country (but not the only one) which has imposed fees on students since 1997. The results have been surprising: enrolments, especially in the most expensive universities, have continued to rise steeply, growing 200% overall between 1997 and 2011. It seems in this case that higher fees attract rather than discourage students, who see them as a sign of a good education. They compete more fiercely for places, leading to the result that a place at a good college can cost $8,000 per year for fees and maintenance.

6   **The use of caution**

(Others are possible)

Modals: might/may/could/should
Adverbs: often/usually/frequently/generally/commonly/mainly/apparently
Verb/phrase: seems to/appears to/in general/by and large/it appears/it seems

7   **Using modifiers**

a)   The company's efforts to save energy were quite/fairly successful.
b)   The survey was (a fairly/quite a) comprehensive study of student opinion.
c)   His second book had a rather hostile reception.
d)   The first-year students were quite fascinated by her lectures.
e)   The latest type of arthritis drug is rather expensive.
f)   This mountain tiger has become quite/rather rare.
g)   The class found the essay topic quite/rather challenging.

8   **Practice B**

(*Example answers*)

a)   Private companies are often more efficient than state-owned businesses.
b)   Exploring space seems to be a waste of valuable resources.
c)   Older students may perform better at university than younger ones.
d)   Word-of-mouth is commonly the best kind of advertising.
e)   English pronunciation can be confusing.
f)   Some cancers may be caused by psychological factors.
g)   It appears that global warming will cause the sea level to rise.
h)   Most shopping may done on the internet in ten years' time.
i)   Online education can be inferior to taught classes.
j)   By 2025 driverless cars might be in common use.

3.8 Time Markers

2   **Practice A**

a)   Recently
b)   until
c)   for
d)   Last month

e)   by
f)   Since
g)   During
h)   After

4   **Practice B – Napoleon**

a)   before
b)   later
c)   at
d)   After
e)   by

f)   later
g)   during
h)   later
i)   After

5   **Practice C – Eating out**

a)   In/Over/During
b)   Since
c)   ago
d)   recently

e)   Currently
f)   by
g)   since
h)   During/In

PROGRESS CHECK 3

1

William Shakespeare was born in Stratford-upon-Avon in 1564, into a wealthy landowning family. When **he** was only 18 he married Anne Hathaway, who was six years older than **him**. **She** subsequently had three children, but **their** only son, Hamnet, died young. Apparently William spent most of his time in London after their marriage, where he acted and started to write plays. **They** were mainly comedies at first, and were very successful. In the early 1600s **his** work became darker, and this is when **he** wrote his most famous plays, such as 'Hamlet' and 'King Lear'. **They** have secured **his** worldwide reputation as a great dramatist and poet. **He** died in 1616 aged only 52, while Anne lived for another seven years.

2

a)	-	f)	-	k)	the	p)	-
b)	the	g)	the	l)	a	q)	-
c)	the	h)	a	m)	a		
d)	a/the	i)	the	n)	the		
e)	the	j)	the	o)	the		

3   *(Model paragraph)*

250 international students were interviewed about their experience of study abroad. Of these a fifth were from China, a fifth from India, a tenth from Nigeria and the remaining half from a variety of European countries. A substantial majority were satisfied with their courses, but a fifth had concerns about the quantity of work required. Just 10% complained about the quality of teaching. Half the students said they found it easy to adapt to a different culture and way of life, but of the others a significant minority disliked the food, a fifth found living too expensive, and a small minority mentioned bad weather.

4   *(Model paragraph)*

Our research aimed to find the best taxi business for campus use, so the performance of six local taxi companies was compared. Companies that had their offices within a kilometre of the campus were selected. The response of each company to requests made at the same time of day (7 p.m.) was timed. Response times varied from ten to 24 minutes. Each driver was then asked to take the passenger to the railway station. The friendliness of the drivers and the length of time taken were recorded, as well as the fare the driver asked for. Overall AZ Taxis were found to have the fastest response and the cheapest fare, but not the most friendly driver.

5

The School of Biomedical Sciences at Borchester University is offering two undergraduate degree courses in Neuroscience this year. Students can study either Neuroscience with Pharmacology or Neuroscience with Biochemistry. There is also a Master's course which runs for four years and involves a period of study abroad during November and December. Professor Andreas Fischer is course leader for Neuroscience and enquiries should be sent to him via the website.

6

a)   Several types of response were recorded.
b)   Three avenues of research were suggested.
c)   One of the groups was eliminated from the competition.
d)   Half the graduates were from Indonesia.
e)   The government was defeated at the election.
f)   The performance of the athletes was improved by his training method.

7   *(Model answer)*

Currently there is widespread concern that significant numbers of people take insufficient exercise, due to sedentary habits such as watching television, which appears to be a major cause of obesity. Yet there is substantial research which demonstrates the mental and physical benefits of walking regularly.

8

a) Dr Gonzalez went to Berlin five days ago.
b) He was in Berlin for two days.
c) During his stay in Berlin he gave a lecture.
d) After leaving Berlin he went to Prague.
e) While staying in Prague he met colleagues at Charles University.
f) By June 10th he had travelled 2,300 kilometres.

PART 4 VOCABULARY FOR WRITING

4.1 Approaches to Vocabulary

4   **Practice**

a) statement
b) anecdote
c) saying
d) euphemism
e) metaphor
f) paradox
g) simile
h) proverb
i) synopsis
j) idiom
k) slogan
l) ambiguity
m) cliché

5   **Confusing pairs**

a) principles
b) lose
c) affect
d) compliments
e) its
f) economic
g) accepted

4.2 Abbreviations

6   **Practice**

a) information and communications technology/higher education/and others
b) genetically modified/for example
c) that is/the World Trade Organisation

d) Note/curricula vitae/Human Resources/September
e) approximately/Before common era
f) The European Union/Value Added Tax
g) Doctor of Philosophy (thesis)/tuberculosis/South East
h) Figure 4/gross national product
i) Vice-Chancellor/Postgraduate Certificate of Education
j) Public relations/approximately/$75,000
k) With reference to/annual general meeting/as soon as possible
l) Doctor/Master of Science/Master of Arts

4.3 Academic Vocabulary: Nouns and Adjectives

2 **Nouns**

(NB: not all these words have close synonyms. This list is a guide to approximate meaning. Students should use a dictionary for a full understanding.)

accuracy – precision
analysis – examination
approach – angle of study
assessment – test
assumption – informed guess
authority – expert
category – type
claim – argument/thesis
controversy – debate
correlation – link
deterrent – disincentive
emphasis – weight put on one area
evidence – proof
exception – different thing
extract – part of a longer work
ideology – belief

implication – unstated suggestion
innovation – new introduction
intuition – understanding without thinking
motivation – incentive
perspective – angle of study
phenomenon – unusual event
policy – formal guidelines
preference – favourite choice
process – series of stages
proposal – suggestion
provision – supply
sequence – series of stages
strategy – plan
substitute – replacement
technique – method
validity – truth

a) evidence
b) proposals
c) intuition
d) provision
e) claim
f) phenomena
g) process
h) correlation

3 **Nouns and adjectives**

(Model examples)

Sherlock Holmes solved crimes by analytical methods; examining each clue.
Although quite famous, the professor was always approachable for students.
Her book is the most authoritative work on the subject.
Even today, the ideas of Karl Marx remain controversial.
Their position was emphatic; the library would remain closed all week.

His performance was <u>exceptional</u>, winning three prizes in his final year.
My objection to the book is <u>ideological</u>, despite it being well written.
California offers an <u>innovative</u> culture, where new ideas are welcomed.
She had an <u>intuitive</u> feeling she would get the job.
In addition to money, praise and recognition are both highly <u>motivational</u>.
The Harry Potter books have been a <u>phenomenal</u> publishing success.
First-class passengers are sure of <u>preferential</u> treatment.
Until it's approved by the council, the agreement is only <u>provisional</u>.
The courses in this faculty are <u>sequential</u>: you must pass one to move to the next.
The general's retreat was just <u>strategic</u> – he lured the enemy into a trap.
<u>Technical</u> support for computer users is available 24/7.
Your bus pass is <u>valid</u> until October next year.

4   Confusing nouns and adjectives

Noun	Adjective	Noun	Adjective
approximation	approximate	particularity	particular
superiority	superior	reason	reasonable
strategy	strategic	synthesis	synthetic
politics	political	economy	economic/al
industry	industrial	culture	cultural
exterior	external	average	average
height	high	reliability	reliable
heat	hot	strength	strong
confidence	confident	truth	true
width	wide	probability	probable
necessity	necessary	length	long
danger	dangerous	relevance	relevant

5   Practice A

a) confident
b) particularities/strengths
c) probability
d) relevant
e) necessary
f) average
g) danger
h) necessity
i) unreliable
j) approximate
k) economic
l) synthesis

8   Practice B

a) irrelevant
b) subjective/irrational
c) Concrete/Relevant
d) approximate/rough
e) relative
f) logical/rational
g) theoretical/abstract
h) unambiguous

9   Practice C

a) strategic – strategy
b) analytical – analysis
c) synthetic – synthesis
d) major – majority
e) cultural – culture
f) theoretical – theory

g) frequent – frequency
h) critical – criticism/critic

i) Social – society
j) practical – practice

4.4 Academic Vocabulary: Verbs and Adverbs

1 Understanding main verbs

(*Approximate synonyms – infinitive form*)

adapt = modify
arise = occur
conduct = carry out
characterise = have features of
clarify = explain
concentrate on = look at closely
be concerned with = deal with
demonstrate = show
determine = find
discriminate = distinguish
establish = found
exhibit = show
focus on = look at closely
generate = create

hold = be true
identify = pick out
imply= suggest
interact = work together
interpret = explain
manifest = show
overcome = defeat
propose = suggest
prove = turn out
recognise = accept
relate to = link to
supplement = add to
undergo = experience
yield = produce

3 Practice A

(*Some other verbs may be possible*)

a) A admitted/accepted that he might have made a mistake. . .
b) B denied saying that women make/made better doctors than men.
c) C stated/claimed/argued that small firms are/were more dynamic than large ones.
d) D agreed with/supported C's views on small firms.
e) E assumed/presumed that most people work/worked for money.
f) F concluded that allergies are/were becoming more common.
g) G doubted that electric cars will/would replace conventional ones.
h) H hypothesised/suggested a link between crime and sunspot activity.

5 Practice B

(*Other verbs may be possible*)

a) L criticised/censured her research methods.
b) M identified/classified four main types of children in care.
c) N commended the company for its record for workplace safety.
d) O interpreted the noises whales make/made as expressions of happiness.
e) P identified/presented wind power and biomass as the leading green energy sources of the future.
f) Q described/portrayed Darwin as the most influential naturalist of the nineteenth century.

7 Practice C

a) Clearly
b) Originally
c) Alternatively
d) Recently
e) Similarly

f) Clearly/crucially
g) broadly
h) factually

8 Practice D

The earliest keys known to history were made by the Egyptians from wood and were <u>significantly</u> improved upon by the Romans, who used metal. Today's keys are <u>basically</u> the same: a piece of metal with teeth, <u>conventionally</u> produced by cutting and stamping. But <u>recently</u> a new technology, 3D printing has made it possible to manufacture much more intricate designs which are <u>virtually</u> impossible to copy <u>illicitly</u>. Although <u>substantially</u> more expensive, these high-tech keys offer remarkable security.

4.5 Conjunctions

2 Types of conjunctions

a) A few inventions, <u>for instance</u> television, have had a major impact on everyday life.
b) <u>Furthermore</u>, many patients were treated in clinics and surgeries.
c) The definition of 'special needs' is important <u>since</u> it is the cause of some disagreement.
d) The technology allows consumers a choice, <u>thus</u> increasing their sense of satisfaction.
e) Four hundred people were interviewed for the survey, and <u>then</u> the results were analysed.
f) <u>However</u>, another body of opinion associates globalisation with unfavourable outcomes.

ii) Result   d
iii) Reason   c
iv) Opposition   f
v) Example   a
vi) Time   e

Biofuels

Conjunction	Type		Conjunction	Type
a) **such as**	**example**	f)	in other words	example
b) but	opposition	g)	Consequently	result
c) Although	opposition	h)	and	addition
d) for instance	example	i)	neither . . . nor	opposition
e) however	opposition			

3 Common conjunctions

(Others are possible)

Addition: moreover/as well as/in addition/and/also/furthermore/plus
Result: therefore/consequently/so/that is why (**see Unit 2.2**)
Reason: because/owing to/as a result of/as/since/due to (**see Unit 2.2**)
Opposition: but/yet/while/however/nevertheless/whereas/albeit/although/despite
Example: such as/e.g./in particular/for instance (**see Unit 2.5**)
Time: after/while/then/next/subsequently (**see Unit 3.8**)

4 Practice A

(Others are possible)

a) After
b) Although/While
c) moreover/furthermore/additionally
d) therefore/so
e) for instance/for example
f) Due to/Because of
g) While
h) As/Because/Since

5   Practice B – Geoengineering

(Others are possible)

a) such as
b) Although
c) either
d) or
e) for instance/for example

f) While/Although
g) due to/because of
h) or
i) Therefore/That is why

7   Conjunctions of opposition

(Example answers)

a)
  i) Although the government claimed that inflation was falling, the opposition said it was rising.
  ii) The government claimed that inflation was falling, while the opposition said it was rising.

b)
  i) This department must reduce expenditure, yet it needs to install new computers.
  ii) While this department must reduce expenditure, it also needs to install new computers.

c)
  i) In spite of being heavily advertised, sales of the new car were poor.
  ii) Sales of the new car were poor despite it being heavily advertised.

8   Practice C

(Example answers)

a) In contrast to America, where gun ownership is common, few Japanese have guns.
b) Despite leaving school at the age of 14, he went on to develop a successful business.
c) The majority displayed a positive attitude to the proposal, but a minority strongly disagreed.
d) While the tutor insisted that the essay was easy, the students found it difficult.
e) Although the spring was cold and dry, the summer was warm and wet.
f) He finished the project before the deadline, yet he still felt dissatisfied with it.
g) She prefers speaking French; nevertheless her English is excellent.
h) Since it was nearly dark they had to stop the experiment.

4.6 Prefixes and Suffixes

1   How prefixes and suffixes work

'Prefabrication' is the process of making something in advance of installation.
'Revitalise' is to give extra strength or impetus to something or someone.

2   Prefixes

auto	by itself	multi	many
co	together	non	negative
ex	(i) previous	over	too much
	(ii) outside	poly	many
fore	in front	post	later
inter	between	pro	in support of
macro	large	re	again
micro	small	sub	below

tele	distance	under	(i) below
trans	across		(ii) not enough

3 Practice A

a) social class at bottom of society
b) more tickets sold than seats available
c) very local climate
d) economy based on information not production
e) not listed in the telephone book
f) disappointed
g) before marriage
h) able to create or control situations

5 Practice B

a) noun – withdrawal of a service
b) adjective – two related events at the same time
c) adverb – without cooperation
d) adjective – related to evolution
e) noun – person who protests
f) adjective – not able to be forecast
g) adjective – able to be sold
h) noun – person being interviewed
i) noun – belief that increasing consumption benefits society
j) adverb – in a way that suggests a symbol

6 Practice C

a) joint production/junior company
b) without choosing to/not hurt
c) able to be refilled/clear and obvious
d) found new times/before school
e) cannot be provided/unusual
f) failure in communication/new order
g) faulty/ridiculous
h) write again/hard to understand

4.7 Prepositions

1 Using prepositions

c) Noun + prep = purpose of/development of/relationship between/decline in/supply of
Verb + prep = contributed to
Adj + prep = valuable for
Place = in Catalonia/in the factory context
Time = in the period
Phrase = In conclusion

2 Practice A

b) adjective + preposition
c) verb + preposition
d) preposition of place
e) noun + preposition

f) phrase
g) preposition of place

h) preposition of time

3 Prepositions and nouns

a) of
b) in

c) of
d) to

e) of
f) on

4 Prepositions in phrases

a) on
b) of
c) of

d) in
e) of
f) on

g) in
h) of

5 Prepositions of place and time

a) Among
b) from, to/between, and
c) in, of
d) in, in

e) in, at
f) On, between
g) around, of/on
h) Between

6 Practice B

a) of
b) in/to
c) to/in
d) among/in
e) from/in

f) between
g) in
h) of
i) in/over
j) between

k) in
l) in
m) of
n) to/in

8 Practice C

a) focused on/concentrated on
b) pointed out
c) specialised in
d) associated with

e) divided into
f) blamed for
g) believed in
h) learned from

4.8 Synonyms

1 How synonyms work

Word/phrase	*synonym*
oil	hydrocarbon
company	firm
in the world	global/internationally
people	employees
Britain	the UK

2 Common synonyms in academic writing

(NB: Some of these pairs are approximate synonyms)

Nouns		Verbs	
area	field	accelerate	speed up
authority	source	alter	change
behaviour	conduct	analyse	take apart
benefit	advantage	assist	help
category	type	attach	join
component	part	challenge	question
controversy	argument	clarify	explain
difficulty	problem	concentrate on	focus on
drawback	disadvantage	conduct	carry out
expansion	increase	confine	limit
feeling	emotion	develop	evolve
framework	structure	evaluate	examine
goal	target	found	establish
interpretation	explanation	maintain	insist
issue	topic	predict	forecast
method	system	prohibit	ban
option	possibility	raise	increase
results	findings	reduce	decrease
statistics	figures	respond	reply
study	research	retain	keep
trend	tendency	show	demonstrate
output	production	strengthen	reinforce

3   Practice A

(*Others are possible*)

a) Professor Hicks challenged the results of the study.
b) The figures demonstrate a steady rise in applications.
c) The institute's forecast has caused a major debate.
d) Cost seems to be the principal disadvantage to that method.
e) They will focus on the first possibility.
f) After the lecture she tried to explain her idea.
g) Three topics need to be evaluated.
h) The structure can be kept but the aim needs to be modified.
i) OPEC, the oil producers' cartel, is to reduce output to increase global prices.
j) The tendency to smaller families has accelerated in the last decade.

4   Practice B

UK – British – this country
agency – organisation – body
advertising campaign – publicity programme – advertising blitz
to raise – to improve
to cut – reduction
before eating – prior to meals

5   Practice C

(*Example answers – others possible*)

build/make vehicles   principal problem
car makers   obstacle

automobile producers
challenges
forecast

energy
produced
vehicles/machines

PROGRESS CHECK 4

1 a, c, d

2
a) lose
b) except
c) site

3
a) International Monetary Fund/Gross Domestic Product
b) Compare/anonymous/approximately/Before common era
c) Master of Science/Genetically modified

4
a) absolute
b) metaphorical
c) subjective
d) precise
e) abstract

5
a) height
b) synthesis
c) length
d) probability
e) relevance

6
a) X claimed/argued that eating spiders is healthy.
b) Y disagreed with X, insisting that his theory was based on poor research.
c) Z agreed with Y's opinion of X's work.

7
a) continuously
b) locally
c) particularly
d) increasingly
e) Traditionally

8 *(Others are possible)*
a) Although
b) since/because/as
c) So/Therefore
d) and
e) But
f) because/as/since
g) Then
h) because/as/since
i) Therefore/So
j) and

9
a) adjective
b) noun
c) verb

    d)   noun
    e)   noun

10

antidote	medicine to counter the effects of poison
correspondent	person you write to regularly
foreword	preliminary section of book
polytechnic	institute where many scientific subjects are taught
proportion	relation of one thing to another
subcutaneous	under the skin
undervalue	assess worth of something too cheaply

11

In the eighteenth century, news travelled as fast as a horseman or sailing ship. It could take weeks for news of a battle in Europe to reach America. By the mid-nineteenth century railways had accelerated the distribution of newspapers, so that they reached distant provinces in hours, and then the telegraph allowed news to be sent in seconds. Today we can be overwhelmed by the volume of news from all over the world which we can continuously receive on our phones and laptops.

12

a) systems/controversy
b) figures/show/advantages
c) option/researching
d) results/strengthen
e) field/study
f) carried out/conduct

PART 5 WRITING MODELS

5.1 Case Studies

1 **Using case studies**

A case study has the advantage of providing a concrete experience/example.

The disadvantages are that it is limited in place and time, and the example may not be applicable to other situations.

Topics	*Case studies*
Methods of teaching dyslexic children	An experimental approach to reading difficulties with children under eight in Singapore
Improving crop yields in semi-deserts	Using solar power to operate irrigation pumps in Ethiopia
Reducing infant mortality	A programme to cut smoking among pregnant women in a Greek clinic.
Building earthquake-resistant bridges	The lessons from Chile – how three structures withstood the 2010 quake
Dealing with reoffending among prisoners	Work and learning – how a Brazilian scheme encouraged convicts to stay out of jail
Improving recycling rates in large cities	The Berlin experiment: increasing public participation in collecting and sorting waste

2 **Model case study**

(*Additional answers are possible here*)

a)

Competition from rivals offering free delivery
Some products (e.g. single beds) not suited to Chinese tastes

b)

Store layouts match Chinese apartments
Products linked to New Year celebrations
Reduced prices by sourcing production locally
Produces thinner but more frequent catalogues
Uses local characters in adverts
Attempts to provide better service
Stores located in downtown areas for public transport

c)

More financial details of IKEA's sales and profits in the Chinese market
More information about IKEA's main competitors in this market

5.2 Literature Reviews and Book Reviews

2 **Example literature review**

a) 2 (content & process)
b) 7
c) 5
d) It is more convenient to use secondary sources in this kind of short literature review. If you were studying just one of these theorists (e.g. Herzberg), you might be expected to use primary sources.

4 **Model book review**

The reviewer might have said what level of student would benefit from reading the book (e.g. undergraduate/Master's/PhD).

5.3 Writing Longer Papers

2 **Example essay**

a) The writer appears to be in favour of nuclear energy.
b) The writer first presents the arguments in favour of nuclear power and compares it with alternatives sources of energy. The safety aspects of the various alternative energy sources are then examined. In the conclusion the writer summarises his/her position ('nuclear energy can be seen . . . fossil fuels').
c) The paper is quite balanced and includes some useful statistical data. But it could be argued that the writer ignores some of the negative aspects of nuclear power, such as the high cost of building nuclear power stations and the difficulty of disposing of nuclear waste. Some of the sources used appear rather outdated.

3 Revision

(Example answers)

a) See Paragraph 1.
b) 'This essay attempts to assess the risks of using nuclear power in comparison with other sources of energy'.
c) 'The main arguments for employing nuclear energy are first considered, followed by an examination of the safety issues around this source of power, including the safety and security concerns connected with nuclear waste'.
d) ' . . . alternative energy sources to fossil fuels (i.e. oil, gas and coal. . .')
e) 'Wind energy and solar power are frequently presented as alternative energy sources to fossil fuels'.
f) 'Mtoe (million tons of oil equivalent)'
g) ' . . . since the Chernobyl accident in 1986 there has been persistent concern. . .'
h) ' . . . burning all three fuels contributes to the greenhouse effect which is causing the world to heat up'.
i) power
j) 'If this increase occurs the total global stock of oil and gas would only be adequate for 250 years. . .'
k) 'It is estimated that in 2003, in the US, nuclear energy prevented the release of 680 million tons of CO_2 . . .'
l) 'However, its opponents argue that it can damage the environment by creating radioactive waste'.
m) Bodansky (2004)
n) 'Lillington (2004) suggests that the cost of purchasing fuel for nuclear energy is likely to remain low compared to other energy sources. . .'

5.4 Reports

2 Essays and reports

1) Essay
2) Report
3) Report
4) Report/essay
5) Essay

3 Practice

Introduction

Due to the recent closure of the maintenance depot, a site approximately 250 metres long and 100 metres wide has become vacant on the west side of the university campus, and is ready for redevelopment. (e)

The aim of the redevelopment is to improve facilities for both staff and students and at the same time enhance the appearance of this part of the campus. (d)

Two alternatives schemes for redevelopment have been put forward, as can be seen in Plans A and B above. (b)

This report attempts to compare the two schemes and to establish which is the more suitable. (c)

The report takes into account a consultation exercise with staff and students carried out last autumn. (a)

(*Example report*)

Proposals

The central feature of Plan A is a circular park area in the middle of the site, which would contain trees and seating. On one side of this is a small car park with space for 40 vehicles. On the other side is a block of tennis courts. The alternative, Plan B, provides a larger car park along the side next to the Access Road with spaces for 100 cars. The other half of the site contains a building housing a café and a range of shops at one end, while at the other end is a swimming pool.

Discussion

Clearly the two proposals offer quite different amenities. Plan A provides some green space for relaxation, along with tennis courts and a limited amount of parking. It is a relatively low-key scheme that could be completed quite cheaply. In contrast, Plan B would be more expensive but would also offer catering and sports facilities as well as extra parking.

Recommendations

It can be argued in favour of Plan B that a swimming pool would have wider appeal than tennis courts, and also that there is a severe shortage of parking on the campus. However, it is not clear that more shops and a café are really needed for the university, and few students actually drive cars. Plan A would also do more to improve the look of the campus by increasing the green space. In view of these considerations, the university should perhaps consider combining the best of both plans and replace the tennis courts in Plan A with a swimming pool.

5 Example report: Student experience of part-time work

a)   conducted
b)   random
c)   questionnaire
d)   questioned
e)   respondents/interviewees
f)   Interviewees/Respondents
g)   mentioned

h)   majority
i)   slightly
j)   minority
k)   questions
l)   common
m)   generally
n)   sample

5.5 Writing Letters and Emails

1   Letters
  a)   Address of sender
  b)   Address of recipient
  c)   Sender's reference
  d   Date
  e)   Greeting
  f)   Subject headline
  g)   Reason for writing
  h)   Further details
  i)   Request for response
  j)   Ending
  k)   Signature
  l)   Writer's name and job title

2   Practice A
     (*Example answer*)

---

54 Sydney Road
Rowborough RB1 6FD

Mr M. Bramble
Administrative Assistant
Central Admissions Office
Wye House
Park Campus
University of Mercia
Borchester BR3 5HT

5th May 2017

Dear Mr Bramble,

Informal Interview: Yr Ref: MB/373

Thank you for inviting me to interview on May 21st. I will be able to attend on that date, but it would be much more convenient if I could have the interview at 12, due to the train times from Rowborough.

Could you please let me know if this alteration is possible?

Yours sincerely,
P. Tan

P. Tan

---

4   **Practice B**

Sender = student/recipient = teacher

A reply is unlikely, unless the recipient needs to comment on the attached paper.

5   **Practice C**

(*Example answers*)

a)   Hi Mark,
     We need to schedule a short meeting tomorrow. What time would suit you?
     See you soon,

b)   Hello Tricia,
     I'm looking for another source for this month's essay. Could you recommend something suitable?
     Best wishes,

c)   Hi everyone,
     It's only a week before the end of the course – what are we going to do to celebrate? Let me have your ideas – I'll pass them on and hopefully get something good fixed up for Sat. 12th!

d)   Dear Tim Carey,
     I've never had this book, so I can't return it. Can you check your records please?

5.6 Writing in Groups

1

a) F
b) T
c) F
d) F
e) T
f) F

2   Making group work successful

1   E.   Get to know the other members.
2   C.   Make everyone feel included.
3   A.   Analyse the task.
4   G.   Plan the job and the responsibilities.
5   B.   Divide up the work fairly, according to the abilities of the members.
6   F.   Select a co-ordinator/editor.
7   D.   Finish the assignment on time.

3   Dealing with problems

a   (i)   The lazy students will learn nothing from this approach, and the same problem will occur the next time they are involved in group work.
a   (ii)   Although it may seem difficult, this is the only positive solution.
a   (iii)   Your teachers are unlikely to help – group work is designed to make these problems your responsibility.
b   (i)   Your teachers are unlikely to help – group work is designed to make these problems your responsibility.
b   (ii)   This will not help you in the long run – you must learn to take part in discussion.
b   (iii)   The right approach. The other members probably don't realise that you are having difficulties with their language.
c   (i)   If everyone in the group takes part, the offender will be forced to accept that their behaviour is unhelpful.
c   (ii)   Your teachers are unlikely to help – group work is designed to make these problems your responsibility.
c   (iii)   You will run the risk that they will get a poor mark and so everyone will suffer.

Index

abbreviations in citations 60–1
abbreviations in writing 187–8
abbreviations, common 186–7
abbreviations, types 185
abstracts, reading 19–20
academic adjectives 193–4
academic style 21, 133, 161–2
academic texts 10–13
academic vocabulary 189–95
academic writing components 6–7
academic writing, format 4–6
academic writing, types 4
adjectives, academic 65, 193–4
adjectives, similar 193
adverbs, academic 196–201
adverbs, with passive 150
American English xxviii–xxx, 155
apostrophes 154
argument 91–5
argument, organisation of 92
articles 139
articles, definite 139–42
assessing internet sources critically 21–22

book reviews 229–33
brainstorming 35

capital letters 152
case studies 225–8
case study, model 226
category words 106–8
cause and effect 96–100
caution 166–7
change, language of 125–6

citation and quotation 56
citations and references 56
citations, abbreviations in 60–1
cohesion 135–8
colons 154
combining sources 64–70
commas 153
comparisons 101–5
comparison structures 101–2
conclusions 76–81
conclusion structure 81
confusing pairs 182–3
conjunctions 202–6
conjunctions, confusing 205
conjunctions of opposition 205–6
conjunctions, types 203–4
counterarguments 93–4
critical approach to sources 65–8
critical thinking 23–5

definitions 106–9
definitions, complex 108
definitions, simple 106
describing visuals 126–7
discussion language 93
discussion organisation 92
discussion vocabulary 91–2

electronic resources, searching
    15–16
emails 249–52
essay length 36–7
essay titles, analysing 34
evidence, providing 94–5

examples 110–13
examples, introducing 111

fact and opinion 20–1
format of academic writing 4–6
full stops 153

generalisations 114–17
generalisations, structure 115
graphs and charts 122, 285
group phrases 158
groups, writing in 253–6

implied language 137
internet resources, assessing critically 21–2
introduction contents 78, 274
introductions 76–81
introduction structure 77–9
inverted commas 155

journals, academic 6

key points, finding 39–45

labelling visuals 128
language features 181
language of change 125–6
language of discussion 93
length of essay 36–7
letters 249–50
library catalogues 14–15
linking paragraphs 74
list of references 61–2
literature reviews 229–33
longer papers 234–41

main verbs, understanding 196–7
mind maps 37, 87
modifiers, using 167

note-making 39–45
note-making methods 42–3
nouns and adjectives 189–95
nouns and adjectives, confusing 191–2
nouns, academic 189
nouns, uncountable 158–9
numbers 143–7
numbers, simplification 144–5
numerical phrases 145–6

opening sentences 79–80
organisation of argument 92

organising paragraphs 71–5
outlines 37

paragraph structure 71–2
paragraphs 71–5
paragraphs, linking 74
paragraphs, organising 71–5
paragraphs, writing in 8–9
paraphrasing 28, 46–54
paraphrasing techniques 52
passives 148–51
passive, use of 149–50
percentages 144
phrases from other languages 183–4
plagiarism 26–32
plagiarism, degrees of 27–8
planning process 33
prefixes 207–10
prepositions 211–15
prepositions and nouns 212
prepositions and verbs 214
prepositions in phrases 213
prepositions of place and time 213
problems and solutions, structure
    118–19
problems and solutions, vocabulary 119
proofreading 82–7
providing evidence 94–5
punctuation 152–6
purpose of academic writing 3

questionnaire design 212
quotation marks 155
quotations 55–63

reading academic texts 177, 179
reading lists 13
reading methods 17–18
reading texts, types of 13
reference systems 57
reference verbs 56
reference words 135
references 55–63
references and citations 56
references, list of 61–2
references, secondary 61
relevant points, finding 40–1
repetition and redundancy, avoiding
    164–5
reports 242–8
reports, scientific 244–6
resources, internet 21–2

restatement 113
rewriting 82–7

scientific reports 244–6
searching electronic resources 15–16
secondary references 61
semi-colons 154
sentence length, varying 165–6
sentences, opening 79–80
sentences, simple and longer 7–8
singular or plural? 157–60
sources, acknowledging 27
sources, combining 64–70
sources, finding suitable 10–16
style guidelines 162–3
style, academic 161–2
suffixes 207–10
summarising 46–54
summarising and paraphrasing 46–54
summarising, stages of 47
superlatives 103
synonyms 216–21

tenses 170
text features 18–19

text types 13
time markers 169–75
titles and sub-titles 18–19
titles, essay 34
titles, understanding 33–8
types of academic writing 4
types of reading texts 13

uncountable nouns 158–9

varying sentence length 165–6
verbs and prepositions 214
verbs of reference 198–9
verbs, academic 196–201
verbs, passives 201
verbs, understanding main 196–7
visual information 122–31
visuals, describing 126–7
visuals, labelling 128
vocabulary, approaches to 179–84
vocabulary, new 180–1

words and phrases from other languages
    183–4
writing in groups 253–6

ALSO AVAILABLE FROM
STEPHEN BAILEY

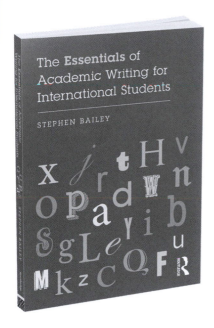

THE ESSENTIALS OF ACADEMIC WRITING FOR INTERNATIONAL STUDENTS

The Essentials of Academic Writing for International Students is designed to help international students achieve success in their written work. This concise book explains the essential skills writing process from start to finish. From selecting and reading suitable sources to note-making, summarizing and referencing, this book provides clear examples and effective exercises. *The Essentials of Academic Writing for International Students* teaches students critical skills such as generalising, referencing, making comparisons and using graphs. All international students wanting to achieve academic success will find this practical and easy-to-use book a valuable guide to improving their written English—quickly!

© 2015 – Routledge • 230 pages // Pb: 9781138885622 • Hb: 9781138885615 • eBook: 9781315715346

2ND EDITION
ACADEMIC WRITING FOR INTERNATIONAL STUDENTS OF BUSINESS

Academic Writing for International Students of Business is a unique and practical book specially designed to assist overseas students studying Business or Economics courses in English. It is an accessible book which explains the writing process from start to finish and also encourages users to practise key writing skills.

This new edition has been thoroughly revised and updated to reflect the interests and issues of contemporary Business studies and there is also now a strong emphasis on how international students can broaden their vocabulary and use it more effectively in their work.

© 2015 – Routledge • 302 pages // Pb: 9781138783904 • Hb: 9781138783898 • eBook: 9781315768434

Routledge
Taylor & Francis Group

Routledge... think about it
www.routledge.com